Calm in the Cauldron
A rugby league journey

John Dorahy

with Tom Mather

London League Publications Ltd

Calm in the Cauldron

A rugby league journey

© John Dorahy and Tom Mather. Forewords © Colin Hutton and Warren Ryan.

The moral right of John Dorahy and Tom Mather to be identified as the authors has been asserted.

Cover design © Stephen McCarthy.

Front cover: John Dorahy when selected for Australia in 1978. Back cover: On the attack with Halifax at Thrum Hall in 1989. (Photo courtesy *Halifax Courier*)

All photographs in this book are from private collections unless otherwise credited. No copyright has been intentionally breached, please contact London League Publications Ltd if you believe there has been a breach of copyright.

A CIP catalogue record for this book is available from the British Library.

First published in Great Britain in November 2010 by:
London League Publications Ltd, P.O. Box 10441, London E14 8WR

ISBN: 978-1903659-54-0

Cover design by: Stephen McCarthy Graphic Design
                           46, Clarence Road, London N15 5BB

Layout: Peter Lush

Printed and bound in Great Britain by
CPI Antony Rowe, Chippenham and Eastbourne

Forewords

John Dorahy was one of the most naturally gifted players that I have ever been involved with.

It seems that our paths were destined to cross, because in 1973 in a game against Leigh at Craven Park I noted and admired the skill of a young centre who scored a smart try against us. I learned that it was John, who was in England for a season with his cousin Tony and I did no more about it.

In 1982 I was in Australia as Great Britain manager to take in the Australia versus New Zealand test series and visited Kogarah Oval to see the St George versus Illawarra game, mainly to see Allan Fitzgibbon who was the coach of Illawarra and who had played for a season in the 1970s with Hull Kingston Rovers and was a family friend.

During the game, it was clear that the star of the show was the Illawarra number 4. Every time he touched the ball something positive happened, and he also kicked the goals resulting in an Illawarra win. After the game, I was invited into the Illawarra dressing room when the number 4 – John – came across to me and said would I consider him if I was recruiting for Hull KR.

I was delightfully surprised—would I consider him! I couldn't get to the phone quick enough to start things moving to get John to England and hull KR. We had a good team at the time, but John was the icing on the cake, and we had a momentous season in 1983–84 when Hull KR became the first club to win the Premiership and the Championship in the same season.

John's performance in the Premiership final against Castleford earned him the Harry Sunderland man-of-the-match award. His try was a gem when he simply nodded at the Castleford full-back to send him the wrong way while John went to the line.

My wife Marjorie and I were proprietors of the Zetland Arms, a local hostelry, and along with other players' families, the Dorahys were frequent visitors, and we became firm friends, and still are. We keep in regular communication through the internet.

I consider it a privilege to be invited to contribute this foreword to what I am sure will be a fascinating book and I for one can't wait for the opportunity to read it.

Colin Hutton
President Hull Kingston Rovers
July 2010

Colin Hutton had a distinguished playing career with Widnes and Hull FC. He coached Hull KR and Great Britain, managed Great Britain, was chairman of Hull KR and was president of the Rugby Football League.

For those of us who were fortunate enough to witness it, John Dorahy's journey from schoolboy rugby league phenomenon to consummate senior champion was as enjoyable as it was inevitable.

It would be unthinkable for me to write a foreword for this book without telling the remarkable story of how our paths first crossed when John was still a 16-year-old schoolboy, so here it is.

John and I were introduced to each other when he was a year 11 student with one year of homework, study and exams still ahead of him. When I reflect on the reason for the introduction, I am still amazed at the prescience of the then secretary of West Wollongong (Red Devils) RLFC Peter (Buck) Buchanan who, when it came to football talent, could separate the wheat from the chaff like no one else I've ever met.

My role in the scheme of things at that time was as captain-coach of West (Red Devils) first grade team and as fate would have it our regular full-back Tony Cull, who was an extremely talented player and a champion goalkicker, had broken the scaphoid bone in his hand. It was only a couple of weeks out from the semi-finals and we were in trouble, or so I thought.

Buck came over to me in the leagues club that night after the game and the conversation went something like this: "Listen old chap I've got just the replacement you need." "Who's that?" I enquired. "John Dorahy." was the reply "The under-17s full-back in the Red Devil's juniors." "You're kidding," I said. "No I'm not. I've never been more serious." said Buck looking supremely confident.

"That's very interesting," I said "so we don't want our 2nd, 3rd or 4th grade full-back or our under-18s lad, we want the under-17s kid?" "That's right," said Buck "but we'll have to go around to his house and get permission from his parents to let him play." Then almost as a throwaway line as we walked towards the league's club door he half turned and looked at me and said "Oh, by the way, he'll play for Australia one day."

Well I was stunned, but I trusted Buck's uncanny ability to pick out future champions so with a bit more spring in my step we covered the short walking distance from the leagues club to the Dorahy's home.

His father Kevin was visibly proud that Buck considered young Johnny good enough to play first grade. The team had already won back-to-back premierships under the captain coaching of former Australian full-back Don Parish so dad considered this quite an honour.

It was a bit different though with John's mother Nola. She was naturally concerned as mothers usually are. She felt that as he was still 16 years old, he might not be able to compete with men so much older and more experienced.

However, mum eventually agreed somewhat reluctantly when I assured her we'd have a good look at him at training in a game of very physical "holding" not full-blooded tackling and wouldn't go ahead if John didn't look capable of handling it.

Well, from the moment the training session began I could see what Buck was talking about. The longer it went the better he looked, confident, skilful, and elusive. This wasn't just some promising kid with potential, we had a rugby league prodigy on our hands. He had absolutely everything in his arsenal of attacking skills. When the session ended I said to Buck "he's good alright, you need a butterfly net to catch him".

To this day it is still a puzzle to me why he was so accomplished at such a young age. To argue he was a product of a wonderful junior development system is to invite the obvious question: where are the other brilliantly gifted products rolling off the assembly line?

Legendary coach Jack Gibson once observed wryly when someone inadvertently risked talking about a player's potential "the beaches are polluted with potential". Jack obviously wasn't interested in what a player might do tomorrow, the only currency he dealt in was what a player could do today.

Juniors are generally afforded the luxury of time to develop physically, mentally and improve all areas of their game. But we were in a tough spot. We had no time for potential. Johnny Dorahy had to be the real deal, goalkicker, the lot if we were going to lift the trophy for a third consecutive year.

I have two outstanding memories of John's first match. One of our second-rowers a tough customer named Dave Hayburn, who was a wood chopper for light recreation in his spare time, deliberately stepped aside and let a big opposition forward through. When I asked him what he was doing he said "We have to find out if the young fellow can tackle before the finals." The young fellow for his part did all right. He dropped the big runaway with a copybook low tackle.

The other memory of his first match was from a scrum about 30 metres out from the opposition's try line. Our forwards won the ball — scrums were still a contest in 1971 — and our schoolboy genius cut through the centres and was planting the ball under the posts just as the front-rowers were disengaging from the scrum.

One of our props, Tony Charlton, a member of the well known Canterbury clan of front-rowers, wandered over to me shaking his head as if he was not sure what he had just seen. "The kid ain't bad," he grunted. From that time onward the team's special name for our boy wonder was "The kid".

As it turned out John had two Illawarra first grade Premierships under his belt when the team won its fourth consecutive title in 1972 and in that year he was selected to represent country firsts against city after playing brilliantly for Illawarra in the country divisional titles.

However, John was destined to unleash his formidable talents on a much bigger stage. Sydney was his inevitable destination. It was only a matter of time before one of the big Sydney clubs in their endless search for quality realised was a priceless piece of football wizardry "The kid" from the "Gong" was.

I have had the privilege of coaching many wonderfully gifted footballers, but of them all John Dorahy, in my view, had more natural ability than any other player I have ever been associated with. Others have acquired high levels of skill but John could do everything at 16 years of age. Why he was so good so young is still a mystery to me.

He could beat a defender with a sidestep off either foot but it was the ease with which he moved not appearing to be going quickly that put him in a special category. He always kept an extra turn of speed in reserve to fool defenders who thought they had him covered.

His composure and confidence under pressure earned him the nickname of "Joe cool" when he went to Sydney to play for Western Suburbs. Older teammates were amazed at his kitbag of attacking skill. He made the chip and regather look so effortless even front rowers tried to copy him at training when he wasn't looking.

John's career is amply covered in this book with support from Tom Mather. That he went on to attain the highest honours of state and national representation was no surprise to team mates who played along side him or to opponents who were so regularly made to look pedestrian by his change of pace.

To his great credit fame has rested very lightly on John's shoulders. Wearing the green and gold of Australia has never affected him like it has so many others who have achieved rugby league stardom. He was always humble and remained so when widely acclaimed as a champion. For that I salute him.

It was a privilege to have played along side John when he was "The kid". Every member of the team realised how fortunate we were to have him in the side. We marvelled at his brilliant skills and smiled knowingly when he left some unsuspecting opponent in his wake.

It was also a pleasure in later years when he had moved on to the big league in Sydney to watch his progress as he went on, as we all knew he would, to play for Australia. Just like Buck had predicted when he was 16 years of age.

Warren Ryan
July 2010

Warren Ryan played for St George and Cronulla before playing for Wollongong Wests. He then had a distinguished coaching career in Australia with Newtown, Canterbury, Balmain, Wests and Newcastle.

Special appreciation to the people who made this book a reality:

Tom Mather, a friend and co-writer of this book, it is difficult to express the level of gratitude my family and I would like to make for the time taken and efforts made to concisely illustrate in words the story of John 'Joe Cool' Dorahy.

Peter Lush and Dave Farrar at London League Publications in England. Thanks for providing the edition of this book for the many UK rugby league supporters wanting to relive the period Joe Cool spent in England and what he achieved on the other side of the world.

Helen Elward from Best Legenz who has, with Tom Mather and Peter Lush, so expertly made the story come to life in a wonderful manner. Importantly I would like to express my appreciation for the time and expert knowledge provided in formatting this book that shows your enjoyment of the game and its participants through words.

John Dorahy
July 2010

About Tom Mather

Tom Mather has written a number of books on rugby league, including *The Rugby League Myth* (with Michael Latham) which put a different slant on the reasons for the break away in 1895, *Snuff out the Moon* which examined the history of floodlit rugby league, to the former Parramatta, Wigan and Auckland Warriors coach, John Monie's biography, *The Iceman*. He has also regularly contributed articles to newspapers and journals in Great Britain.

Tom and his wife, Janet, live in Lytham on the coast in the North West of England. Now retired, he was for most of his working life a school teacher and spent 16 years as head of psychology in the largest school in Lancashire. On retiring from teaching, he has spent his time writing and has recently published *Best in the Northern Union*, an account of the first ever tour to Australia and New Zealand by the British Lions rugby league team in 1910. He was also instrumental in getting the English rugby authorities to use a replica of the 1910 tour jersey when they meet New Zealand in the 2010 Four Nations Competition to celebrate the centenary of that visit and the first ever test between the two countries to be played in New Zealand.

He is the father of Barrie-Jon Mather, the former Wigan and Perth Western Reds player and now head of player performance for the RFL in England. He first met John Dorahy in 1993, when he coached Barrie-Jon and Wigan to a cup and league double, and they have been firm friends ever since. Tom and Janet spend a good deal of their time between Australia where they have two children living in Sydney and England where their other two children live.

This book is the latest effort to come off the production line and he was delighted when John Dorahy agreed to it being written and allowed him to bring John's remarkable career to the wider rugby league loving public both in Australia and Great Britain.

There are very special people I want to dedicate this book to for showing the confidence in my ability to go on with the job, and giving me the time and space to achieve.

To the most wonderful people in my life: my wife Linda (née Mitchell), who has had to put up with so much more than the average woman; my children, Dane Anthony, Jason Kurt and Cara Lea, who have provided Linda and me with an enormous amount of joy and pride in what they have achieved in their lives, while having to put up with constant change in their young lives. Without their unconditional love and unending acceptance of travel, I would not have achieved nearly as much success from this life as a rugby league player, coach and manager, father and husband.

To my parents, Kevin and Nola (1929 to 1995), who gave me the early opportunities to pursue my love of rugby league.

To my sister Lesley and brother Rob, who had to endure being placed second on so many occasions, never complaining but proud to stand by and be proud of my achievements.

I thank each and every one of you for your unending love, affection and support through the highs and lows that are life in the world of rugby league.

I was so lucky to have the chance to participate in the game. My life would not have been complete if I didn't enjoy it over the years, during times of excitement and adversity.

Rugby league has been an astonishing journey through the highs and lows that come with involvement in sport especially at the highest level when the stakes can be higher still. The words that best sum up the life of John 'Joe Cool' Dorahy in rugby league are:

"When the dream is right for the person and the person is right for the dream, the two cannot be separated from each other."
(John C. Maxwell)

Acknowledgements

Our thanks to everyone who supplied photos for the book, Steve McCarthy for designing the cover and the staff of CPI Anthony Rowe for printing it.

This book has been a joint project, with Best Legendz in Australia and London League Publications Ltd in Great Britain working together, sharing information, photographs and much more. We would like to thank Helen Elward for all her support during the project, and for publishing the book in Australia.

Finally, thank you to Tom Mather for his sterling work on the book, and John and his family for all their input as well.

Peter Lush and Dave Farrar
London League Publications Ltd

Contents

1.	Starting out	1
2.	Second season honours	17
3.	Freezing in Leigh	25
4.	Western Suburbs	31
5.	Test honours ... and twins	45
6.	Leaving Wests	57
7.	Manly	65
8.	Illawarra Steelers	77
9.	Hull KR and the Steelers	87
10.	So close at Wembley	107
11.	Red Devils and a Rovers return	117
12.	Problems at Halifax	129
13.	Home and away	149
14.	Wigan	163
15.	Perth Western Reds	183
16.	Warrington	193
17.	Finale in Australia	199
18.	Our Dad, our hero	207
19.	And finally... a special thank you	215

Appendices:

1	Rugby league memories	220
2	Statistics and records	221

With Linda.

1.   Starting out

John Dorahy went by the nickname of 'Joe Cool'. It was a pretty good description of the man and the rugby league player. During his career he was called up for his first international match just 72 hours before kick-off. He lost a Rugby League Challenge Cup Final at Wembley with the last kick of the game. In Sydney he played in a finals play-off game with a depressed fracture of the cheek bone that he had received in the previous round and kept the injury secret from his team mates and the opposition, only entering hospital for the surgery after the match. In a representative City versus Country game, he got carried from the field paralysed and was told by a doctor, "Don't move your head, it may well fall off!" He took on the Australian Rugby League in court on a matter of principle. As a coach he steered Wigan to a cup and league double only to be sacked just five days later. To survive such setbacks in a career you needed to be cool. All of this occurred when the game was played in a very different way from today.

* * * * *

I was born in Wollongong Hospital on 28 August 1954. My parents John Kevin and Nola (née Arblaster) Dorahy had a new son. I had an older sister, Lesley, and a younger brother, Robert.

I grew up in Unanderra, a suburb 4 miles (6.5 km) west of Wollongong, about an hour's drive south of Sydney. I attended St Pius X Catholic Primary school, just a punt kick across the road from our house, which was terrific because I didn't have to leave too early, at least during primary school years. Unanderra was a working class suburb. Both my parents were hard working people. My dad was a butcher in the family business; mum worked in the post office. We didn't see dad go off to work because he was at it before the sun rose on the new day. Mum did just about everything around the home at 14 Maynes Parade, situated behind the Western Suburbs Leagues Club.

My father's nickname was 'Puff' because when he was a young man he would get out of breath easily, but was a quick runner. I saw this when the family company used to have their annual Christmas picnic down at Gerroa. Dad would participate in all the day's activities – three legged race, 100 yard sprint, wheelbarrow race and others. He used to win all the individual races with his pace.

Before she got married my mum was a very good bike racer, but stopped to look after dad and the family as we all came along. Mum's brothers, Eric and Bob Arblaster, both played for Port Kembla DRLFC. Many people told me over the years that Eric especially was a fine first team player. Eric went on to become Port Kembla's club secretary and in recent times was asked to sit on the selection panel to choose the Illawarra Team of the Century, which will be announced sometime in 2011 as part of the celebrations of 100 years of Illawarra Rugby League. I am proud to say I have been chosen as an ambassador to represent the Illawarra Rugby League in 2011. I am humbled to think that I represent the hundreds of men who have gone before me and those currently involved in this NSW Country Division.

My first game of rugby league was as a five year old boy in my first year in kindergarten. This was in 1960 and the under-4 stone team was coached by Mr Vienney and Mr Gardner, two local parents who gave their time freely to coach a young team of five and six year old boys. My first game, at Lindsay Main Oval, was unflattering. I had received my first pair of boots as hand-me downs from my cousin, Tim Dorahy, for which I was extremely grateful. They were ankle high 'Featherweights' with nailed studs. Over time the nails protruded into the boot. This caused blisters and it was not the done thing to complain about some little old nail burying itself in your foot. I vaguely remember my introduction to the game of rugby league, but have been informed on numerous occasions that when I was passed the ball I immediately headed for the goal line. Unfortunately for me, and the team, it was the wrong end. I thought I had scored, but had placed the ball behind our line for a goal line drop-out. What a beginning

Once I had played I was hooked. I wanted to play everyday with friends in the front yards of our places, or in the park down the road just two punt kicks away, or maybe one if the ball bounced and rolled correctly. During lunch time we either played rugby league or a game of British bulldog that allowed us to practice our attack and defence trying to stop runners making the other side of the school grounds.

One of the toughest tacklers in this game was my cousin, Greg Dorahy, who became an absolute tough nut in football defending like tomorrow depended on it. Fortunately, later in life I had only to play against him once. Luckily I was never tackled by him.

My sister was a good field hockey player. Every other week she played hockey down the road and I went down there to watch. Well, my school mates and I would make out we were there playing touch football while watching the game and all the pretty girls in their short skirts. I remember having to practice hockey with Lesley at home. She would make sure my legs were never in close range of her stick because you would receive an almighty whack on the shins or ankles that was always an accident. Ha ha, sure it was. This was a life lesson – never take on girls at a game they are good at. I also remember going to school one Saturday to play touch football with my mates and being asked if I wanted to fill in for a missing player in the school netball teams. I duly obliged and soon found out that watching this stop-start game was very different to playing. It did teach me a lot about finding a player in space and passing the ball to them before they could be covered by a defender. I kept a close eye on one player, Ann Mawson, who was my first girlfriend. She ended up marrying Peter Nolan from Thirroul who went to St Paul's College in Bellambi. They had several children and live on the Gold Coast in Queensland.

Hockey also taught me these skills. In that game it is important to know that to create an advantage it is crucial to create the space, have a support player run into space and get the ball to someone in a better position than you to get the ball to the goal.

My younger brother Robert was just over two years younger than me. He tried rugby league, but his asthma cruelly stopped any chance of him playing too much. Rob thoroughly enjoyed playing tennis and could have gone on to be a good player if he had had the discipline to continue.

One of my favourite people in those early years was Sister Mary Hugh, the Principal of St Pius X school from my first day in 1960. Sister Hugh taught me in sixth class in 1966. She loved rugby league and encouraged all the boys at the school to get involved if possible. I remember my brother starting school in 1962 and because we lived across the road he ran away from school to home during the lunch break. Mum brought him back. I came over to see what was happening and stood alongside Rob when mum was leaving the school grounds and Rob in the hands of Sister Hugh.

To placate Rob Sister Hugh arranged for him to have a complimentary sausage roll. When he was handed it he threw it at Sister Hugh, hitting her fair in the middle. Poor Rob was then marched off to receive some well needed instruction and a couple of whacks on the backside. Rob never again ran away from the school yard. I certainly learnt it was better to take the heat and get on with life than to fight too much.

In primary school I enjoyed rugby league playing under the unlimited tackles rule. As most children did back then we threw the ball around and with the game played on a full size field it was generally all about the quick players running around the outside of the team and to the try line. I had a bit of pace and managed to score a few long range tries.

My first and only school yard fight was in 1962 when a little jealousy erupted between me and a kid named Greg Potts. I was soundly flogged by Pottsy, but won the war with Ann Mawson sticking by me not Pottsy. Greg later became a referee and ran the line in the local Illawarra competition – bad luck Greg, some people are drawn to fights but refereeing wasn't your forté.

Looking back there were, I suppose, two major events that impacted on me and my rugby league career. The first was when I was around 10 or 11 years old and was identified by a number of people as being a youngster who had some ability in the game with one of the most desired skills – speed. They went out of their way to play me at district level, develop the talent they had seen in me and take me to a higher level.

I had played with the St Pius X School for six years before leaving to attend high school in Bellambi, a northern suburb of Wollongong, and enjoyed playing with my school mates. I was invited to play with the Wests team in Wollongong in a knock-out comp in Gymea for the under–12 side, a year above my age group. This was a big learning curve for me as a youngster playing with and against players more mature and experienced than me. Similarly, a year later I was again invited to a knock-out comp in Nowra playing above my own age group. It was then I decided to play junior rugby league for Wests, where I enjoyed the game immensely with newfound mates.

Sister Hugh heard about me playing and asked if I was going to play with school or play with Wests. I replied "with the school" although I also wanted to play with Wests. She was not 100 per cent happy, but as long as I could play for the school all was okay.

This was when mum became a winter taxi driver, taking me around all over the place from one game to another on Saturdays. I remember

1965, first rep team, Illawarra Catholic Schools 5-stone-7-pound team. I am in the front row, second from left.

one day in particular. I played for Wests under-12s at 10am against Thirroul at the northern end of Wollongong, and mum had to race all the way out to Reid Park in Dapto where the school team was playing at 11am. Mum got me there about 15 minutes into the game. The coach had kept a reserve spot available for me. All I had to do was sign the play sheet and dress for the game. There was some uproar from the opposite coach about the lateness of a player signing, but all was well after some heated conversation. St Pius X School went onto win the match against St John's Dapto and I scored a couple of tries. The Dapto team coach was not pleased afterwards, but hey, I enjoyed playing that much I would have played all day as long as there was a game to play. As kids do. We would arrive home after Saturday morning footie and have lunch, before heading off to the park at the bottom of the street to play more touch football and kicking games such as forcing back which taught me to kick.

When I left primary school for high school my parents sent me to St Paul's College in Bellambi, 12 miles from Unanderra. I had to catch an early bus at 7.15am into Wollongong station for the 8.10am train to Bellambi and an 800 yard walk to the school. The school closest to our home was Edmund Rice College. Both schools were boys only, with strong sporting histories, but mum and dad thought going to Bellambi would be best for my academic education and so it proved. Though I wanted to leave school in Year 10 and become a builder, my parents

5

had other ideas. I went on to year 12, passed the Higher School Certificate and studied accountancy while working for the family company. At school my first coach was Father John Burke in the under 7 stone team. We were well drilled in football discipline. The team went on to win the local schools knockout carnival followed by the NSW state schools knockout at Moore Park, alongside the Sydney Cricket Ground. The Under 7 stone 7 pounds team was also successful in the local knockout a year later under the guidance of the late Father Lionel Dean, although his real love was cricket. Father Dean coached the cricket first XI to some success and was coach when I played in the team, taking us to Geelong Victoria by train to play against our sister college, which no longer exists. A great time was had and we went along to a Victoria Football League game between Geelong and Collingwood. It was from this match that I then began supporting the Collingwood Magpies. In the AFL Collingwood are one of those teams people either support or support the team playing against them. Like Manly in rugby league, they are the team everyone hates to see win.

The second major event that had an impact on my career was when as a 16 year old I was catapulted into first grade with Wests. This came as a complete surprise to me and possibly many others. There were a number of players in my age group who really could have been outstanding players and gone onto higher honours, but did not make it to Sydney first grade. I wonder if it is all to do with timing and opportunity through the eyes of others – likely it is and the 'sliding doors' that life presents when someone has an option to choose to go one way or another.

One of the oldest clichés in sport is the one that says 'one player's misfortune is another player's opportunity'. In my case it was certainly true. I was 16 years old in 1971 and the first grade full-back Tony Cull broke a scaphoid bone in his wrist just seven weeks before the finals series. It was so bad that he was expected to be ruled out for the rest of the season. Tony lived just two doors away from me. I remember speaking to him on the front drive as he was heading off to training and found he was quite sad because of his misfortune. Tony also mentioned that he didn't think Dennis McGoldrick, his potential replacement from second grade would last long before being replaced. The clubs' player-coach was the now well known Warren Ryan, coach extraordinaire. He was left with a problem – he needed a full-back at the business end of the season. There were just four matches left. The

6

club was hoping to win its third Grand Final in a row and had brought in Dennis McGoldrick, another Unanderra lad to replace Tony Cull. In the two games he had played, he had failed to impress Warren Ryan, who was pondering what to do to fill the problem full-back slot.

I had been playing very well at College and for Wests, but it never entered my head that I would even be considered for the role. The club secretary, Peter Buchanan, was the instigator of events that would ultimately change the whole course of my life. He, unknown to me at the time, convinced Ryan that I was capable of stepping up to first grade and solving the full-back problem for the club. To this day I am not sure which was the harder job for Buchanan, convincing the coach I should play or talking my mother into allowing me to step up to first grade as a 16 year old lad.

The club contacted my mum and dad when they had decided that I should be given the first grade opportunity. Mum and dad sat down with me and told me what Wests were planning and asked what I thought. I was mad keen, of course, to take the opportunity. However, I remember mum piped up and asked how was I going to be able to play against men while I was still a boy; keep up my studies and have the energy to play at that level? She told me in no uncertain manner that she would not be going to watch me play in any such matches. I believe mum was trying to look after my best interests and ensure I completed my schooling satisfactorily and wasn't put into a situation against adult men playing a tough sport.

I had more or less reluctantly agreed with her that I would not play so as to not upset her, but on the Wednesday, which was a training night for Wests I had just scoffed down one of her best lamb baked dinners. It was an unusually early dinner, although I reckon mum and dad were aware of a visit happening that evening.

There was a knock at the door and there stood Peter Buchanan and Warren Ryan. They proceeded to tell mum and dad just what an opportunity it was for me. Ryan relayed to her how he had known of players who having been given an opportunity, not taken it, and were lost to the game and a bright future. Eventually they talked her round after Peter Buchanan said how I could handle the rise in standard and be protected at the same time. I would be playing behind Ryan, who was a formidable centre for Wests in the Illawarra competition, and a strong team. It also provided another time-worn cliché 'if he's good enough, he's old enough'. I was then asked by mum reluctantly: "John do you want to play?" I quickly replied "yes". This was a huge opportunity which allowed me to go on and enjoy the highs and live the lows that is rugby league as a professional player.

I was then driven to training, directed to the changing room, introduced to the backroom staff, changed and met my new team mates who were already out on the field waiting for the coach to get to training Though I didn't realise at the time Ryan had organised a short game of touch footy to start the session. He wanted to watch how I handled being amongst senior players, what I could do with the ball in hand and whether Peter Buchanan was correct about me having the vision, positional skills, speed and step. I remember playing alongside Warren and David Waite with the ball coming to me often, planned I reckon, and I was able to do a couple of steps, beat the defender and set up a couple of players with simple two-on-one plays or inside passes.

I guess it all went okay because we started training. Warren and our trainer, Les Anderson, a former Cronulla Sharks conditioner had cooked up another test for me with a sprint session of twenty 100 yard sprints under 13 seconds per sprint with a jog back of not less than half pace. I was teamed with David Waite, who was a speedster, to test my pace across the 100 yards. After about 8 sprints I remember throwing up my dinner that mum had so lovingly prepared, thinking I would do as she wished and not go to training. The coach must have agreed with Buchanan's assessment of me as he decided to go with me on the Sunday.

I was confident of my ability to handle the match, but was made more so after the training session and meeting my team mates. It was a class team, tough as nails with forwards that every backline player would want to play behind. Ray Staff and Ross Standring were in the front-row, holding up Shane Day, a classic hooker from the South Sydney district. In the back-row Wests had possibly the toughest combination ever with Dave Hayburn, a strong, thickset player who did not take a step backwards, Klaus Reh, a wiry, strong no compromise style forward and Dennis McCulloch at lock who was a Ron Coote style player – tall, lean with excellent ball skills and speed across the ground. I wasn't afraid to go into my first match after watching these guys prepare for the Corrimal versus Wests match. There was a tough, uncompromising defensive attitude in this pack, something that showed strongly in the next four matches.

The backs were all class with plenty of try scoring ability. They were headed by Warren Ryan, a big, strong centre with a massive chest of which Atlas would have been proud. His partner on this occasion was Terry McCarthy, who was also a strong centre, making his mark. The wingers, Darryl Smith and John Lumsden, could finish off any backline move with aplomb. One of the halves was a centre cum five-eighth (stand-off) Owen Smith. Although not a classic player for this position, he was again a strong defensive player who got the ball to Warren Ryan quickly and supported from the inside. The half-back, Greg Rodgers, was my next door neighbour and one of the best halves to come out of the Illawarra who didn't play senior rep football. David Waite was also in the team, but due to injury was not available for this match.

Like any 16 year old when given the chance, I was desperate to play at the higher level and was so relieved when all of the persuasion finally managed to get mum to bow to the inevitable. I was ecstatic being involved with the local first team and enjoyed the opportunity to test myself at the higher level. Mum had threatened to throw me out of the house if I agreed to play first grade. The following Wednesday evening, when the weather had cleared, I finally got the nod that I was to play on the Sunday against Corrimal. The match was played at the Wollongong Showground in the 'Match-of-the-Round' as was customary in the early 1970s.

It is hard to say just when the nerves kicked in, if they ever did. It is one thing to play College footy in finals and knock-out competition finals, but the pressure is nowhere near as intense as that I felt as game time approached. These were men, men who got paid to ply their trade on the paddock and they played with such intensity, guys who had played in the NSWRL competition, the premier comp of the day and I had never experienced this before. I was confident that I would be able to cope with everything that would be thrown at me. Training had been good and felt I settled in to the team pattern. The rain delay had helped me get an understanding with most of the players I would rely on to run off or look after me in tight situations. The press did not help when before the game I read headlines like 'Key role for Wests youth', 'Schoolboy full-back in big test' and 'Wests gamble on youngster'. They had a field day with a big story.

One thing I was disappointed about when all this occurred was that I was destined not to go back and play with my mates who I had played with for the past five years. I had great friends in the junior grades, people like Peter 'Mont' Marmont, a solid, tough half-back with a wicked humorous side to him. I remember the day in under-13s on Figtree Oval No.3 playing against Towradgi. Now Towradgi were a good team, solid across the park, but with a terrific robust centre called Mark Bell who had the speed and strength to bust timid tackles. At a scrum set about 30 yards from the Towradgi tryline and Peter feeding, the ball went in and came out fast at which time Mont picked up the ball and pointed to the sky saying "look at that!" He took off between the scrum and the five-eighth as everyone looked skyward. Fortunately for Towradgi, but unfortunate for Peter, Mark Bell didn't take the bait and proceeded to try and cut off Mont before he could score. The next thing that happened was sickening to anyone watching and most of all to the players. Mark hit Mont with an almighty tackle side on and absolutely splattered him in one of those tackles usually seen on television in senior league. Mont went into a muscle spasm and shook like he was doing a Richter 10 earthquake. The Zambuck (ambulance man) had to be called quick smart and Mont was taken to hospital for observation and treatment. It was the first and last time Mont tried this trick, but it was moments like these that made the person and his mateship with his team mates.

Back to the story...

It was 5 September 1971, just a week after my 17th birthday, when I ran out onto the Showground to make my first grade debut against the third placed team Corrimal. If I was to be disappointed about anything in the lead up to the match, it was that this game should have been played a week earlier when I was 16, but the rain washed out the match until the next week. However, it was a blessing to have the extra week to train with the team, get a little more knowledge of the plays and when to chime into the line.

In the pre-match atmosphere the opportunity was rammed home when my uncle, Eric Arblaster, then the Port Kembla secretary and a former player for that club, came into our change room and asked if I was nervous. I was not really nervous at all, just enjoying the moment. I sat there as I always did before games in junior football and thought about my part to play as I had done since being a young player. I sat with my eyes closed and visualised the step, change of pace, goalkicking from all angles and how to make tackles along with the myriad of new plays I was to be involved in. When asked how I was feeling, was I nervous, I got the feeling uncle Eric was expecting the reply, "yes, real nervous". I duly replied "yeah a little nervous" and off he trotted saying "you'll be fine kid, just go out and do your best".

The team gave probably their best performance of the season and we thrashed Corrimal 26–5. We scored eight tries that afternoon and in the blustery conditions that Wollongong showground can throw up I only managed to convert one of them. I did, however, play well and the players and club officials were delighted with my debut as were the press. There was one moment in this match that I thought "Geez what I'm in trouble here". It was the moment a hulking Kiwi prop forward, Oscar Danielson, broke through the defence and was running at me, the last line of defence. Because of the windy conditions I was standing about 25 yards back. Everything seemed to slow down and provide the time to make the correct decision on how to make this important tackle. Should I wait for Oscar to run to me or should I advance to him? Oscar would have scored had I missed the tackle. I moved towards him to cut down his options, waited until the last moment and rather than try and be the hero and go high, I instinctively dropped low to make a perfect tackle on Oscar with him trying to run over me. I reckon Oscar believed he could run over the top of me and score, so he didn't even look for the support that was coming with him.

I was delighted to keep my place in the full-back spot for the following game, against Thirroul again at the Showground. However, both I and the team came up short, going down 11–7 in a match best described as 'dour'. Thirroul had some very good players led by the diminutive John McCarthy as half-back and coach. He just happened to be my school first XIII coach during the week. And didn't Macca give it to me at training for the school team and on the previous two Wednesday sport days when the school team played against other local High Schools. Once again the press had praise for the defensive efforts I made in the game. I did spend a worrying few days not knowing if I would keep the jersey or not. There was a moment in this match when I decided when returning the ball upfield to make a short kick over the defence coming towards me and try to retrieve it before the full-back, John 'Slappy' Air could get to it. Unfortunately, I put a little too much weight on the kick and Slappy got to it a fraction before

I did. At least I made the tackle on him in their half. Warren Ryan, spoke to me after the game and said though I did well, it was something to try these things, but in a close game as this was sometimes it is best to just return the ball and take the tackle. A good lesson learnt for tough games ahead.

Looking through my mother's scrapbooks reminded me that I was not the only family member playing at this time. I had two cousins playing for Collegians RL in the same competition, Tony Dorahy and Eddie Dorahy, who were both back-rowers. They were strong and tough, who were taught not to take a backward step from anyone and always played well for Collegians.

We were in the major semi-final and were to meet Thirroul yet again. However, there were injury worries at the club. I was happy to find I had done enough to keep my jersey at full-back. I now had yet another worry, because the papers were writing about talent scouts being in Wollongong to watch me play in the heat of finals football. It was pressure I could have done without. My dad told me to forget about it all and just play the way I had done the last couple of games. That was not easy, given my third game was a major semi-final. Early in the game we got a penalty and I was able to slot it over which settled me down. By half-time we were 12–4 up and I had kicked three goals. By the end we had won 19–7, I had five goals to my credit and the team had scored three times with tries then worth three points each. The press went into overdrive and said I was in first class form. The result meant I was to play in a Grand Final in my fourth game in first grade. More scouts made the trip down from Sydney.

I was getting more and more plaudits and yet I had played only three games at first grade level, I thought it was crazy. My school mates were riding me hard, especially as I attended a college in the northern suburbs where Thirroul was situated and several mates lived. Added to that, the press were writing that the final was a foregone conclusion and the trophy was already in Wests' cabinet. *The Sun* on 29 September printed a story by Peter Peters, a former Manly and Wests Illawarra player, which gave me great wraps. He wrote: "Not since Graeme Langlands burst on the local scene in 1962 has the Illawarra Rugby League had a draw card like the current pin-up boy John Dorahy... Every Sydney club will have talent scouts in Wollongong to check over Dorahy following glowing reports recently about the young full back..."

I didn't read papers in those days, although mum kept an excellent diary of events and as we now know she wasn't keen on me playing at this level even if I had gone okay in the early games. I was able to put the reports to the back of my mind as I was more worried about playing in a Grand Final. I did get a big lift when the team was selected because it was announced that Tony Cull, who had initially been ruled out for the season, had recovered sufficiently to play in the Grand Final. He was, however, selected to play on the wing and I was to keep the full-back berth and once more Thirroul who would be the opposition. That was another defining moment in my early first grade career. Tony Cull was a family friend as well as a team mate. The coach could have gone with him back in the number one shirt and my career could have lasted only three games. He didn't do that, showed faith in me and my ability, and left me in the team. I also believe it was a smart ploy by the coach as Tony Cull was a prolific goalkicker within a 40 yard range. I think Tony was up around the 82 per cent to 85 per cent accuracy rate as a kicker – he was that good. And Tony was a 'toe poker', kicking the ball as I did with the toe of the boot, not like most of today's round the corner style.

On the day of the Grand Final, Warren Ryan had arranged for the team to meet at Wests' home ground, Figtree Oval. We all changed and then hopped on a bus to the ground only to arrive 20 minutes before the match was due to start. To say the officials were unhappy was an understatement, but the plan worked as the opposition were informed Wests were not at the ground and no one knew why. This possibly unsettled them a little and provided a psychological boost for Wests before the kick-off.

Wests received a terrible blow in the first half when the dynamic David Waite received a nasty shoulder injury. He had to leave the field and be replaced. However, in a very strange twist, Warren Ryan selected the front-rower Ray Staff to play at five-eighth which was an absolute genius move. Ray outshone his counterpart easily and laid a great foundation for the backs to play well. Little did many people know that Ray had played this role many times as a younger player even though it was many moons ago.

We beat them again, this time 18–11, to win the Grand Final. It was Wests' third successive Grand Final win. I had won a Grand Final blazer although I had only played four games. I wondered when the fairy tale was going to end, but as the saying goes, the rest is history.

13

1971 Wests Red Devils Premiers – John's first premiership at 17 years old. Top row: John Dorahy, Owen Smith, David Waite, Tony Cull, Greg Rodgers, Graeme Simpson; middle: Terry McCarthy, Dave Hayburn, Peter Buchanan (secretary), Tony Brown (manager), Bill Murphy (president), Ray Staff, Shane Day; front: Darryl Smith, Klaus Reh, Geoff Pol, Warren Ryan (captain-coach), Phil Charlton, John Lumsden, Dennis McCulloch, Ross Standring, Greg Buchanan (ball boy).

Those four games set me on a course that was to lead me pulling on the green and gold shirt every Australian player dreams about. Had Peter Buchanan not seen something in me, had Warren Ryan not been convinced by the arguments Peter put forward and not put me in the team, who knows just what would have happened to me. Would I even have had a professional rugby league career?

With the final won, the scouts began to put more pressure on me to go up to Sydney and I hadn't completed school yet. Mum and dad had other ideas and insisted that I complete my education before I did anything else. They had plans for my education outside football.

The coach of Thirroul and our school first XIII coach, John McCarthy, was a former Balmain player. He had advised Kevin Humphreys, Balmain's secretary, to speak to my parents and me about an opportunity to move to Sydney and play in the Tiger colours of black and gold. Humphreys visited our home and spoke about the terrific opportunity to live and study in Sydney while playing at Balmain. However, I was a quiet country lad and was not keen on leaving home for an uncertain future in the big city. I declined a very good offer and stayed at Wests Illawarra for my first full season in 1972.

At the end of season awards night held at the Coniston Hotel I was extremely pleased to see my mother and father receive an unusual award for 'production' with my sister Lesley looking on in admiration.

I played in the school's open weight league teams for two years in 1971 and 1972. We played in the final of the local schools knockout competition against Dapto High School where several of my Wests Red Devils mates played. We won both times with a very strong team in each year. This carnival attracted the best teams from across NSW and sometimes further afield such as St Gregory's College Campbelltown. They had several Islanders and Papuans attending school, so they had these big hard boppers who would cause havoc among some of the lesser teams.

I remember the two finals almost like yesterday, because they involved friends and team mates from my Wests Illawarra club in the opposition team. During both finals I reckon I was lucky not to be sent off. In 1971 I spear-tackled Chris Stocker, who lived just 400 yards up the road and Wayne Green, who lived directly behind us in the next street. He was a close friend then and still is today. The guys on the other team were livid. I would make this tackle, but it just happened when I ducked at the last second to drive with my shoulder and the momentum had them heading head first into the ground.

I guess it was either I made the tackle or I would have been bumped out of the way and looked like a sissy tackler. This taught me to tackle with better discipline because I certainly didn't want to maim any player especially mates.

The final two years of school were a hoot and though I didn't study as well as I should have, I was earmarked as someone who would get through okay. And so it proved. I achieved a well earned higher school certificate and left knowing I wouldn't have to study for a wee while. With football on my mind and had played a full season plus four games, represented the Illawarra Division, played for NSW Country on a tour and against the might of the NSWRL competition I was now at 18 years ready to push myself towards being a better player and work hard in the family business learning the meat trade from an office desk.

However, rugby league had got in the way of my dream job in the final two years at school, which was to live in Canberra and attend the Royal Military College in Duntroon, for officer training. A school friend,

Joe Wilson, went to Duntroon and I caught up with him by chance many years later. He had achieved the rank of Major and in some ways I was a little jealous, but was certainly pleased that Joey had achieved in his chosen profession. In fact Joey was a very good rugby league half-back. I didn't get the chance to ask if he played rugby union in the forces, but I am sure if he had done he would have been a success because he had a quick mind and was a capable captain in the local junior competition as a lad.

2. Second season honours

It is often the case with newcomers to the game that they suffer what is called 'second season syndrome'. That is when they fail, for whatever reason, to live up to their performances in their debut season. I never seemed to suffer that problem simply because my first season comprised only four first grade matches, I had nothing to live up to really, yet there was a weight of expectation surrounding me. It was not from me or the club, it came more from both the local and Sydney journalists. They were writing up their expectations of me and then expecting me to live up to them.

In the lead up to the 1972 season I received much more pressure from my mother who wanted me to have a year away from football and concentrate on school studies as it was my final year of high school. Dad was okay as long as I did not shirk any studies or waste time when it was study time. I also received plenty of pressure from school to consider the advantages of concentrating on studies to achieve my goals. I even had a visit at home by my favourite teacher, Father Dean, a Kiwi who loved his cricket and rugby and coached various schools teams. The year got going and I was doing it all – school studies, football at school and of course playing for Wests. Life was very busy, but fun at the same time.

That said the season did not start very well because I picked up a knee injury playing in a knockout comp in Shellharbour which caused me to miss the first game of the season. I had injured the knee playing cricket for the college and aggravated it at Shellharbour. The injury took longer to clear up than anticipated and the press boys went into a frenzy. One guy even wrote that my future was in doubt. I was only 17 and he was writing me off. Looking back, the injury was probably the best thing that could have happened to me as it meant that when I did return the season was well underway and there were other things for the press to focus on.

I got back into the team after four weeks out and it was as if I had never been away. I thought I played well. The press, however, felt that I was a shoo-in for the Illawarra rep team to play in the first round of the New South Wales Country Championship. I was just happy to be back playing for Wests and expected nothing more. When Bill Simpson of the *Illawarra Mercury* picked his squad I was in it at full-back. However, he did not pick the rep side, the selectors did.

When the side was selected I was one of eight Wests players in the squad to meet Monaro in Queanbeyan the following Sunday. On 16 April 1972 I made my rep debut for my home division, Illawarra, and I had played only a handful of first grade games. Prior to the game the *Sun Herald* wrote: "Much attention will be focussed on John Dorahy... Many regard him as the best full-back prospect since Graeme Langlands."

It was great praise to be compared with Langlands, but I thought it was a bit over the top. I was just glad to be pulling on the scarlet red rep shirt for the first time for the Illawarra Division at this level. Our coach was Tony Paskins, a strong looking man with a reputation for being a tough centre for Eastern Suburbs Roosters and, for the greater part of his career Workington in England. Tony went on to coach Easts in Sydney the following season. During the lead-up to this match, we stayed overnight at the Royal Hotel in Queanbeyan. We had a pre-game meeting on the Sunday at 12.30pm. Never before and never since have I had such a novel, but interesting, preparation for a young bloke. Tony gathered us all around, spoke to us about how to play the match and then asked everyone to partake in his own style of pre-match preparation. He had arranged for four dozen eggs, a box of Glucodine powder and three bottles of sweet sherry. Gee, I was 17 years old and never a drinker, but was subjected to having to do what each of the other players had to do and drink this concoction. Mind you I used to love the egg flips my mum would make which weren't too far removed from Tony's concoction with milk instead of sherry. The promise behind it was to open the lungs.

Tony made the drink himself – two eggs, a tablespoon of Glucodine powder and a good swig of sweet sherry. I managed to get it down, but I abruptly returned it straight back to the floor. It opened everything up alright, with plenty of laughs for my new team-mates before we promptly left for the ground.

One point from this match defined how I wanted to play, I received the ball about 20 metres from our line on a short side with little room to exploit options, so I ran straight at the left winger and made a small right foot step followed with a big left foot step immediately. I went past the winger without a hand on me, the full-back was out of position towards the middle of the pitch waiting for the play to swing to the open side and I took off for the tryline. That 80 yard run gave me a great deal of confidence for the rest of my career and was certainly a highlight in my first rep game. We managed to beat Monaro and I was delighted to keep the shirt for the semi-final against Western Division back in Wollongong.

In the semi-final I managed to score a try in our 23–18 win over the Western Division team at Wollongong Showground. The Australian selectors Ernie Hammerton and Henry Porter were at the game and seemingly were impressed with the performance I gave. I had not played a dozen first team games and I was going to play in a Country Divisional Final.

In the final Illawarra were to play Northern Division in Tamworth and I was selected again to play. We travelled to Tamworth on a very old DC3 plane from Sydney airport, reputedly one of the safest planes to fly. I had visions of the Munich air disaster involving the great Manchester United Football team of the 1950s, but we arrived safely. In a one sided affair we beat Northern Division 32–15. With a try and three goals I was more than happy with my contribution. I was even happier when it was announced I was in the NSW Country squad that was to go on a three match tour to Queensland playing against North Queensland, Central Queensland and South Queensland.

I was sitting quietly at the Wests Tamworth Leagues Club after the match drinking orange juice. I was too young to have a beer. I was waiting for the team announcement and for us to leave and return to Sydney. I had to keep asking myself when the bubble was going to burst. Could I keep going at this rate? I had achieved more in six months than many players do in their entire careers. People had been telling me I would be selected, but I really didn't believe I would be. I took it all in good stride because I was totally unaware of the importance of this selection. I was happy that Warren Ryan was to be the Country captain and another three players were chosen to tour: Barry Hulbert, Kevin Goldspink and Shane Day.

This opportunity to tour with the Country rugby league squad was an eye opener to what life holds for achieving standards. The first match against North Queensland was a cracker and I was fortunate to play well. I scored a try and kicked three goals in a well drilled team coached by the legend Arthur Summons. When the team was to board the plane for Rockhampton to play Central Queensland an unbelievable situation occurred. We were delayed due to a bomb scare. Yes, back in the 1970s there were fools about who tried to create havoc in the same way as today's terrorists do. Fortunately nothing happened and the plane carried everyone on to Rocky for our next match. In the lead up to this match the Central QRL announced they would not allow the NSW Country trainer Les Griffin on the pitch to attend players when they were injured. They said an ambulance man could attend the players. Les was going to leave the tour and return to Wollongong, but Shane Day, Barry Hulbert and I encouraged him to stay on and complete the job. This was important for both Shane and Barry as they were injured. I also received great assistance from this legend of trainers. We won 24–0 and moved on to the final match of the tour.

This was against South Queensland and saw some familiar names pop up – Wayne Bennett, Col Weiss, Jim Murphy and John Lang. they were all well known players with Wayne Bennett and John Lang going on to become first class coaches in the NRL competition. In a tough match the NSW Country team, though starting as underdogs, won a close encounter 20–14 at Lang Park. It was the first match in which I had to receive treatment for a cut over the right eye. That was okay, but when I was taken to the changing room for stitching I was given a lesson in being tough. The Doctor completed the stitching without an anaesthetic to ease the pain of the needle being pushed through my skin on 10 occasions. I was then given clearance to go back and join the fray, which I duly did and thoroughly enjoyed it.

The press, of course, had a field day. It seemed to them that I could do nothing wrong and people were continually linking me with the great full-backs who had left Wollongong and gone on to first grade football and higher honours in Sydney. These included players who I had and still look up to, Graeme Langlands, Keith Barnes, Colin Dunn, Bob Smithies and others. People were forgetting I was still at college completing my final year of High School and was not yet 18. Tony Paskins even said I was a 'cert' to play for Australia. I was happy playing for Wests and college at this stage in my life and if I was selected for higher honours then it was a bonus. Credit should go to the players I played with and Warren Ryan who was so instrumental in buffing my abilities to the point of where people were making such positive comments.

I thoroughly enjoyed the NSW Country tour to Queensland with some seasoned players with Sydney experience and quality country players as was the case in the era before full-time professionalism. Country had won all three matches and a highlight of the tour was getting the chance to play on Lang Park. The selectors had taken two full-backs on the tour which was not something they normally did so I guess there was some apprehension about playing a 17-year-old player at that level. I handled all that was thrown at me comfortably and came away form the tour satisfied I had achieved the goals set prior to leaving.

On my return my name was being linked to a number of Sydney clubs. Both Canterbury and Newton let it be known that they were interested in signing me. I was getting ready for what was to be the biggest game by far of my career to date.

I had been selected at full-back for the NSW Country first team to meet Sydney at the holy grail of footy, the Sydney Cricket Ground. Mind you, the guy wearing the full-back shirt for the opposition was none other than the legend Graeme Langlands which was a bit disconcerting. When we got back from the Queensland tour we went into camp at the Bondi Hotel opposite Bondi Beach. I wondered why they would put country lads opposite a beach, but hey everyone enjoyed the opportunity to go for a walk on the beach or a surf if they were game enough to take on the cold water of late autumn in May.

On the day of the game we travelled down to the SCG and I remember sitting in the sheds trying to come to terms with just where I was. I remember the referee calling us out. The Country team always took the field first. We ran the down the steps from the SCG rooms onto a ground full of sunshine and cheering fans because hundreds of people had travelled many miles to see their beloved country lads put one over the city boys. I ran around to get a feel of the place with my team mates in their country maroon shirts with the two gold vees. Then the City team ran onto the paddock. The sun seemed to accentuate the brightness of their gold shirts and glistening two blue vees. I thought to myself that they looked awesome, huge, twice the size of our boys, larger than life. It was only then I realised that my knees were trembling and knew I was in a big match.

Not surprisingly we got a bit of a drubbing, 35–8, from the internationals in that City side. Back then the difference between the two sides was no where near as great as it is today. Then players in the Country did not always want to go to Sydney and so there were some great players in our team such as Johnny Greaves, David Waite and Allan Fitzgibbon. However, on the day we simply could not hold the City boys.

I was pleased with my performance as were some of the press. The greatest experience of my rugby life up to that point was scoring the try for Country at the SCG against City, the feeling that gave me is difficult to describe even now. The try was as a result of a set move that was a bit revolutionary at the time. We set up a situation where it appeared that we were going to move the ball infield from the touchline, but at the last second Warren Ryan and I swept back onto the short side to create a three-on-two situation. It worked like a dream and Ryan went through with the ball, got smashed by Langlands, but slipped the ball to me in the tackle and I literally coasted in. The feeling when I touched down was a bit surreal but certainly very enjoyable. It was even more pleasing as it was the first try of the game and all the Country boys were ecstatic.

There were some journalists who felt I had let myself down while others thought that I had been put into the side when I was too young. I was more concerned with what the players thought as they are always the best judge. Graeme Langlands gave me some good wraps and that was all I was bothered about. He said "He is exactly the same mover as Les Johns... I have no doubt Dorahy has earned his Country firsts rating, but given more experience he would have had a bigger impact.... I told him after the game that he had only to stick to the game and he will enjoy a great football future." At the time I had no idea just how prophetic Langlands's words would be.

Interestingly during this match a peculiar, but important, learning event occurred. When running the ball forward north toward the Paddington end I was tackled by Graeme Langlands and Mark Harris. Nothing much about the tackle but... after playing the ball I was punched by Changa which stunned me a bit, although it was not strong enough to knock me over. With the punch Changa said "welcome to rep football". I was gobsmacked, but laughed at the time and just jogged back into my position as I had no answer other than to play as well as I could.

The rest of that second season went pretty much as my first season had. The only difference was that it was much longer for me in the first team. We met Thirroul in the Grand Final once more and overcame them 23–9. The other important event was in early July when I was in the NSW Country side that played the touring New Zealand team at Queanbeyan. If there was such a thing as second season syndrome then I would have to experience it in what would be my third season in first grade. Every thing in the second season had gone pretty much as it had in those four weeks in my first one. I was still on cloud nine and at that age you do not think it will ever come to an end. It did as once the Country verses City game was over the school holidays came to an end and it was back to my real job, trying to get through my finals at school.

The big Sydney clubs were all clamouring to get me to sign for them, but they lacked the firepower my mum had. She was in no mood to change her stand on my education. As far as she was concerned finishing school was not negotiable; football took second place to education. When I was in year 11 in 1971 and I was a big Balmain fan Kevin Humphreys, the Balmain secretary, came with an offer to sign for them, everyone was shocked when I turned it down. In 1972, Tony Paskins, who had coached the Illawarra Divisional side, went up to Easts as coach and the following year he asked me to sign for them, but I did not want to leave home so turned them down as well. It was all getting a bit crazy. I said I wanted to finish school and play country football for another year before even thinking about Sydney and the reporters were all over me. *Rugby League Week* in May 1972 ran the story with a front page headline of "Wonder boy! – And he's strictly hands-off!

What should I do? I considered all options and met various people who would give free advice, but the decision I made was the best at the time. I felt I was not ready for Sydney or its football and people who I respected in the game advised me to spend a little more time at Wests. With hindsight it was the best advice I could have been given. There was a great deal going on in my life at that time and trying to fit it all in and break into Sydney football would have been just too much. I do know one thing, whenever people ask me what was the luckiest break I ever got in footy I would have to say it was the break to the bone in Tony Cull's wrist because it really did set me on a career in the game. I would go on to play until I was into my 30s and love every minute of it.

For me these opportunities and decisions were all part of the growing and learning phase of life and I wouldn't at this stage have changed anything. Mum and dad were right to have me stay in Wollongong to complete school and then worry about the rest of life as it would unfold.

Enjoying my 21st birthday celebrations with mum, Nola, and dad, Kevin.

With cousin Tony Dorahy at Leigh.

3. Freezing in Leigh

My third season was in many respects a case of *déjà vu*. Once again I was fortunate enough to represent the NSW Country side at the SCG in the annual City verses Country game. I felt exactly the same second time round, even though the result was the same – a 33–17 drubbing. Once again I was lucky enough to cross for a three pointer, as did another Country boy who went on to become a legend in the game, Mick Cronin. Mind you, there were one or two in the opposition who made a mark in the game a well. Langlands skippered the side and it included Bob Fulton, Tim Pickup, Tommy Raudonikis, John Quayle and Arthur Beetson, not a bad line up in any generation. Overall, the City team was chock full of stars and it was a true test of character and ability to face them a second time in 12 months.

The papers were still writing that this club or that club wanted me to sign for them. They were also telling me that I needed to move to a Sydney club if I was to further my career. There was all of this speculation and I was only 18. It is interesting to recall what it was like in 1973 given the size of the contracts flying around today. I have a note detailing my end of season payment from Wests. It said:

First Grade

13 ½ wins @ $60	$810
5 losses @ $20	$100
Incentive	$200
Total	$1,110
Make Ups	$160

Deductions

Shorts	$4
Club membership	$1
Donation D.H.	$20
Minor League	$20
Photo	$14

Total Payment   **$1,211**

That was payment for the whole season and I had to buy my own shorts to play in.

For the second time I made the front page of *Rugby League Week* under the banner headline: 'Dorahy! – He must come to Sydney'. The introduction to the story read: "Two of the greatest full-backs Les

Johns and Keith Barnes agree that John Dorahy the 18 year old full-back from Illawarra club Western Suburbs is a future international."

No pressure there then. At the time it seemed everyone knew what was best for me and were quite happy to tell me and anyone who would listen also. If there was any chance that I was going to start believing all that was being written about me it was quickly and frighteningly dispelled.

We were playing Corrimal at Ziems Park in a first versus second in the ladder clash. We had been playing about 30 minutes when I was hit with a two-man heavy tackle. As I hit the ground the world simply blacked out. I could not see a thing – it was as if my eyes had stopped working. As I was led off the field it was the scariest experience I had had on the footy field up to this point. Thank God once I got into the sheds my sight slowly came back. It was then I realised just how fragile a career in footy could be. The press boys could write what they like, but a player was simply one tackle away from disaster. It had a chastening effect on me and certainly stopped me believing what was written in the papers.

The second thing to knock me back was that Wests lost the Grand Final at the end of the season. In what was billed as the best final seen at Wollongong Showground, Thirroul pipped us at the post to win 8–6 and take the trophy. It was the first time I had been on the losing side in a final in my three years in first grade. Warren Ryan had vacated his role as coach of Wests with Klaus Reh taking over the reigns. I am sure in hindsight we missed Warren greatly, although at the time as a young player I just got on with playing as best I could.

The disappointment I felt was tempered a little by the knowledge that I had the opportunity to go and play footy in England. I thought it would be a great experience and remove me from the hot bed of the Sydney press and their speculation about me.

I had known for a little while that the chance to play in England was on the cards. Dave Cox, who was coaching Castleford at the time and an uncle of mine, Bill Beedles, an Englishman who married my father's sister, were both good mates and helped set up the move. They had already arranged for my cousin, Tony Dorahy, to go for a couple of months and they stepped in and got me a spot. Having talked things over with dad, the decision was that it would help me both on and off the field. Things had been crazier than usual in the lead up to the Grand Final. The papers were full of stories about how I would have to miss the final if I was selected for the tour to England by the Australians. I may well have dreamed of getting the nod, but my chances were very slim, given the quality of players ahead of me.

At the time Graeme Eadie was playing first grade with Manly and I always felt he was in the driving seat for the full-back berth on the tour. I realised that if I were to play the off season in England I would need to leave as soon as I could after the Grand Final if we got there.

It was a bit of a shock for the Wests' executive committee when on the eve of the final, I had to go to them and ask for clearance to play in England. They had no idea that I was even considering such a move, but negotiations were well down the track with a First Division club there. At that stage, because things had not been finalised, I did not want to say where I was to play in case it did not work out and I was left with egg on my face.

Of course, everyone expected that I would stay in Wollongong and sign for a Sydney club, so it was a surprise for them when they found I was to play the off season in the old country. I wrote to the secretary of the club and clearance was really a formality, but it came as a shock when I finally revealed I was to play for Leigh. The other thing no one was aware of was that I had more or less decided that I would sign for Western Suburbs Magpies in the NSWRL for the following season.

It was a great time to be an Australian footballer having a stint in England, because the Australian Kangaroo side was going to tour. I had not made the tour squad, but was still travelling over to play first grade in Lancashire and, if the chance arose, I could go and watch the Australians play in England. The fairy tale, if I can call it that, seemed to continue once I got to Leigh. Tony and I met Dave Cox at Heathrow Airport and before we could say anything Dave had us at a bar downing a "pint" of lager. Well, both Tony and I almost choked when taking the first mouthful as it was warm and not cold like Aussie beer. Enough said that we soon became accustomed to warm beer once living in Leigh.

When Tony and I arrived at Hilton Park met the club secretary, John Stringer, and went to watch the club play in a floodlit midweek game. We stood on the terraces, sort of incognito but, unfortunately, not wearing the correct footwear. As the game wore on we were freezing from the feet up. I had never been as cold in my life. I played in reserve grade the following Saturday and quickly got called up to

27

the first team on the Sunday as a substitute. It was then I learned a very important rugby lesson. We travelled over to Hull to play Hull KR.

At the time two of the Hull KR players were Australians – Allan Fitzgibbon and Bobbie Smithies – both of whom played in the comp against me in Illawarra for the Dapto Canaries. Of course I had played with Allan in the Illawarra rep team. The lesson went like this: the previous season I had played against Smithies as a centre alongside Warren Ryan. As Bobbie was passing the ball he put out a hand to fend me away. I knocked it down and tackled him high with a good one under the chin that stunned him a wee bit. Bobbie never got the chance to repay the compliment, but at Hull he did. I had not been on the field long when I chimed into the line from full-back and Smithies was waiting. He struck, my lights went out and I remember nothing more of the match. I did, however, learn that if you dish it out you have to be prepared to take it back. You may well have to wait a while for the repayment, but it will come. Of course, on the other side of the ledger, you have to be patient for your chance to square up.

One highlight for me in England was having the chance to play against the Australian tourists for Leigh. We began well and at full-back I had played quite well in the first half. We left the field 4–3 in the lead. I was unimpressed with the Australians' performance and felt that the forwards were perhaps lacking some discipline and took it a little easy on Leigh. The coach and skipper 'Changa' Langlands must have felt that there was a possibility that they could lose, so he brought on Bob Fulton and Arthur Beetson.

That change made the difference as they had too much class for the Leigh lads. Leigh were a capable team playing a good brand of football with some good lads such as Jim Fiddler and Mick Stacey. I found out from David Waite, my Wests team mate, that before the game Bobby Fulton had been pumping him for information about me, the way I played and if I was as good as the press made me out to be. He had played against me in the City versus Country match in May. To his credit, Waite told him "Look, he is a good young player just trying to make his way in the game".

Tony and I took the chance to drive to London to watch the England versus Australia test at Wembley and loved the beauty and history of the stadium. Unfortunately, on this occasion there were only 10,000 singing spectators all gathered in one corner of the ground. It was interesting when the singing or yelling began it echoed around the stadium like down a canyon. A good time was had and it was a game that the English team were well up for winning in fine fashion. Tony and I bought an old Austin A40 in which, when driving down the M1 we were passed by the big lorries often and the poor old car shook as they passed. We stopped off at Heathrow at 4.00am after leaving Leigh around 12 midnight so we could get a little sleep on the benches in the terminal.

I soon worked out that the English game was a strong game and very enjoyable as it was based around using the ball to create the advantage by getting it into space. Unlike Australia which had by now started to restrict players' options and lessen possible mistake opportunities. Of course, the grounds were soft under foot due to playing in the autumn and winter months, but I found this equally invigorating as it was different to Australia. As it turned out I didn't stay as long as I would have like to because I had to get home to begin training for the upcoming Sydney season.

If I was to compare the two competitions at this time I suggest the English game was still enjoying the benefits of open attractive ball-playing football where the supporters would be involved through their singing and chanting. I thoroughly enjoyed that aspect of the English game where the supporters got involved. Also the Leigh management were very good to us Aussies during our short stay.

While I was in Leigh, events were still going on back home. Don Parish, who had coached at Wests from 1968 to 1970, was now the coach as Western Suburbs Magpies in the NSWRL competition. He was keen to sign me. I was now happy to sign for the Magpies and ready to test myself in the premier competition in Australia.

Other clubs were coming in with offers to pay me the maximum $2,000 signing-on fee plus $200 a game, which was the maximum allowed by the NSWRL at that time. It was a rule that had only been introduced that season. If I had gone to Sydney earlier then I would have been earning a great deal more than I was for the Magpies.

I was happy to be going to the Magpies simply because I knew they would give me a chance at first grade footy quicker than some of the bigger clubs would. The problem was that history was about to repeat itself again, with the same outcome as before.

At the mighty Wests Magpies.

4.   Western Suburbs

When I arrived home from Leigh early in 1974 I met the Western Suburbs people, coach Don Parish and club secretary Neville Bayfield along with my father Kevin and a surprise guardian, Warren Ryan. Parish was quite surprised that I brought Warren along, but given the maximum payment structure and nowhere else to move to I eventually signed to play for Western Suburbs. It was a huge relief to me to have it over and get ready to attend training. Once the deal was done the Sydney press got off my back a little and I got down to serious training. As mentioned, it was only as the season was beginning that history repeated itself. The club had arranged to play a friendly game back in Wollongong against Port Kembla. When we trotted out onto the paddock there was a large crowd there. Most of them had come to see me playing with the 'big boys'. I did well because I wanted to impress all my friends. I was delighted when I crossed for a three pointer and then made another. In addition, I kicked five goals from as many attempts, but it was all going too well. Late in the game I went to make a tackle and felt a sharp pain in my thumb when I smacked Greg Rose on the top of his head. I played on for a little bit, but after the game my hand and thumb were really sore.

I later found that the thumb was broken and needed to be pinned. I would have to miss the whole of the Wills Cup comp; the estimate was that I would be out for five weeks. In retrospect, it was a very good injury – if there is such a thing – simply because it kept me out of the press spotlight, but still allowed me to do most of the hard pre-season training. One factor I had never considered, however, was the travel involved in getting to and from training each week and on game day. I reckon I was clocking up around 500 to 600 kilometres a week.

In March that year tragedy struck home and showed me the fragility of footy in general and life in particular. The guy whose broken wrist kick started my football career sadly passed away. Tony Cull was involved in an accident in the local Mount Kembla mine where he worked. The continuous miner machine he was operating backed into a wooden prop. The impact of the collision forced his head onto the controls of the miner and he suffered severe head injuries and brain damage. Sadly, he never regained consciousness and died. He was only in his early 20s. His passing saddened me greatly, not just because he was a former team mate, but was also a friend and neighbour.

When I was fit to play, full-back Tony Ford, a long term Wests Magpies player had been playing very well. However, Don Parish stayed true to his word about getting me to play first grade as soon as possible. He selected me to play in the centre, which I didn't mind as I had played centre for much of my first two full seasons in Wollongong. I have to say that the team was not going well. We seemed to lack consistency and were unable to string two good games together. Don Parish persevered, but then decided that changes had to be made if we were to start to climb the ladder. It was in mid-June that the decision was made to give the youngsters their head. Against Cronulla Parish picked a very young side and it paid dividends because we turned them over 16–6, when no one expected us to. It was a defining moment in the club's and my own season because we went from strength to strength from that game onwards. We had some experienced players in the squad, but there were young reserve grade players who progressed to such an extent they simply could not be ignored. The coach gave them the opportunity and they took it

As far as I was concerned, I seemed to have one of those purple patches of form players have, but in my case it seemed to last for a good length of time. What I did find was that the press were quick to pick up on any perceived mistakes I made as well as the good things I did. One headline read: "Dorahy Puzzle for Wests. Brilliant, mediocre."

Jeff Collinson wrote: "But while his attacking play was outstanding he missed vital tackles and twice wasted penalty kicks by failing to find touch." This was after we had beaten Parramatta 14–8; I wonder what he would have written had the score line gone the other way?

We strung together a series of wins which put us into the top five on the ladder and into the play-off spots. At the same time, generally speaking, I was getting good wraps for my performances. I remember going to Lidcombe Oval to play the mighty Manly team which contained at the time both Mal Reilly and Phil Lowe from England. We put on a performance which had everyone harping back to the Wests teams of the early 1960s. We beat Manly 22–17. I remember managing to cross for a try at a crucial time in the game which more or less secured the win. Reilly was not a happy bunny because he received his marching orders from the ref for the second successive game, this time for a tackle on Tommy Raudonikis.

Everything was going well for me and the club. In just 11 appearances I had scored 91 points and it looked certain I would top the ton by the end of the regular season. Certainly the coach was delighted that his faith in me had been justified. More importantly he had turned the whole season around and done it with a bunch of youngsters at that.

Mind you, my season could be summed up in one word: travel. One writer reckoned that in scoring 100 points in my debut season I had notched up 13,600 miles in travelling back and forth to Sydney. I was working as a salesman in the family meat business, having moved out of the office as a trainee accountant. I had to make the 110 mile round trip three or four times a week. It did not bother me when we clinched a play-off spot at the end of the regular season. For me, the fairy tale was still going on. In my first season in the NSWRL I was playing in the play-offs. Some players go through their entire careers and never achieve that. To make the finals for the first time in 11 years, we needed to get a result against Cronulla at the aptly named Endeavour Field. We were 8–7 down when we went into the sheds at half-time, but were confident because we knew we had wind advantage in the second half. We used it to keep the pressure on Cronulla and came away with a 20–8 victory.

This was a defining game for the Wests Magpies club because it provided the springboard for a successful period over many years. With the inclusion of the younger breed, including Mick Luibinskas, Pat Hundy, Geoff Foster, Trevor Reardon, Trevor Scarr mixed in with the older tough breed, Tom Raudonikis, John Elford, Jim Murphy, Shane Day, Steven Knight and Robbie Parker, the old Wests' formula was being left behind.

It was strange to be going into training while others were heading off for the surf. It was not like being in Wollongong as we prepared for the game against South Sydney in the preliminary semi at the Sydney Sportsground. None of the team had experienced such preparations before and certainly never the weight of expectations the fans had for success. Back then the ground ran from east to west so you either had the sun at your back or in your face. Souths played the first half with a slight wind in their favour and once again we went to the sheds at half-time 8–7 down. As we left the field we could see a storm coming up and by the time we returned to the field there was a southerly gale blowing in our favour. As in the Cronulla game the previous week we came home with a win, this time 24–8, to set up a gigantic clash with the mighty Manly club. It could be said that the weather won the game for us that day. Few people, if anyone outside our supporters, expected us to win that Souths game. We were a young, relatively inexperienced, outfit and they had a wealth of experience in their side. For my part, as the season had worn on, more and more of the Sydney press were concentrating on my style of play and coming to the conclusion that I always seemed to be cool under pressure. The nickname 'Joe Cool' was given to me by two team mates at Wests, Jon Clarke and Geoff Foster, for the way I nonchalantly returned to retrieve a ball kicked downfield or took a high ball before heading back upfield to regularly beat the first defender.

I certainly was not feeling cool when we took the field in the match one paper billed as: 'The Manly Princes versus The Wests Paupers at the SCG'.

Having played in a couple of Country versus City games at the SCG I thought I knew what to expect, but nothing prepared me for that minor semi-final. I had never been more nervous, in an emotional way, in my career and I think that was because I loved playing footy and would have played for nothing. To me, it was simply playing that was important, not if we won or how big an occasion the game was, although winning made a great difference when all was said and done. That semi was a big occasion, a 40,000 plus crowd had swarmed into the SCG. I believe I had my best game of footy of the season that day as we turned round a 15–4 deficit. As the game wore on we kept the scoreboard ticking over until we were 23–15 in front with the game seemingly in the bag. So we thought. With eight minutes to go Bobby Fulton had other ideas and raced over for a try in the corner. To make matters worse Graham Eadie added the conversion with a real pressure kick to take the score to 23–20. We managed to hang on for the victory in those last few minutes.

I believe to this day it was skipper Tommy Raudonikis's efforts that won the game for us, but the press will always favour the younger upstart and the headlines read 'Dorahy slays Eagles'.

What was not in doubt was that it was a superb game of footy for a bumper crowd. We were through to the preliminary final to face Easts and another big occasion. In my four seasons in first grade footy I had reached a final in every season. We had not achieved anything yet. We still had to over come Easts and then Canterbury in the Grand Final if we were to become champions.

Another crossroads in my life – what if I had taken the chance to play with Easts when Tony Paskins asked me to join him in Sydney for the 1973 season. Would I have been playing against Wests? Would I have still been in Sydney? I would never know as my decision to play on in Wollongong was reward enough and the choice I made was still exciting.

We went into the final against Easts full of hope and expectation and left full of despair and dejection. We simply did not perform and were blown away by Easts, and the weather for that matter, 23–2. It was a terrible let down for the players, club, supporters and me. We were never in the game. Towards the end the heavens opened and we played in a torrential downpour which finally washed away what hopes we may have had of salvaging the game. Not that I knew anything about that. Sadly I got injured late in the first half and was unable to take the field for the second. There was no comeback this time, it was a game too far for us and we would watch the Grand Final from the sidelines. For me, the season had been a great success. I had raced to one of the quickest 100 points in a debut season and made the play-offs. But after all the travelling I had done I was glad to put my feet up and await the grind of pre-season training once again.

At season's end the club arranged for a trip to Townsville in North Queensland to play an exhibition match against the local rep team. There was a large crowd in attendance and a win for Wests. Unlike some modern day players that fall foul of the constabulary and life's expectations of good morals I can say that this team were well behaved with no problems of misbehaviour to report. All they wanted was a relaxing moment with a drink, to tell some stories from the year past and for those moving on enjoying a last session with their mates.

In 1975, as in my first season at Wests, prior to the season's main comp we played in the Wills Cup. In pre-season I did not pick up any injuries. We did not have the easiest of draws as we met Canterbury in the first round, given that they were beaten Grand Finalists I think everyone felt they were the favourites. We ran out winners 7–2 and that set the press boys off once again. This time the talk was of representative teams and me being in the driving seat for the number one jersey for Australia. By now I was used to the 'tripe' from the press. I just got on with playing and enjoying the footy. If the first round of the Wills Cup was a toughie to win, our reward was a game against Easts, who having beaten us in the Preliminary Final in 1974 had gone on to win the Grand Final. There was the revenge factor of course. We continued with the form we had shown against Canterbury and came home with a 15–2 win. We had a lot of confidence that we could go even further this coming season. Maybe this was the catalyst for Wests to shake off their lethargy and go onto win the 1975 competition.

Unfortunately, it was not to be and the Wills Cup and the season itself were not the success everyone hoped for. With hindsight it is easy to see just why that was. We did not make the play-offs. In the following season, 1976 the young team that had made the play-offs in 1974 simply failed to kick on and develop.

In my opinion the reason was due to the mentality of the Wests board, that of being the perennial poor relation in the league. They either could not, or would not, splash out the cash to bring in players who would have taken us to the next level and enable us to compete with the big clubs in Sydney.

It would be true to say that in 1975, my second season in Sydney, I did experience that dreaded 'second season syndrome'. Teams were more and more setting out to target me and if possible get me out of the game. I would like to say more by fair means than foul, but that was not the case. The nature of the game back then was different and a lot more garbage was allowed to go on than it is today. We played Newtown in the Amco Cup and on at least four occasions, I went up to take high balls and got clattered while doing so. I found that I was releasing the ball in a pass and seconds later would be tackled off the ball, elbows would be left raised as a tackle was made on me.

In that game I needed treatment four times after illegal tackles. The press were quick to jump on the fact that I was being targeted. I would like to say that it didn't bother me, but of course it did, and my form suffered a little. My goalkicking form dropped away. I was missing more kicks at goal than I was hitting and it needed addressing sooner rather than later. I remembered what Keith Barnes used to do to address such problems and it was something I had done myself in junior footy. As a 'toe' kicker, it was deemed an excellent method of improving your accuracy. I went back to practicing kicking along the sideline trying to ensure the ball travelled from my boot in a straight line and I soon had my technique as fluid as I could. It must have worked as I got back on track.

In the May 1975 I was invited by Trevor Reardon, a guy who was by now a very good friend and team mate, to visit the Concord RSL club on the Sunday night after the match for a couple of drinks and review the local 'culture'. It had taken me some almost 18 months to venture out into the nightlife of inner west Sydney, but it was lucky I went out that night.

It was on that night I met my future wife. I was stood around the bar with the lads enjoying a really sociable evening with team mates and my friend from Wollongong, Sean '007' Connolly, who was good enough to travel with me on this night out. If the truth be told, I was absolutely out of my depth as I was still the shy country guy just playing football and working in the family business.

It was not long into the night, say 8.30pm, when I noticed this young vivacious girl at a table on the right of the room as you look away from the bar, probably 12 metres away. I felt I had to make a move and meet her! I said to 'Double O' "Mate, see that good sort over there?" questioning his eyesight. I should have known Sean would have seen her before I did, but he had also seen Linda's friend, a blonde girl who happened to be my team mate's sister, Jenny Rigney. I then sought Sean's assistance by getting him to ask this beautiful woman to a dance and suss out what she was like. Initially Sean said no, but I coerced him into it by threatening not to drive him home to Wollongong that night.

Well, Sean went over asked this girl for a dance, only for her to ask me to look after her handbag while she danced. To my surprise it didn't last more than two minutes and Sean was back to our group. I went across to speak to her and introduce myself because I had to know who this woman was. Both Linda and I had decided that we wanted to meet.

Linda hadn't wanted to go out, but was encouraged to by her mother Ida, and have some fun. Linda worked two jobs then and spent her time in bed all day on Sundays and did not go out at night. I guess it is another crossroads – if I hadn't gone to the Concord RSL that night and Linda hadn't taken her mum's advice – would we be together? I don't know. But I do know I wouldn't have had the chance to have the three wonderful children we have now if I hadn't gone out that night.

After Sean had come back I built the courage to go over to Linda to have a chat, and the rest is history. As I was the quiet one I was more nervous than at any time in my career when I was sitting with Linda and talking. I was about to take my leave and go back to the lads without asking Linda out – even though I was desperate to do so – and she asked whether I would like to go with her to an engagement party in six weeks time. I then reciprocated and asked Linda out the next weekend to the football at Lidcombe Oval and watch Wests Magpies play.

Linda said "Yes" and now I had to find her place in North Strathfield on Sunday morning and take someone unknown to me to a game, which doubled my nerves big time.

I drove into Wellbank Street, North Strathfield on the next Sunday morning in my Holden wagon. As I slowly moved up the street, I cacked myself and turned around to drive to the ground and not pick her up. It could have been so different. Here I was, a first grade rugby league player, unable to drive to a beautiful girl's parents' home and pick her up to go to the football. I thought "you fool what are doing, just turn around and go to meet her." Funny thing was though when picking up Linda on this day and the next few Sundays there was never anyone else around. I would sheepishly walk up to the front door, knock and wait nervously for either one of Linda's parents or her siblings to open the door to greet me. Well, I needn't have been worried because when Linda opened the door and invited me into the lounge room, no one was about. Linda would pick up her bag and we would leave with me none the wiser.

We arrived at Lidcombe Oval parking in the player's car park and walked over to the North-West hill where my parents, friends and some players gathered before games to talk and watch the two lower grades sides play before going into the change room for our preparation.

I introduced Linda to my parents but as luck would have it Linda then sat down on my mother's left side, which was her deaf ear. I left shortly after to go to the change room and left Linda to fend for herself with my Wollongong friends and my parents. When Linda tried to speak to my mum she had no reaction because of mum's deafness. As I later found out, Linda at first wondered if meeting the parents of her new friend was a bad dream. However, she tapped mum on the arm and the explanation was given, so Linda then sat on mum's good side.

I soon found out that the Mitchell family were died in the wool Magpies supporters, but Linda detested rugby league and hadn't gone for years. She preferred to stay in bed all day and read a book after working a second job on Friday and Saturday nights. All that changed pretty quickly. Linda's Nan, Rita Mitchell the matriarch of the family was a proud Wests supporter and told Linda to treat me better than the other boys she had dated. Linda duly did and after a quick three months going out, mostly to the footie, we were engaged.

The season went along similar tracks like my first and we continued to surprise teams and the press alike. We won more than we lost and along the way I seemed to be scoring regularly which kept my name in the spotlight. I had a good run of form and people were claiming I must be the best full-back in the world, high praise but I wondered what criteria these people used? I had other problems to bother about. My two year contract with Wests was coming to an end and they were keen to sign me to a long term deal. Other clubs were aware of the situation and they were interested in getting me to join them. Wests offered me a five-year deal worth $40,000, but I was only interested in a two-year deal. Also, I was beginning to come to terms with just how much I was worth to clubs and set my sights on a $10,000 a year deal if I could get it.

If that were not enough we had the World Cup comp going on in Australia and people were tipping me to be selected for the green and gold. This time I did feel I was in with a chance and was desperately trying not to let it affect my game. Then Wests let it be known that while my contract was up at the end of the season they had an option on me and they were so desperate to keep me they would consider going to court to enforce the option. All I wanted was to play footy. Eventually I settled on a three-year deal with Wests. One reason for doing so was the desire I had to play an off-season in England again. I felt they would be more amenable to such a move than would a new club for which I had just signed. There was a chance that I could go over and play for Castleford because Dave Cox was coaching there.

As we got to the business end of the season once again there was one event which left a nasty taste in the mouth. We had gone to the Belmore Sports Ground to play Canterbury and managed to get a tough, uncompromising 7–7 draw. The Canterbury secretary, Peter

Moore claimed we had used an ineligible player when the coach, Don Parish had sent Mick Luibinskas on as a replacement. Moore contended that as Luibinskas had not played a full reserve grade game he was unable to take the field. The one point we had grafted for was taken away by the NSWRL authorities who upheld Moore's claim. The loss of that point dropped us down to fifth in the table and made us vulnerable to not making the play-offs. Sadly, as I said earlier, we failed to make the finals and set off for a holiday sooner than we had the previous season.

Earlier that season I had planned to go around Australia with my best mates from Wollongong, but this came to a thundering halt after I met Linda and fell head-over-heels in love. It was either Linda or the trip and wisely I chose Linda. By this time we had been going out together for just on three months and decided it was time and we wanted to get married.

We met in May 1975 and in August I sought Linda's parent's permission to take her hand in marriage. The wedding was set for March 1976, just before the start of the season. All Don Mitchell could say was "I could take the ladder from the shed if I wanted." We had a fantastic summer and were looking forward to a great 1976, getting married and setting up house while continuing to play football for the mighty Magpies.

The 1976 season began with the customary pre-season competition. We had to play Parramatta at the old Parramatta Oval. This was not the best of grounds to play at. It was almost devoid of grass and hard as rock. During the first half I went into tackle John Peard, the Parramatta stand-off who was a very clever player with a deft kicking game, especially bombs that seem to hang for minutes before descending to a player about to be smashed by a quick following defensive team. His kicks often resulted in a try for Parramatta either from a dropped ball or a mistake by the catching team. While making the tackle on Peard, my right leg went under his body and all I remember is a crack of the bone in the ankle. There was little pain, but I couldn't stand up and knew it was serious. This was not good because Linda and I were due to get married in two weeks.

I was carried off the field on a stretcher to the change room and then moved to another room away from the players who were about to come in for their half-time break. The ambulance soon arrived to take me to the nearby Parramatta Hospital for X-rays and specialist treatment. This was not good for Linda because she had to drive my car. It had manual gears, something which she had never driven, and it was a powerful V8 as well. Linda swapped the car with someone she knew who drove it back to the Mitchell's and she drove an automatic. It was safer for her to do this than to try and drive a manual V8 car. I was later to find out that it would have been suicidal for her to do so without me alongside her.

I thought this was the end of my season. How was I going to get married with a broken ankle? The ankle break was a classic Potts fracture type two and required surgery to put it back together. The prognosis was average to good and depended on how well I healed. Fortunately, I healed well and hadn't lost any pace. If I had lost my speed I would not have been as effective as before which would have affected my future prospects.

More importantly, I was due to marry Linda on 5 March at St Augustine's Catholic Church in Balmain and had a broken ankle. We managed to get through the service, but it ached like nothing I had previously experienced. Father Murphy, who presided over the service, was Balmain mad and made some jokes about our predicament and how I should have taken the path of least bother and played for Balmain when I had the chance.

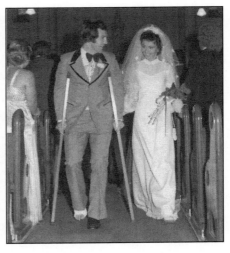

The service was a lovely occasion and as I hobbled down the aisle on crutches the MC, Noel Rogers from Concord, said during his speech at the reception that "no one has mentioned it today, but it is the first time he has ever seen the bride lead the groom down the aisle by the crotch (crutch)". Of course, he brought the house down with his quick wit and the party began. My only disappointment of the day was that I was unable to do the bridal waltz with Linda, but had the chance to catch up on this activity when our children were married in later years which was equally as exciting.

41

Linda and I went off to our room at the reception place, Windsor Gardens only to be woken at 7.30am by Linda's father Don who decided it was a good time to pick us up for breakfast back at their place. Gee, we didn't even get to sleep in on our first day of married life. One of our guests at the wedding was Reg Gasnier, a relative of the Mitchell family. Reg was a popular guest as you could imagine, but one of the funny stories from the after party back at Mitchell's Concord home was when Linda's brother's friend, Robert 'Nobby' Evans, went up to Reg and asked "Was he up for a signature?" Reg replied "Yes" and the response from the friend was "Have you got a pen and paper and I will sign it for you Reg". Everyone laughed and someone should have knocked him out for being a smart alec, but Reg took it in good spirit and laughed it off.

Linda and I moved into our new Wollongong apartment in the suburb of Fairy Meadow. It was on the third floor, all stairs and no lift. To say Linda was miffed would be an understatement because it was a struggle for my little lady to carry our worldly possessions up several flights of stairs while I was laid up in the lounge with a broken ankle. Up to 30 trips were made that day and when I mentioned "did she want a hand?" All I received was a curt "NO just sit there and don't say anything". I genuinely felt for her, but this was possibly the start of how hard Linda had to work during our time together as a footballer's wife. There were many occasions when I was not around to assist which didn't help inspire what marriage was all about. That said it is about managing situations and that is what occurred so many times. And I loved Linda for all her efforts in making life as easy for me as she could so I could do what I loved to do, play footie. Linda even gave up her love of netball to ensure the home fires were always burning and strong.

When I returned to the field it was through the under-23s team. I remember it well because we played Eastern Suburbs at the Sports Ground at 12 midday, which I hadn't done for five years since playing for the under-17s in Wollongong. Easts were undefeated and playing well, but it was the boys from Western Suburbs who got the money that day. I was surprised to learn that the players enjoyed playing alongside a first team player who was able to provide some direction in the match which improved the way they played. I also remember playing against Manly the following week in the under-23s. I then came on to play for the first team on the wing, a position I would never want to play again.

Bob Fulton was at his menacing best on this day and I copped the brunt of it. He either ran at me or side-stepped me several times to score three tries down the right side defence. Fortunately I then received a call up to the first team the following week and my season was back on track.

As the season progressed my form was getting back to its best and the selectors were again taking notice of not just me, but how well the Wests players were playing in a winning team. The wins didn't really start to come together until the second half of the season, but it stood us in good stead for the upcoming finals.

However, we didn't do as well in the finals as we would have liked there was much to celebrate when three Wests players were chosen to tour with the combined Sydney squad coached by the legend Noel Kelly, a former Wests Magpies and Australia hooker and prop. The Wests players were the great Tom Raudonikis, John Donnelly and me. I had picked up a slight knee injury during the finals, but was able to pass a fitness test done by the rugby league doctor, Bill Monaghan. He was a good doctor and asked me a straight question: "I know you were injured, how is it and would it stop you from playing at your best on tour? Tell me the truth because if you don't it will be the last time you have a chance to pass this type of medical test." I can honestly say I s..t myself at this and replied: "I am okay and yes, I could play at my best."

We travelled to Auckland and quickly settled into the Auckland Hotel where a funny incident occurred. I am not sure if the culprits would have got away with it today, but they did then. During one lunch Dallas Donnelly was at the fish tank behind the wall to the reception area trying to take a fish from the tank with his bare hands.

It wasn't working and down came Tommy Raudonikis who also had a go at trying this technique. Along came Ted Goodwin from St George who asked "what are you guys doing?" He said he could catch a fish and, as surprising as it is, Ted of Kiwi background placed his hand over the tank and quick as a flash dipped his hand into the tank and came out with a wriggling fish held tight in his big fist. At this point it got worse. Dallas says "give it to me Ted" which he duly did and within the blink of the eye Dallas had taken one big bite of the live fish and thrown the other end back into the pond. Not to be outdone, another player said "give me that other half" and proceeded to eat the portion that Dallas had left behind. I witnessed all this and was amazed. Everyone went to lunch laughing and joking about how these three guys retrieved the fish, ate half of it and demolished the other half.

We headed off to the Waikato district and came away with a win before heading down to Christchurch to play the Canterbury region that ended up being a tough match. I was rested and witnessed a torrid affair against some tough Kiwis. Paul Hayward was the stand-off and as a boxer was in his element with all the punch-ups during this match. Of course, Paul became more famous in a few years time for trying to smuggle drugs from Thailand to Australia, getting caught and being jailed before returning home and dying of Aids. We returned to Auckland to play a combined Auckland team and there were a couple of interesting moments during and after the match. During the game a scrum was packing down and Ted Goodwin came over to the full-back position from his left centre spot to talk about the game and what we should be doing. Ted was oblivious to the need to return to the centre position because the scrum was being fed by the Auckland half-back. When they won the ball and tried to get away down their right side it was important for Ted to react and try to stop the player from going too far. Fortunately, they didn't score on that occasion, but it was just one of those funny things that occur with certain players. The second interesting point from this trip was when three players took the liberty of grabbing a bag full of Auckland playing gear and distributing it among the team on the coach back to hotel. There was a bit of an enquiry, but nothing came of it other than most of the gear being returned to its rightful owners.

This was the first occasion I spent time away from Linda when we were a married couple and much as I enjoyed the tour and the camaraderie that comes from these trips, I sorely missed my new wife and longed for the chance to return to Sydney.

Following the New Zealand trip Linda and I had already arranged to move to Sydney into a lovely townhouse on Burwood Road in Burwood. My parents and the in-laws were not happy that the move occurred while Linda and I travelled to England for a belated honeymoon, also visiting many European countries. We were happy as the move had been done and all the furniture was in our new home. Thanks to all my relatives we only had to move our clothes and settle in before I started training for the 1977 season.

5. Test honours ... and twins

The new season saw the club appoint a legend of the mighty Western Suburbs Magpies, Keith Holman, as head coach for the 1977 season. He was a favourite son of Wests. He had played through the 1950s and 1960s, won representative honours for Australia and NSW. He was a half-back of enormous strength and courage and was now given the tough task of providing the current playing register with the guidance to achieve some silverware. No easy task for any coach.

Pre-season started went well. We put together a good set of results in the Wills Cup. The second major comp of the season was the AMCO Cup, a made-for-television event with the games played in four 20 minute quarters under floodlights on a Wednesday night at Leichhardt Oval, Balmain Tigers' home. Having got past Manly in the quarters and Canterbury in the semis we played Easts in the final. The game was worth $60,000 to the winning club and we wanted to put one over on Easts, who had convincingly beaten us in the 1974 finals.

The final was a tough, tense, low scoring affair. With three minutes to go we were leading 6–2. All our points had come from three penalties I managed to put over before half-time. Everyone thought it was going to be a tryless final, but Artie Beetson and their full-back Russell Fairfax had other ideas. Unfortunately, I was off the pitch at the time having succumbed to a knee injury just on half-time and been unable to return for the second half. Artie Beetson slipped a brilliant pass to Fairfax on the half-way line who then chipped the ball over the full-back and gathered to score. As the Wests players stood behind the posts and the throng of Wests players and officials on the sideline gasped I felt the cup had been snatched away from us in the dying moments. But then I watched Fairfax's conversion sail wide to the left of the posts. Their recognised goalkicker, Kevin 'Stumpy' Stevens was overlooked to take the all-important kick. As the whistle blew for time I screamed with delight as did all the Wests supporters. Fairfax cried! The club had won its first silverware since 1965 – it had been a long time between drinks.

The season was not all downhill, but for the first time in my first grade career I found out what it felt like to be dropped. It was in March, and the team and I in particular were not responding well enough to the methods the new coach was employing. After we had managed to snatch defeat from the jaws of victory against a 12-man

Canterbury side I was one of a number of players dropped for the following weekend.

I realised I was not playing at the top of my game and took it is as a motivation to play well in the second team to ensure I returned to first team duties quickly – and so it happened. Only one game in the second team, but that was enough to never be dropped again. Another now well-known coach wanted to drop me for a lesser player when I was playing ok, maybe not quite at to the top of my game but certainly better than the option mooted to take my place. I will return to this story later.

The season seemed to go on forever. Even though I was still enjoying my footy in many ways, I was glad we did not make the finals. In another twist, as occurs with a change of coach, Keith brought in a couple of his own players to bolster the team. One such player was Peter Rowles – a former rugby union player – who had played rugby league down at Port Kembla in 1976 and was considered to a very good player when he came over from union. Keith approached me to see if I would mind giving up the kicking duties in favour of Peter. Of course I was not keen on giving up the prestigious role as Wests' kicker. I was averaging about 75 per cent and didn't think I deserved to be asked to pass on the role. So when I was dropped it was an easy decision for the coach to make when Peter took on the duties for one game, kicked very well, and took his chance to impress the coach and selectors. I missed out on kicking for most of the year unless Peter was injured, that is almost 200 points I could have scored as a kicker. This would have increased my record substantially. But saying that, I played in a team and being just part of it I made sure I didn't let the team down with any sulking sessions. I just got on and did what needed to be done to win. It was another lesson: either put up or go and do not cause the team or the club any problems. As they say a happy team with happy players makes for a winning culture.

As the season ended Keith Holman decided it was not his place to be coach and moved on. They had a young coach who had taken the under-23 side to the title that season and felt that he was ready to step up to the plate in first grade. His name was Roy Masters and through his innovative psychology methods he would transform the side the following season. Warren Ryan was brought into take over the coaching of the under-23s team from Masters. This was an excellent choice by the club's management because Warren assisted Roy enormously which gave him a terrific springboard to launch his first team coaching career.

With a family on the way I felt I should get a proper job. Having worked in the family meat business since starting playing professional footy, I took the plunge and bought a butchers shop in Lidcombe with my brother-in-law, John Mitchell. I felt at least I would have less travelling time to the training and games, although start and finish times were going to be tough as butchers started work early in the day, mostly before the sun rose.

At the end of the season it was time to take a holiday. Les Boyd, his girlfriend at the time Judy who later became Mrs Boyd and with Linda and I took a two week driving holiday north to Queensland in October. Little did we realise at the time Linda was expecting twins, but gee we could have guessed as much with her being so big in pregnancy.

As we left Burwood, Les, being a bit of a punter, wanted to place some bets at the Royal Sheaf Hotel on the corner of Burwood and Liverpool Roads. We drove up the coast on holiday with our best friends as we listened to the race channel on the car stereo. Low and behold the trifecta that Les and I had taken gets up, yee haa, the car was noisy for some time. We stopped for a late afternoon break at Coffs Harbour where Les cashed our trifecta ticket in. Well the result was great, but the return was $10 for a $6 bet. Not being a punter I gave it to Les and wanted to know why the return was so low when all you hear about trifectas was the big payouts of $1000s. Easily solved Les says, the horses we backed were all low odds and little return was gained. Oh well, it re-enforced to me that gambling was never what it looked from the outside.

We arrived in Ballina late and after a terrible ride for Linda, who was most uncomfortable during the long drive north, we settled into the motel for a good night's rest. Mind you we drove some nine hours almost continuously and with her as big as she was it was credit to her she lasted as long as she did. Those two little bundles of joy were giving Linda a right kicking in that tummy. After a well earned sleep, we drove on to stay at Coolangatta where we enjoyed a day or two of sunshine and beach. It was here that a funny thing occurred. We wandered onto the beach and Les and I both went for a swim. Les got out before me, as I was enjoying the body surfing so much, and made sure when he got back to the girls he sat on the far side of Judy away from Linda because he didn't want anyone to think he was with a big pregnant woman who was in a bikini, which was not a done thing back then. I stayed in until I was almost prune-like and Linda asked if I was embarrassed to sit with her like Les was. Of course not was my response. From Coolangatta we drove on to Noosa and thoroughly enjoyed the next week of our holidays before returning to the grind of work and football training for the forthcoming season.

In December 1977 Linda's and my world turned to gold with the birth of our twins, Dane and Jason. They were born at 30 weeks, some 10 weeks early, and were in grave danger of not making it. Our gynaecologist was Doctor Bob McInerney, the Wests club doctor and a Macquarie Street specialist. He was made for this event and provided the best of conditions for the lads to survive. It was a marvellous occasion and stressful going through the next 10 weeks with them in hospital, seeing them wired for monitoring. Their legs were no thicker than my finger which worried me that they would grow to only 2 foot tall but I was put at ease by the paediatrician who said these strong little guys would grow to be good footballers like their dad to which their mum curtly said they'll play golf or tennis. We shouldn't have worried as Linda's mum Ida was a teacher at the St Augustine's Catholic Primary School in Leichhardt. She had the sisters praying for the twins' survival, and a bright future for the new family. One of the sisters was Sister Mary Hugh, the former principal from my primary school, St Pius X in Unanderra. She was an absolutely marvellous woman with energy to burn. It was great knowing that the twins would be at home as the 1978 season began. It was the start of one of my best ever seasons.

However, 1978 also proved to be a greatest disappointment for me and the other players. Masters was a new breed of coach and I think was a little ahead of his time in using psychology and how to motivate individuals and teams. He analysed the opposition, although there was nothing new in that. Where he stood out was that he also analysed the players he had under his control. He was able to work out how to motivate individual players to get the best out of them. He also knew how to motivate players in a different manner depending on the opposition that weekend. He worked with Warren Ryan to be at the top his tactical approach to the game as well, and the players responded to his methods in a way they never had for Holman.

As a current school teacher in Penrith, Masters had the opportunity to use his pupils as a tool to provide his motivation for the players. One Thursday training night Masters sat the team down and began to speak about the Magpie – Wests' emblem – and how it protected its territory in a vigorous way. The point being rammed into our heads was that if Wests were to make the finals in 1978 the team had to win our home matches and at least 50 per cent of away games. He pulled out a large cardboard project reputedly done by a student on his or her own volition, but in reality masterfully orchestrated by Masters, their teacher. This project portrayed how the magpie would fight tooth and nail to secure its nest and immediate territory when mating and when its eggs were laid.

Personally, I had big doubts whether the student did this project without some direction from their teacher. I was proved to be correct later that year when after speaking to Masters at a social event he came clean when pressed and admitted he had instigated the project. It worked, that was the point. It helped Wests become a formidable team and one to be feared under Masters's control. Wests maintained a clean sheet at home and were crowned minor premiers in his first year in charge.

Another innovation was his infamous face slapping psychological idea. This was well documented after an airing on television. It was before a big match when Masters employed this motivational ploy in front of the Channel 9 television cameras from *A Current Affair*. It was one of the most unusual motivational methods I have ever been involved with.

Masters asked the players to pair off with someone about the same size. The players spun around as directed to team up and I was lucky on this occasion to be standing next to Graeme O'Grady, a lock forward – loose forward in England.

The luck came in when Masters asked us to face each other and alternate between punching each other in the stomach for about 30 seconds, then slapping each other's face for about the same time. I've never known 30 seconds to go on so long. We were told "don't hold back", you're going out to play a team of thugs who are going to belt you and this won't be as tough as that. Well I said lucky. Graeme O'Grady was a tough player, not big in stature, but tough as teak. He was a very good runner with the ball, support player and had an uncanny ability to provide excellent ball-playing options and importantly, someone to be standing next to when the face slapping began. Graeme, for all his toughness, wasn't much into this new motivational technique, which suited me right down to the ground as I didn't care for it much either. So we just made it through with a bit of 'patter cake' type slapping. Thankfully.

This was not the end of the face slapping technique as the next game came upon us. I was not impressed when before one match I turned to Graeme O'Grady and was disappointed because he had already found a partner in Les Boyd! I turned the other way to be met by big John 'Dallas' Donnelly. Scared? Definitely!

The outcome was that Dallas said to me in his husky voice, "Joe, you go first". I started with the belly punching and all Dallas could say was "Hit me harder Joe!" So I absolutely s..t myself when it was his turn. The best way to describe the belly punching from Dallas was: I was much closer to the doorway after the 30 seconds than before it.

Unfortunately for me, there was still the face slapping to come. I slapped Dallas first, only to be met with "hit me harder Joe". I wasn't looking forward to my turn receiving... Well I did receive plenty of head-turning slaps that almost knocked me out before going out to play. It was the only occasion I have ever been in tears before playing a match.

We quickly felt the effect of Masters's approach to the game in an early training session. Masters had us in at 6pm. We walked off the training paddock at 9pm. Three hour training sessions were unheard of at Wests. During that session, Masters gave us a break to listen to a lecture from a player from The Harlem Globetrotters professional basketball outfit. Masters was breaking new ground, but he believed in what he was doing and results showed he was right in his approach. A lot of hungry blokes left that training session as I recall, thinking they could bounce a ball like the legend 'ball player. It was interesting to see team mates trying to bounce the rugby league ball and the lack of control with this ball.

The other problem we had that year was that the club was all but broke, which hampered progress, but did focus our minds. Roy used this in an unprecedented manner. Early in the season for a game against Balmain in the Craven Mild Cup his motivational speech was short, sharp and to the point. The $1,000 prize money was urgently needed by the club, so get out and win the game. We did. Mind you, we did not go on and win the trophy. However, as the season progressed we suddenly found that teams coming to our place seemed to be going away without the points.

That was good because I had a couple of reasons for wanting to keep playing well, sons Dane and Jason. Linda and I now had the twins to focus our minds. It is amazing how your outlook changes with other mouths to feed. I was waking at 3am to 4am to feed two very hungry lads before heading off to work in the butchers shop at 5am.

As the season got into its stride I seemed to hit a good stretch of form. I think this was due to the way Masters allowed us to play. He wanted us to play a fast, open attacking style which suited me. Then, as before, injury struck and I was laid up with yet another ankle injury. Luckily it was not as bad as I first thought and I was not out for too long. I got the opportunity to observe Masters at work and the way he motivated folks.

He was instrumental in talking Mick Luibinskas into remaining at the club, when other clubs were making him good offers. Mick had copped a lot of flak a couple of years previously when he was held responsible for us losing a point against Canterbury when he was ruled to be ineligible to play. Masters told him things would get better for him, he stayed and had a good year. Our prop John Donnelly had always struggled with his weight. Masters set him a target weight and if he crept over it, each pound cost him a $10 fine. Funnily enough his weight problem disappeared. It was a measure of Masters's approach that he did the same with reserve grade prop Bruce 'The Sloth' Gibbs. This meant that even reserve grade players felt Masters was interested in them, but the truth was that Roy had earmarked Sloth as a first team player before others had.

We may have played attacking football, but we also could play it tough when we had to. Wests had gone to Melbourne to play Manly in an exhibition game before the season had begun and Masters had decided one or two of the Manly pack would not fire if the going got rough. His game plan when Wests faced Manly was to play a tough forward game, intimidate their forwards and stop their go forward. John Donnelly took Masters's words a little too literally and in the opening minutes launched himself at Manly's enforcer Terry Randall. The result was chaos as a pitched battle erupted. After that the Manly players were more intent on trying to hurt us than beat us at footy, they did not succeed at either and we got the win.

51

With Wests going well, once again the press began to look in depth at Joe Cool, particularly when I was overlooked for the City versus Country game. They analysed every play I did and made great play of my supposed inconsistencies. Whenever I got the ball I was always willing to try something different, to spring a surprise on the opposition. Sometimes it worked, and the press would sing my praises. On other occasions I bombed and they criticised me. I would rather play adventurous footy than play safe all the time, and the only person I had to worry about was the coach, not the writers.

By June we were sitting on top of the pile and had been for some time. It was unusual for Wests to be looking down on the rest of the ladder, usually we were struggling to climb it. Tommy Raudonikis, our inspirational captain who had a way with words, was asked why Wests were on top. He replied: "Because we are like starving dogs".

The truth was a little different. We were at the top because of the way Roy Masters had got us playing the game. I now had the extra responsibility of captaining the side whenever Raudonikis was injured or on international duty. I thrived on the responsibility. The Kiwis were over on tour and the press were saying that my form was such that I was the shadow full-back for the national side. Frank Hyde wrote that if the Australians clinched the series by winning the second test then I would start the third. As he did not pick the team I took little notice of him. It was then that fate took a hand in the Dorahy career just as it had when I was a 16-year-old.

The Australian team for the second test had been selected with Graham Eadie at full-back. The squad had flown up to Brisbane to go into camp for the game. The team were having a public training session when Eadie pulled up with hamstring problems. At the time it seemed I was the last person to know I was being called into the squad. Once it was decided that Eadie would not be fit to play, the Australian RL president Kevin Humphreys tried to contact me. He rang the butchers shop in Lidcombe and my brother-in-law John answered the phone and told Humphreys that I was at the bank. John then rang Linda my wife with the news. Linda rang my mum in Wollongong. All of this was happening while I was going to-and-from the bank. Of course, back in those days there were no mobile phones so I was oblivious to what was happening in my absence.

When I got back to the shop I thought John was winding me up and told him there was no way I was ringing Humphreys. Eventually, I reluctantly made the call, thinking all the time of how embarrassed I would be, but Humphreys told me to get on a plane for Brisbane quick sharp. The pleasing thing for me was that John Donnelly was in the team so there would be at least one friendly face for me.

Of course, I was over the moon about being selected to replace Graham Eadie as Australian full-back in the test team to play the Kiwis. I was emotional on the plane there, finding it hard to believe that John Dorahy was catching a flight to represent our great country. But yes it was true and I settled into the week. Frank Stanton was the coach and I soon learnt it was Frank's way or the highway. All the same Frank knew how to strategise for a win. He was known as a cranky red head and his manner came out often enough to understand why.

It was Saturday 15 July when I ran onto the field in a green and gold shirt and looked over to see the Kiwis' black and white. Every player dreams of playing for their country and I was no different. This was the proudest moment of my career to date. I was not going to let it go by without giving my best, especially knowing that by playing well I could challenge for the full-back role on the upcoming Kangaroo tour at the end of the season. My family had travelled to watch me play for Australia. I was extremely proud to have them in the stands enjoying the moment as much as I did.

I had the dream debut that one can only dream of because we blitzed the Kiwis, winning 37–7. From the first scrum we took the ball and I came into the line and created the overlap that allowed Steve Rogers to put the other debutant, wingman Nev Glover, in for a try. In the 20th minute I managed to put Ray Price through a hole and he scored at a canter with a couple of Aussies in support should he have needed them. The really pleasing thing for me was that the Kiwis did not cross the line for a try. The one they were awarded was a penalty try when ref Eddie Ward ruled interference when the Kiwis kicked through. I walked from the field as high as a kite. For me it was the perfect debut game and in the sheds I was reluctant to take the green and gold shirt off.

During the first half I had identified an opportunity on our right side and called to Rod 'Rocket' Reddy for the ball. Rocket duly obliged and I made a break from which a try was scored by Ray Price. However, at half time Frank Stanton was not impressed because the team had a play set up down the short left side and I was told not to take the game into my own hands. Gee, what a tough call I thought, because we had scored. But hey, Frank's the coach and so in the second half I made limited calls for the ball that weren't drilled for.

The press seemed to be pleased with my performance and were already writing that I was on the plane to the tour to England and France at the end of the season as number two to Eadie. They never seem to grasp the fact that footy is a rough, tough and dangerous game. Anything can and will happen on and off the pitch. All I wanted was to find out if I had done enough to impress Frank Stanton and keep the jersey for the third test. Luckily I did, and in the match managed to cross for a three pointer that gave me the greatest pleasure I think I have had on a footy paddock. It was not a good performance although we won 33–16. It shows how fickle the press are; suddenly I was not showing the gloss of my first test. The team did not perform so Dorahy was not performing, footy is a strange world.

With the series over it was back to the bread and butter world. After leading the ladder for seven weeks we had suffered a couple of losses away from home and dropped to second. On the paddock we were getting back on track and beginning to churn out the results Roy Masters wanted. My problem was that the lacklustre performance I had put in the third test was due to me getting a bad injury to my neck and back.

I was diagnosed with a couple of displaced vertebra and the pain was constant. Before each game I had to have the chiropractor manipulate my spine or I could not turn my head. Mind you, when you are top of the ladder the pain seems to be a lot less than when you are at the bottom. We ended the regular season in number one spot after winning at Cronulla in the last round. We had a week off and two chances of getting to the Grand Final; sadly we blew both of them. We meet Cronulla in the major semi. It was real tough rough play-off footy. With just a few minutes to go we were tied up at 10–10. Unfortunately two late penalty goals saw Cronulla go clear to win the game 14–10. We were all sick, but the coach picked us up telling us we still had a get out of gaol card against Manly.

We felt we could still make the Grand Final because we had done well against Manly during the season, having won one and lost one. On the day we just could not get over the line and lost 14–7. It was a heartbreaker for all of us. What was particularly upsetting was that in the second half we had two tries wiped off by the referee. Having gone so well during the regular season, we had come up short once again when it really mattered. While I was pretty down, there was always the tour spot that I may well be able to grab, sadly even that was not to be.

It is interesting to note here that referees are only human, make mistakes and do not see everything. But when some referees get their dander up because of a player's bad attitude and lack of discipline it is easy to see some penalties take place in curious positions and times that belie the game momentum. Some people would accuse the referees of deliberately providing advantage to one team over another or not giving one team a fair go, but it would be difficult to prove in the game of rugby league when there is a million opportunities to make a decision that can be construed two ways. A mistake by me midway through the first half made it difficult for the team. During the early part of the match Manly put up a bomb that was just a normal catch in any match, but on this occasion I didn't catch it. It slipped through my open arms that would normally have been like a fish net catching a prize big fish, only to see the Manly stand-off Alan Thompson run through to pick up the ball and score from a short distance.

Having gone so well during the regular season we had come up short once again when it really mattered. While I was pretty down there was always the tour spot that I may well be able to grab, sadly even that was not to be and probably off the back of two games where two mistakes possibly swayed the selector's minds.

During the season I had been spoken to by one of the representative selectors, a chap called Jack Hampstead from the Balmain club who informed me that "I had a ticket" on the plane. If there was one thing I had grown accustomed to over my years playing rugby league, it was to not take notice of selectors until you heard your name read out as part of the official team. I even received a call from my wife's uncle, Ian Middleton, who had also received "good information" that I was chosen already. Well, as the history books show, John Dorahy missed out on selection. I was not unhappy because I had really been prepared for a summer at home, not one in the north of England. The full-backs chosen were Allan McMahon and Graham Eadie from Manly. So I did not feel disgraced, but was happy to know that I was mentioned as a worthy option. Though it is an interesting, but mute, point that Allan was the Balmain full-back and maybe had I signed for and played with the Tigers it might have been me on the plane instead of Allan, given the politics of selections and the influence of certain club CEOs

At end of the season and on Les's return from his trip with the Kangaroos he got married to Judy in Cootamundra on 16 December. Linda and I were excited to make the trip to Coota for the wedding; I was to be one of Les's groomsmen. It was a great wedding, but Linda and I had to rush back on the Sunday because it was our twin boys first birthday. Definitely a weekend to remember.

6.   Leaving Wests

Having experienced the euphoria of winning two test caps, I put the disappointment of two failed attempts to make the Grand Final and missing selection in the Australian Kangaroos tour team behind me. I tried to enjoy the off season and get back into pre-season training. However, missing out on the Grand Final caused great problems and ultimately lead to a souring of relationship between me and Wests. At the end of the 1978 season I was halfway through a two year contract with the club. I had a clause in my contract that said that it would be reviewed at the end of the first year. My understanding of that clause was that if I had performed well the club would look to increase my income, sadly the club viewed it differently, particularly the club president, Bill Carson.

I felt that during 1978 I had more than fulfilled my half of the bargain. I had been a big part of the team and helped the club to the finals again. Ok, we had failed at the last two hurdles, but although I had made a couple of mistakes leading to tries by the opposition it was a team game, not up to the individual. In addition I had been capped twice by my country, so I felt that a 25 per cent increase in what was a pretty low contract payment was not unreasonable. Unfortunately, the board saw it differently and the secretary told me and the press that the board had twice reviewed my contract as they were required to do and had decided not to increase my contract payments. Their view was that my contract stated that they "only had to review the contract without detriment to the player'. They had done that and not reduced the payments, so there was no detriment to me. When I signed on at Wests it was during a payment crisis in rugby league when clubs were restricted to a cap of $2,000 sign-on fee and $200 per win. I certainly went to Sydney at the wrong time if I wanted to receive what would have been considered fair reward for my ability.

That said, I was never in it for the money. I enjoyed playing the game and would have done so if it was amateur league... at least until this point when I had a family and felt I should maximise my earnings in a supposedly professional sport.

I was both hurt and disappointed with the club's attitude after what I had given to them in the five years I had been there. I was not on the biggest of contracts by Sydney league standards. What I was asking for was not really that great an increase compared to what many people in the game suggested. Also I was one of the top three players in the club.

As pre-season went on, I was becoming more-and-more disillusioned with the club's attitude towards my contract and the lack of movement to conclude the situation. For the love of the game and knowing I was better than what I was being served up, I placed it all to the side put my head down and thought about how I would best help the team in the 1979 season.

At the start of pre-season I had been really excited as the coach, Roy Masters, had taken me to one side and told me he agreed with my suggestion to play me in the centre rather than at full-back in the forthcoming season. I had broached the subject with him because I felt in the centre I would be much closer to the action than at full-back and could improve the team in this role.

I was excited by the challenge of playing at centre and with some new blood in the team the 1979 season was looking promising. However, I was concerned that the club had lost a very good coach in the ranks when Warren Ryan left to become coach of the Newtown club. I asked Roy Masters for the contract matter to be resolved as soon as possible so that I could get down to being fully prepared for the season. Roy did his best to get the board to resolve the situation.

With the pre-season upon us, the pressure placed on me to commit saddened me a great deal – the club I spilled blood for was not forthcoming with a reasonable response to a player with the qualities most clubs want. This was my first professional club and one I had great respect for, where I was prepared to do almost anything to achieve the premiership silverware it longed to win.

We seemed to be deadlocked over the contract when the secretary, Gary Russell, told me that the board were prepared to increase my contract payments provided I signed a new two year contract with the club. My solicitor wrote to the club and told them that, because they had refused to re-negotiate the last year of my contract, they were in breach of contract and therefore I was open to offers from other clubs. Wests knew full well there were plenty of other clubs who would be prepared to pay me the 'peanuts' they were paying plus the increase I wanted. It was all very sad and about not a great amount of money really. For me it was the principle rather than the cash.

I was selected for the Craven Mild Cup game against Balmain, but the secretary again said to the press that the club would struggle to meet its contract payments to the players that season. The implication was that my demands would push the club over the edge. In my opinion that was rubbish. When pushed to say how much of an increase I was looking for, I told the press boys $4,000. My contract was $11,000 and I was asking for it to be increased to $15,000. It was then that the club came up with a scheme to save face. They said they would pay me a bonus, but only if we made the finals at the end of the season. They were going to add an addendum to my existing contract to allow this to happen. It was their way of getting around the claim my solicitor was making that they had not really reviewed my contract as they should have done.

It was then that matters took a turn for the worse and soured my relationship with the board to such an extent that it was beyond repair. I was told that at a meeting Bill Carson said that the two handling errors that I had made in the semi-final games the previous season had robbed Wests of a spot in the Grand Final. I was also told he had said that he did not care if I played for the club again or not. I felt that after five years with the club that was a real kick in the guts. I was well aware that I had made errors in the finals, but that could happen to any player. Over the course of a game, errors may or may not affect the outcome or result. Also, there were more mistakes in the games than the two I had made. What he was doing was putting the blame on me for the team's failure which I strongly felt was unfair.

In the end, I had a gut full of the whole affair and decided I would take the $2,000 bonus the club was offering if we made the semi-finals and play out my contract. I was, however, more determined than ever that I would do everything in my power to get that bonus. I set about getting to grips with the demands of playing in the centre and the team went as well as it had the previous season. Mind you, we had that young and innocent forward Les Boyd playing as well as ever and he never took a backward step. In fact, he would take too many steps forward at times and there were a number of confrontations with the opposition that season. The press boys claimed, as did our skipper Tommy Raudonikis, that opposition players were baiting Boyd. Take it from me he did not need baiting. He could cause a riot in a graveyard, no trouble at all. Later in the season it led to another first for me.

I was enjoying the greater responsibility of playing in the centre and took great satisfaction every time the press wrote that I had played well.

The Sun newspaper had sponsored a competition in the regular season matches, *The Sun* Medal, the best three players from each game were awarded points and those points were tallied up each week. In my first league game at centre at Parramatta I was voted man-of-the-match and received three points towards the *Sun* Medal. We were once again everyone's dark horse to make the end of season play-offs. Each game I played at centre I got better and better. This was testament to Warren Ryan, who I played centre alongside at Wests Illawarra in my early years of professional rugby league as a schoolboy. I had learnt so much about the options available in this role and the defensive qualities required of a centre in the frontline. Throughout the season I remained in the top three in the *Sun* Medal award, made the NSW team to play the touring Great Britain team and the club were in a play-off spot. The press once again started writing that I was worth a test spot, this time as a centre, they never seemed to learn. I just continued trying to enjoy my footy.

As the club was unbeaten at the time, the fans naturally figured that I would automatically re-sign. I said I would see what was out there and would not make a decision regarding my future until January. A lot of fans were not happy about the decision, but I was determined I was going to do what was best for John Dorahy at the end of the season. In the meantime I continued to get good wraps from the press and more importantly from the coach. I made the City 2nds team as centre in the annual City versus Country weekend that year, but as it was my first season at centre I was more than pleased to do that.

At the end of May I was selected for the NSW team to play Queensland and we blitzed them 30–5. I kicked six goals. The guy who played against me for the Maroons was a youngster by the name of Mal Meninga. We all know what he went on to achieve in the game. It was not all sunshine and roses, however. When the test side was announced to play the Poms I was overlooked. That was bad enough after the way I had been playing, but the reserve back was Allan McMahon, who I thought had not been playing anywhere near as well as I had. However, he had toured with the 1978 Kangaroos and it was common knowledge that the team didn't change much unless absolutely necessary. Roy Masters blasted the selectors and the politics that went on at that time with team selection for the national side. I tried to put it behind me, but with all that had gone on that year it was a bitter pill to swallow.

I was, however, selected to play centre for NSW against Great Britain alongside Peter Mortimer after we both played well together in the City 2nds game. Peter and his family were to become close friends over the years. The Great Britain team included Steve Norton, John Joyner, Mike Smith and George Fairbairn. It was a tough game as you can imagine. Great Britain won the match and I was impressed with how they played the game. It had me privately considering how I could get back to England and play there.

This option didn't happen for several years due to the international rule of not allowing player exchange between Australia and England after the Australian game had secured the playing services of such players as Malcolm Reilly, Steve Norton, John Gray, Mike Stephenson and Bill Ashurst. Of course, any team, including an international team, would miss the quality of these players and so the International Board placed a ban on players moving between Australia and England.

As luck would have it, as often happens in footy, the following week we played Balmain. I was up against McMahon and had a cracking game, scored two tries and kicked the goals in a 17–15 win. It did not alter the fact that he was the reserve back and I was out in the cold, but I did get some satisfaction from showing the selectors how wrong they were. It was well known that the chairman of selectors, Ernie Hammerton was not a John Dorahy fan though several of the other selectors were. So, unfortunately I missed out on selection, especially when the vote came down to a choice decided by the chairman in selection meetings.

Meanwhile, at Wests, typically, they were moaning about how much our wins were going to cost them as players were due for contract renewals. They wanted to re-sign the star players and it was their way of trying to ensure they got them for the least amount of money. They acted like the paupers of the league and that was how people and players perceived them. This perception is still put forward today by many people at the club.

As we were getting to the business end of the season once more I was playing as well at centre as I had at full-back. I was enjoying being closer to the action and I certainly saw more of the ball. Back then the game was a good deal more violent than it is today and, on a number of occasions, some of our games got a little out of hand. We played Cronulla and lost 22–12. However, the Cronulla coach, Norm Provan, claimed after the game that his players had been subjected to the worst violence he had seen in 25 years. I am not sure about that, but Norm was known for being able to dish it out a bit, so I must respect his judgement. However, worse was still to come.

We went to Belmore Sports Ground to play Canterbury. To this day, I am not certain what kicked it all off, but it did not take long. We kicked off and Ray Brown, our new hooker from the Griffith Waratah NSW country club, was penalised on the very first tackle by referee Braybrook. Two minutes later, a bit of a 'blue' started, and the Canterbury prop Greg Cook ran in swinging punches. He walked out swinging his arms as he was sent to the sheds for an early bath. Then on 14 minutes our prop, John Donnelly, made the same walk after punching a player on the deck in the tackle. I am not sure if Donnelly had reached the sheds when I was following in his footsteps.

I was following a high bomb I had kicked when the Canterbury full-back Stan Cutler came in to take the ball. I was committed to going for the ball and followed through with a jump for the ball. My forearm hit Cutler square across the neck and chest area. He went down as if hit by a sniper's bullet and the referee was lifting his arm and pointing to the dressing sheds. We had not even played a quarter of the game.

I was devastated. I had never been sent off before. The press had a field day as this was the third rough house match Wests had been involved in and they played on that. The board told Roy Masters to say nothing to the press after the game to allow tempers to cool. Sadly, no one told Les Boyd who launched a gob full at the press boys for the stories they had written about the team.

The papers on Monday had pictures of my tackle on Cutler in stages. They say the camera can't lie, but those photos did not tell the full story that's for sure. I was up before the judiciary the following Wednesday and copped a four match ban. I felt it was a bit harsh because it was my first time up before them. I guess with the amount of news emanating about the Wests' brutality in matches an example was made of the players sent off in this game.

Worse was to follow. Unknown to me, one of the radio stations, 2SM, covering the judiciary meeting claimed that I had spat at a television camera crew when I was leaving. I believe it was another player who did this, certainly not me. I let my solicitor deal with it. They later retracted the allegation, but the damage was done. As they say, mud sticks. The shop had my business telephone number which was in the public domain. I copped a load of abusive calls during the run up to and after the hearing. Sadly, my wife Linda and her mother also copped some of the calls. The radio station 2SM involved admitted their mistake, read out a statement retracting the allegation and apologising for their action, but as I said the damage had been done. The club launched an appeal against my four match ban, but with no success, after all this was a Wests player and the club had been involved in big bust ups on consecutive weekends. I had no chance.

The lay off could not have come at a worse time as we were struggling to make the play-offs. Knowing I was inactive prompted a number of clubs to inquire about my plans for the next season. Back then agents were relatively unheard of and I did all my dealings with clubs through my solicitor. He received an offer from Penrith for a three-year deal worth $90,000, which was a fabulous offer. However, I had a business to run in Lidcombe and the prospect of travelling to Penrith to train and play was difficult. Also, Penrith were a struggling team and I didn't fancy going to a club to battle against the odds each week. Once the press got the story, headlines sprung up again about me leaving. Wests made me an offer, as they had to Les Boyd, but I told them and the press I would make a decision after the season ended. The offer was not even close to what I felt the market value was for a player of my stature. The club set a deadline for the acceptance of their offer to Les and me, which we ignored.

Any chance that I may have had a change of heart went out the window at the end of August. We went to play North Sydney and it was my 100th game for the club. It was an achievement I was pretty proud of as were my family and the club's supporters. The whole family travelled to watch the game and help me celebrate. There was no mention made of my achievement by officials at the North Sydney Oval. The club's attitude shocked me, but I suppose they had by now made their minds up that I would probably leave, so why bother? Peter Peters broke the story after the game when an irate fan phoned him, disgusted with the snub given to me by the board.

Almost three weeks later Wests did something, but only after news got out that I had been speaking to Ken Arthurson and Manly about the following season. I received a letter from the secretary, Greg Russell, which I still have. It read: "Am enclosing a cheque for $2000 in recognition of your playing 100 First Grade matches with Western

Suburbs. I would like to thank you for your efforts over the past six seasons as you have given our supporters many thrilling moments and much enjoyment..."

The letter was from the secretary, not the board, and was delivered by mail and not from the Wests executive. However, I was entering a new phase in my career. After six seasons with the paupers of the league I was about to experience life with the princes of the league.

I would like to mention what occurred to the business in Lidcombe after I moved to Manly. We had a very faithful customer base on the retail side aligned to the Wests Magpies. Many of the customers said they would always continue to buy meat from the shop because they received excellent and friendly service at a competitive price. However, one of the customers took it to an extreme when she came into the shop one rainy day. My brother-in-law and partner, John Mitchell, called me to the front of the shop to meet someone giving me an absolute mouthful for leaving Wests Magpies. This was not all; she actually leaned over the shop counter and tried to hit me with her umbrella not once, but a few times. It was funny as much as disappointing to know how passion can turn ugly. The worst impact from my signing at Manly, and John had warned about it, was when I turned out for Manly in my first competitive match. The next weeks at the shop saw business drop by 30 per cent. That was a very strong statement by the loyal Wests Magpies supporters who happened to be customers.

7.   Manly

Colin Love, then the Manly and Australian RL solicitor approached me about joining Manly. They were the club I was really interested in because they seemed to have a professional outlook to the game and its players, had won competitions recently and had a stable of first class players. Unfortunately, I found out that their coach, the very well respected Frank Stanton, intended to step down. I was a bit wary of signing for a club not knowing who was going to be coaching me. I spoke to the Manly secretary, Ken Arthurson on a number of occasions. He made it clear he wanted me to come to the club, play centre and not to worry about the coach because he said the club would only appoint a quality coach. He also said that he was keen to get Les Boyd and Ray Brown into the club as well. The terms they were offering me really did make Wests seem like paupers. It was hard to keep the talks out of the papers and, of course, once it became known what Manly were up to Wests' board went ballistic. They accused Manly of everything from ruining the game to causing World War Two.

The meeting of the three Wests players was arranged by Colin Love to take place at his office in Macquarie Street, Sydney, the home of the top surgeons and lawyers. At the meeting in Colin's office were Ken Arthurson, Ray Brown, Les Boyd and me. We were provided with the ins-and-outs of signing for Manly as a trio, all on the same contracts, because they felt we were close enough as mates and players to know Manly believed we should all receive the same deal. Interestingly, Arko told us we wouldn't have trouble with match officials again as we did at Wests Magpies because Manly was always considered a better behaved team than Wests. It may have been a tongue in cheek comment.

Again, interestingly, at an earlier meeting Arko said how I had been mistreated on the representative stage and suggested it was unlikely it would happen at Manly. He said I should have toured with the 1978 Kangaroo squad and made the 1979 Kangaroos who played Great Britain. I was comforted in the knowledge that Arko was a strong administrator and wanted me to sign a contract. As time would have it, I was to be selected in the first of the rep teams for 1980 and was thrilled I could unseat a player like Steve Rogers.

65

The three signings prompted one of the Wests committee members, Bill McCabe, to pen a letter to the papers stating that the money moguls were destroying the club and taking players that the club had turned from 'no namers' into internationals. For my part, I was looking forward to enjoying the off season and starting life with a brand new club. Wests, however, were determined to keep the furore going in the press and Gary Russell, their secretary, claimed that Les Boyd and I would be earning around $78,000 over two seasons. He went on to say that if Boyd and I had been retained it would have taken up 60 per cent of the leagues club grant the club received. It was the club's way of getting out of a sticky situation. They were trying to justify our loss to the fans by claiming we were trying to rape the club financially which was rubbish. We were only interested in receiving market value and providing a return on their investment. I was more concerned about my customers' reaction now I was a Manly player because our shop was in the heart of Wests territory.

These were interesting times because I never fully thought I would leave Wests after making so many good friends and setting up a successful business in the local area with my brother-in-law just two years earlier. Also, I had shed much blood and endured pain for the mighty Magpies. I had really envisaged being at Wests during my whole career because I was not brought up to change without good reason. But, as we now know, I ended up a kind of gypsy and enjoyed the changes that were either thrust upon me or the challenges I took up. Gypsy fits the bill and I would not change too much at all, if anything.

When I turned up to the first pre-season training session the club had a new coach in Alan Thompson. Alan was a former Manly player, originally from Newcastle, a school teacher, and thought he could deliver the coaching required by this team of quality players. The truth is Alan was a good bloke, but couldn't coach this team to its potential. I must say in his defence, we were fit, bloody fit. Alan had one exercise he continued throughout the year that had the team always ready for battle. He would have the squad line up on the try line, sprint at no less than 80 percent to the 90 metre mark, then sprint 100 per cent to the next try line before going into an exercise such as push-ups or burpees then turning for the other end jogging at no less than 50 per cent. We would have to do at least 20 to 30 of these runs. Try them yourself to know how fit Manly were in 1980.

However, it was in the area of game strategy and opposition awareness that I felt Alan didn't fare well. The players provided many of the tactical moves. Alan only lasted one year.

In hindsight, had I known that Alan Thompson was to be coach I probably would have strongly considered the Newtown offer with Warren Ryan as coach, but Arko had assured me, Boyd and Brownie that a suitable coach would be in place before December 1979 to begin pre-season training.

Linda and I quickly became friends with the Manly players and their partners, none more than Graham and Barbara Eadie. We are close friends still today, and our families enjoy a get together or two during the year. The Christmas holidays spent together are a blessing for all. Mind you, Barb has been trying to get Linda and I to travel to Bali for a holiday for sometime now, but there is no way I am visiting those countries where strife has occurred and is likely to occur again. I get as much enjoyment from a holiday with the family and Linda in Australia as I would spending additional money on airfares and waiting in airports. The Australian holiday opportunities are boundless and deserve to have a visit from us here in Australia.

My first encounter with John Dorahy was around 1976 to 1977. It was a Manly versus Wests game on a wet cold day at Lidcombe Oval. During the game John's mates (who I shared several drinks with in the years to follow) were on the hill and very vocal about certain things that occurred in the game — living up to my fiery red hair temperament I decided not to hold back in my responses.

Not too long after, John joined Manly. Could this actually work? A fibro joining the silver tails! As our children were similar ages I offered my help with kindergarten for the boys and other necessary local services. Little did I know that this would lead to a special lifelong friendship which has spanned over 30 years not only for John, Linda and myself, but our six children who are all extremely close and now our grandchildren who plan to continue this wonderful family connection.

During this time we were also very lucky to spend several winters in the North of England together and still holiday together each Xmas on the north coast, something we all look forward to each year.

I would just like to say if there were more guys like John Dorahy involved the NRL today the game would be in much better shape — a perfect gentlemen, mate and friend.
Barb Eadie

Back to the real story... We played trials in February 1980. One I remember vividly for two reasons. It was against Easts at Brookvale Oval, Manly Sea Eagles' home ground.

Graham Eadie retrieved a ball from behind our try line ran to 10 metres and passed it to me on the right side of the field near the hill. From here we passed it to each other twice more down the right side and when I passed it back to Graham on the 50 metre line he raced away to score in the right hand corner with a couple of Easts players on his tail. Graham, after scoring, threw the ball to me and said "you can kick, Joe". Graham was absolutely shattered as was I, but a kick is a kick and I felt confident. I took the ball back just over the quarter line and placed it on the sand mound we used then. Everything seemed fine. I took my customary six steps and strode in to kick the ball. When I kicked it, I looked up to where the ball was going instead of ensuring I had made correct contact with the ball. The ball flew off the boot towards the posts and all of one metre above the ground. I was totally embarrassed and could have jumped into one those holes you look for when something doesn't happen how you expect it to. Anyway, the crowd cheered and I jogged back to take up my position for the kick off. But didn't I receive plenty of cheek from the players and supporters alike.

The second incident in this match was that I copped an almighty knee from Noel Cleal during a tackle. It knocked me silly and caused major pins and needles down both my arms and a very sore neck. The Manly club doctor, Bob Higham, said the sensation would go away and that I was okay to play the next week because I had got through the match without further bother other than the pins and needles. This was to be a problem as the season went on.

As the pre-season got under way, some players have peculiar methods of welcoming other players to their club. During one training session Terry 'Igor' Randall left the training pitch early and while he was inside the change room did a devilish act and smeared an amount of Deep Heat massage cream onto a player's jocks. When the team completed the session I ventured into the change room, showered and proceeded to dress. At this time I did the customary thing when putting my jocks on, I ensured my 'family jewels' were comfortable. I then had occasion to feel uncomfortable and repositioned the family jewels. For a third time I did the same thing as I began to feel the heat from the cream. I can honestly tell you my whole area was burning like Vesuvius during a volcanic eruption. I whipped off my pants and jocks and went for the shower to cool down. I was told by one of the trainers not to get under the shower because it would make the area worse by increasing the heat. Another trainer said "you will need oil" and when I went for the trainers massage oil he told me to stop as it was laced with liniment. My reaction was to get into the car and drive as quick as I could to get some cooking oil from home on my by now burning family jewels.

I raced out of Brookvale Oval with just a towel wrapped around me, drove through a couple of red lights in Dee Why and straight up to the door at home in Wheeler Heights. I jumped out of the car and banged on the front door for Linda to open it. Linda's reaction upon seeing me rushing in the door with little more than a towel around me asking for cooking oil was one of disbelief. I quickly found the oil and to my utter joy and amazement the heat subsided quickly with almost instant relief.

Interestingly, I never did get the chance to repay Igor for this act of lunacy. Maybe it was because Igor was such a large player, towering over me and as strong as a bull, or maybe he thought Les Boyd would get a bit more volatile than me if he was the recipient and he was probably correct. It sure was an unorthodox welcome to the club.

Once the season started I seemed to carry on where I left off at Wests. I was a little concerned about the patterns of play Manly ran and how I would be expected to play, but I seemed to blend into the Manly style easily. It was easy playing with a team full of quality players. We were playing in the pre-season Craven 'A' Mild Cup comp and after a couple of wins the press were again including me in their headlines. We got to the final and there met Balmain who went into the sheds at half-time 12–5 up. The second half was a different story as we powered up our play and ran away from Balmain to win 21–12. I had silverware after less than a handful of games with Manly. I also came away with the man-of-the-match award that pleased me even more. I think Manly had added a new dimension to my game simply because of the support play style they adopted. I was able to become a provider as well as a scorer. I have always enjoyed my footy, but at Manly I was enjoying it even more in a winning team. I can't imagine how much better we would have been with a Frank Stanton level coach in charge. To this day, my fellow centre partner Russell Gartner says he provided all the chances for me to score because I ran off him or he completed all the tackles so I would not get tired in the games... Russell and I are still good friends and work in the gaming industry.

It was always on the cards that when we went back to Lidcombe Oval to play Wests the three 'turncoats' would be on a hiding to nothing, and that was how it turned out. They put us through the grinder, scored five tries and Manly could not cross their line. It was a typical Wests display of tough, hard defence built on resolute play and taking the chances as they came. I copped a bit of flak as well with late tackles and the like but then I expected nothing less.

In one incident during the Wests versus Manly match I made a break down the right side only to be covered by a Wests player, who had read the play really well. However, because he got to me on the touch line, he wasn't concerned that I kicked infield to provide an opportunity for the support to pick up the ball for a possible try. He was only interested in belting me good and proper. And wow, he did just that. I hit the deck hard from a swinging arm and when I rose to my feet my right leg gave way as though I didn't have one. Coincidentally, the match officials missed it. All I had for it was pins and needles down my arms as had happened in the earlier trial match against Easts. This time I was raced off to hospital for a check up, cleared of any danger and advised that it would ease and have no impact on my ability to play rugby league.

As the City versus Country game loomed onto the scene all the press were tipping me for a centre spot. In my first season in the centres I played in the City Seconds, so was delighted when the teams were announced and I was to play in the centre for City Firsts. As it turned out, I would have been better to have missed the game. Though I was absolutely chuffed to know I had displaced Steve Rogers who was selected in the Seconds team, but did not play. Rumour has it he dodged it because he was unhappy that he had missed selection for the first team.

We had only been playing for 15 minutes when I took a pass off Rod 'Rocket' Reddy near the edge of the ruck and met Country second-row Paul Graham head on. To say I came off second best is a bit of an understatement. I ran into his chest area with my head and felt a pain in my neck. I went down and don't remember anything about the tackle except that I couldn't move, except my head from side to side. Fortunately, our hooker that day was the Canterbury player Doctor George Peponis, who strongly suggested not to move an inch and said that help was on the way.

They put me in a neck brace, carried me off the field and took me to St Vincent's Hospital. Following X-rays I was moving freely and felt quite okay until a registrar doctor came to my emergency room and with my wife Linda beside me I was informed "do not move your head". I asked why and was promptly told that it could fall off my shoulders. The initial x-ray showed up a line across what is referred to as the 'hangman's bone' in my neck. The doctors feared the worst and that I had broken my neck. I knew there was something wrong the moment I hit the deck.

The initial pins and needles were something I had experienced earlier in the season on a couple of occasions following a bang to the head. It was when I lost the feeling in my arms and legs that I got worried. When the medical people at St Vincent's thought I had broken my neck I really did begin to fear the worst. Luckily that was not the case, and after a couple of days the feeling came slowly back to my limbs. As I was recovering I began to get confusing medical information and advice. The specialist came into my room in St Vincent's and seriously asked: "Do you not want to play rugby league?" To which I categorically replied: "What do you mean? Of course I want to play." I then sought opinions from other neurological specialists. They told me I would be out of the game for three or four weeks, although one specialist said I should never play the game again. It was confusing for me and the Manly secretary was also baffled. He sought legal advice as to what should happen if I got medical clearance to play and then suffered the same injury again. It was a worrying time for both my family and me.

I took my time to return to the training park and games because it was important to receive the right advice. I surely didn't want to end up in a wheelchair. Having a wonderful wife and two beautiful boys to raise, I couldn't picture myself being disabled and not partaking in their lives in a meaningful way. Fortunately, the prognosis from most of the specialists was correct and the option to play was there. I returned to the paddock and unbelievably not too long after my return to the game I received another bad injury. This time it was a medial ligament rupture and I missed the rest of the season. I visited Doctor Richard Tooth, a Macquarie Street orthopaedic specialist, who was a former rugby union international, so he knew a thing or two about

71

knees and footballers. He operated and did a fantastic job because I returned in 1981 with the same pace I had before being injured.

Despite all the set backs of this season, I did however receive an amazing award from the National Panasonic Cup. I had been nominated for the Golden Try Award and reached the last four tries to be judged. On final night Linda and I were in bed watching the final and they announced the winner of the Golden Try – they began with fourth runner-up – no not me, then third runner-up – no not me, then second runner-up – no not me. Well, that could only mean one thing – I had won the Golden Try for The National Panasonic Cup 1980. And what a prize it was from Tynan Motors – a brand new two-door Sports Volvo.

1981 was a good year for Manly, a new coach – Ray Ritchie, former Manly first grade winger who brought a different edge to the team and was prepared to try and innovate. Manly was successful and made the 1981 final series where we came up against a Newtown team with an attitude.

One of the biggest fights occurred on a fateful day in September 1981 against a team lead by Tommy Raudonikis. Yep the 'madman' was playing against Manly for Newtown. Tommy was providing their coach Warren Ryan with the necessary grunt needed to make a big challenge in this competition. Of course, it was well known that Tommy absolutely hated Manly and would play them every week if he had the chance to as he loved to belt them, encourage his team mates to do likewise, and verbalise them in a way which cannot be written in these pages.

Manly had a new recruit in 1981, Mark Broadhurst, a tough uncompromising prop from Christchurch in New Zealand. Mark had played for the Kiwis and received glowing reports for his tough play and forward progress with the ball. Mark, his wife Ann and daughter Stacey moved in across the road from us in Wheeler Heights. This was as good for Linda as it was for Ann, because they became good friends from living close. We continued this friendship for many years when we played together at different clubs.

During the season Mark was a tower of strength on the field with his tough playing, never-say-die attitude. But poor Mark got his come-uppance in the semi-final against Newtown. The reason for this fight started earlier in the week at training. Max Krilich brought the team

Playing for Manly with Les Boyd in support.

into a huddle and strongly suggested that Manly start a stink early in the game to unsettle the Newtown team. Well, there were some pretty mixed emotions at this call. Mark was dead set against it as were several players including me, because I couldn't fight my way out of a wet paper bag. Unfortunately, at the end of the session it was agreed reluctantly Manly would start a fight in one of the early scrums. Well... what next?

As the ball was fed by Johnny Gibbs and sent out the backline, the scrum erupted because someone had thrown a punch. From this there were several skirmishes carrying on and although several players from both sides tried to quieten things down it was clear it was mayhem. As I turned from pulling one fight apart another would be growing. At one time I backed away and bumped into a player, none other than Graeme O'Grady. As we turned and looked at each other with a stunned look we just went to another fight. We had been mates at Wests for several years and didn't want to fight at this time. However, I know Graeme would have cleaned me up easily.

I turned away from Graeme and saw Mark Broadhurst in a great deal of trouble with big Steve Bowden, Newtown's prop. The interesting part here is both Mark and Steve were renowned fighters with experience in the ring, but Mark did not know Steve Bowden had the vital street fighter advantage. By the time I jumped on Steve Bowden's back and pulled him away Mark's face was a mess. The extent of his injuries was woeful with fractured nose, cheekbones and eye sockets. In the heat of the moment it was easy to jump on Steve Bowden, but when he threw me off like a rag doll I fell to the floor and covered up as I saw Bowden approach. He was bending down to absolutely belt the crap out of me.

As I covered up and waited for the inevitable I heard an almighty crack. Terry Randall had seen me pull Bowden away from Broadhurst. As Bowden came down upon my foetal positioned body Randall let go with a big size 12 boot into the side of Bowden's head. Bowden fell over and Randall took to him like a bee to a honey pot. From this episode within the fight everyone came in to try and stop the carnage, thankfully because it must have gone on for several minutes.

The referee blew time off and received the touch judge reports, though I am not sure how they could gather all the information to provide the correct feedback to the referee. To cap it off the referee sent Bowden from the field for instigating the fight and Randall for kicking. Everyone else stayed on the field to complete the match with 12 players aside.

At the next penalty restart Tommy Raudonikis took the free tap, ran straight at Les Boyd and in the run to the defensive line threw the ball to the ground and attacked Les Boyd. Miraculously, Tommy was allowed to stay on the field and it proved a winner for the Newtown club as they went on to outplay Manly in a tough encounter.

That was the end of Manly's season and the completion of Joe Cool's time at the club. This move started during the previous season when I had received two terrible injuries and provided little return for the Manly club. Arko had made it known that I would not figure greatly in their plans for the 1982 season unless I took a 50 per cent cut in my contract. I had bought a second butcher's shop in Wheeler Heights, just up the road from our home. We had settled in nicely and the family were enjoying the beaches and new friends immensely. It was also not a great time to change clubs with Linda heavily pregnant with our daughter, Cara Lea, who still has her daddy wrapped around her little finger. She is now happily married and working for the WIN Corporation as NSW publicity & promotions manager. Well done girl.

Our need to consider all options took us to Queensland where I met the legendary Ron McAuliffe, chairman of Queensland RL. Initially I was to meet Nick Pappas from the South Brisbane club. He was keen to get me there and was also able to set me up to run a hotel in Brisbane. All this sounded great, except Ron McAuliffe had other ideas and suggested I speak to Redcliffe club where I met another Queensland legend in Dick 'Tossa' Turner. We drove out to Redcliffe, met with Dick and Arthur Beetson, Redcliffe's coach at that time. We had a terrific chat about how I and the family would fit into the club and area which was really attractive. But there was hitch...

A new club was being put together in Illawarra with Bob Millward as secretary – CEO in today's terms. Bob and his hardworking team had secured the coaching services of Allan Fitzgibbon from the Dapto club who had played for the Tigers in their 1969 Grand Final win against South Sydney Rabbittohs.

This was a really tough time because we had enjoyed living on the coast in the Manly district, had a second shop trading very well and were not really looking to change. However, as happens in rugby league "the meat sometimes is considered stale and must be thrown out". Well that was Arko's choice and so I left.

My choice at the end of the day was to move back to Wollongong and play for the Illawarra Steelers who were making their debut in the NSWRL competition. It was a tough call because Dick Turner had put a great deal on the table, but it was the tyranny of distance from family that swayed the decision. Wollongong to Gerringong or Sydney was not as far as Redcliffe to Sydney or Gerringong. And besides, Linda had a close family that would drop everything to look after the Dorahy twins and promised to do likewise for the new addition arriving in December.

Again being by choice or forced upon me a decision had to be made to better the family. We moved with a fresh mind to a new adventure. Wollongong here we come...

8.   Illawarra Steelers

As we progressed through the contract talks in Illawarra, the coach Allan Fitzgibbon approached me and asked how I felt about captaining the side. I was delighted to be offered the job, but I had not captained a side since I left Wests and then only as a stand in for Tommy Raudonikis when he was injured. I had captained teams through my junior rugby league days and was confident I could handle the on field role and be a good leader off the park for the club. The board accepted Fitzgibbon's recommendation and I got the job. It was a huge accolade for the experience I brought to the club and team and that was how it was conveyed to me by Allan Fitzgibbon and Bob Millward. To say I was excited would be an understatement. The feeling I took from this was one of immense pride that I was to be the captain of the inaugural Steelers first grade team in the Sydney competition. Equally important was that the players to a man totally supported me getting the job. We trained hard under the tutelage of Ken Boothroyd, a trainer who had a wonderful history training the St George team through their purple patch in the 1970s. I felt that we were as fit as the boys up in Sydney by the time the pre-season trial games arrived.

However, both the board and I were under no illusions as to what lay ahead for both ourselves and the other newcomer to the competition, Canberra. We were going to find it tough. Most of the players at the Steelers were looking for an opportunity although I knew we would match the other teams for fitness. Having got through the pre-season games with few injury worries we were ready for the competition to start. Having sold the shop in Manly I was unemployed when I returned to Wollongong and had to find work. I started work at Tancred Brothers wholesale meat depot and worked from 4am till 3pm as a wholesale meat salesman so as to have my evenings free to train.

The Steelers' first trial was against the South Sydney Rabbitohs who came to Wollongong with a strong team. During this match I snatched an intercept on our 20 metre line and started the long sprint to the try line. Little did I know when I started out that big Peter Smith was lingering in the back field and was quicker than I thought. As I hit the 50 metre line I saw big Pete coming from my left side at 100 miles an hour although I had really expected to continue on my merry way to the line. At this point my legs seemed to be going up and down in the one spot and I knew I was a goner because Pete caught me with a good tackle from slightly behind me. Didn't I get it from the players, being chased down by a prop forward, but Pete was a quick man over 40 metres or so. Funnily Peter Smith joined the Steelers the following year and become a team mate. Of course when he came into our ranks he gave it to me severely, but could never do it again – catch me in a sprint.

Off the field, my family had begun to settle well in Figtree. Our daughter Cara was born in Sydney and was just 10 days old when we moved from Collaroy to Wollongong. We had new neighbours, the Creightons, who over the years became dear friends and a rock to us all. Not to mention that they had four beautiful daughters, with the eldest Jenelle offering to be our immediate babysitter and Penny a wonderful friend and playmate to the twins.

Under Bob Millward and Allan Fitzgibbon's watchful eye the team and extended families were bonding and enjoying the atmosphere of a fresh new club. Nancy Millward, Michelle Fitzgibbon and Judy Russell were the backbone for the new wives and girlfriends of the club, helping them to settle and feel at home in the Illawarra setup.

At the end of February 1982 I arrived at Wollongong Stadium for our first match, only to find in my nervous state I had left behind my car pass to enter the ground. The gateman, ever vigilant on his first day, turned me away and I drove back to Figtree to retrieve the forgotten passes for myself and family. Interestingly, Kevin Humphreys and Keith Nolan were in the car behind me awaiting entry, seeing me turned away, they asked the gateman did he know who he just refused entry? After they explained, he was very nonchalant in his reply "well he didn't have a pass to get in".

I lead the team out onto the Wollongong Showground that day at a few minutes before 5pm for the Steelers' first competitive game. We faced Penrith that afternoon at a ground that had undergone $100,000.00 worth of improvements. All of the players were a little nervous and it showed. The Penrith captain on the day was big Darryl Brohman, who is far bigger today than he was as a player and goes by the moniker 'The big marn' working on the 2GB rugby league programme *The Call Team* with Ray Hadley.

We gave Penrith a bit too much respect and as the first half came to an end we walked to the sheds 14–0 down. We had never really

Opening game for Steelers at Wollongong Showground 1982 versus Penrith.

troubled the scoreboard or the Penrith defence for that matter. As we went out for that second half the game, season and club could have gone either way. It could have turned into a rout had we let our heads go down. The boys showed real character, however, in front of 9,652 supporters that afternoon. The referee, Michael Stone, gave us a sign of things to come in the season when one of our forwards, Martin Cavill, was felled by a high shot. He struggled to get up, but managed to play the ball and collapsed in a heap. The ref believed he was feigning injury and ordered play on. Cavill had to leave the field, so I don't think he was feigning anything because we were fighting back and the score was 14–7. However, we lost our way a little after he departed. It was typical of the treatment we got from refs as a newcomer to the comp because I firmly believe even in the modern game referees have a theory that the so-called better teams should win and do not do some of the things that the lesser teams are penalised for. That said, it was a game we could have won in the second half, we simply could not get across the try line enough and went down 17–7. But a good start all the same.

We had to wait until round three before we got our first win in the comp. We beat South Sydney 20–10 at Wollongong in a downpour. We played well and were worth the win, scoring four tries and never really lost command of the game. I think that was one of the sweetest victories in my career, the first for a new club and I was captain to boot. It was made even better as the previous week Easts had put 40 points past us and the coach could have made great changes. He didn't, showed faith in the boys and got his reward for the courage he showed. Fitzy was an excellent coach and really had the players working for each other throughout the season.

We just could not match the consistency of the established clubs week in week out which was always going to be the major concern in the first season. We could win a game, but the extra effort we needed to cross the line took its toll and the following week we would be lacking a little in our game. When the club went up to Manly everyone was on a high, I think because I had just left the club, and we played brilliantly. At one stage we were winning 15–7 and I thought we were going to put one over on Arko. Early in the second half we lost our hooker Barry Jenson and the young bloke who replaced him simply could not win the ball at the scrums. Back then the scrums were contested and the half-back had to put the ball in almost the middle of the tunnel anyway. We were having to play without the ball and with 20 minutes to go we were still leading, but the ref took a hand once more. Our loose-forward, Wayne Springall, was sent off for a tackle on Les Boyd and Manly took full advantage, stealing the match 19–15. That loss hurt me a lot because I would have loved to put one over on Arko and Manly that afternoon.

The one thing that was becoming more and more apparent as the season was progressing was that referees were not going to give us newcomers an even break. This was brought clearly into focus when we played Parramatta in Wollongong in the second weekend in May. We thought that the ref had an absolute shocker. The crowd were incensed and he needed a police escort at the end of the game. We were winning 11–8 when I took the ball up to the line and copped a knee in the head from Ray Price. Given my recent history with head and neck injuries I was far from happy. As I played the ball I gave Price one for his trouble. While I was doing so the ball had been shipped out wide to the left and we had scored. The score would have taken us out to a 14 or possible 16–8 lead and we could have kicked on and won the game.

As the team were celebrating the touch judge had run on the field and made a report to the ref. Funnily enough, he had not seen the knee from Price but had seen the punch I had given Price. I argued that the incident while wrong had no bearing on the try being scored and so the score should stand. The referee disagreed, disallowed the try, and gave Parra a penalty. Later in the game he bumped into one of our players who was covering across the paddock to make a tackle to stop a try. Again when I pointed this out he ignored me and awarded the try. In the end we went down 23–11. What added insult to injury was that the Refs advisory board member attending the game supported his display, saying that he thought the ref had given a good display. It really came home to me then that we were in for a long hard season from the refs.

Later in the season when Wests came to our ground, a brawl broke out after just a couple of minutes. The ref said that our player, Greg Cook, had been the instigator and sent him off 'for causing a brawl'. When the case went up before the judiciary Cook was found to have no case to answer and was cleared. However, we still lost the game.

During that season we had some good wins, but lacked consistency. On reflection I think we did as well as we could. We struggled when we got injuries and that showed up our lack of depth in the squad. We also got a taste of things to come at the City versus Country game that year. There was not one rep from either the Steelers or Canberra in either team. They may have let us into the comp, but they sure as hell were not going to let us into the rep teams as well. It was a long season, but there were one or two bright spots for me personally. Colin Hutton was at that time the Great Britain team manager and was in Sydney on a spying mission. He came to watch us play St George at Kogarah Oval and I had a particularly good afternoon. Hutton was quoted in the *Daily Mirror* as saying: "If John Dorahy is not one of the best centres running around in Australia, I'm a bad judge."

Little did I know then that he and I would cross paths again which would result in my career taking a change of direction and cause the rugby league authorities to change their international transfer rules.

The other high for me came when we faced Manly in the second round of matches. With time running out we were locked at 25–25.

81

The Steelers had lived up to their name that day and really played out of their skins. In what was probably going to be the last set Illawarra got to carry the ball up into the Manly half and from a play the ball I had stepped back to take the ball. As I received the ball to the right hand side towards the western stand, Les Boyd flew up knowing full well what was going to happen. I let him come as close I dare then feigned a right foot step to step back to the right as Les went past me on the inside. I let fly with my boot on the ball with one my best ever drop-kicks. I hit it sweetly from 35 metres out and watched as it flew over the cross bar to give us a 26–25 lead. There was no time for Manly to come back and we walked off with the victory. I think that win showed everyone that the club, new as it was, was here to stay.

A number of senior players signed for the fledgling team. Barry Jensen was a hooker from the Newtown club. Unfortunately for Barry, he succumbed to a bad neck injury during our first year and didn't play a great deal though his experience was much appreciated by all in the team. Brian Hetherington was a centre, also from the Newtown club. He was a NSW representative player and originally from the Illawarra region which meant that he was coming home as well. Brian was a strong player and real asset to the Steelers' ranks. He joined me at Halifax in 1989 for a season which will be covered later.

Shane Mackellar was a winger and another recruit from Newtown. Fox, as he was affectionately known, had a habit of running cross the pitch and trying to beat the tacklers infield rather than down the touch line where he had exceptional pace. If he had been more confident he could have scooted past defenders many times. Peter Ryan was a prop forward from Cronulla. He was one of the funniest lads you could want to meet. His jokes were hilarious and he was forever taking the mick out of other players. Paul Thompson was one who especially copped it from big Pete. Peter was a solid prop who was willing to take on the opposition combined with a willingness to make yards and tackle like a demon. Although he was at the end of his career he was a mighty tower of strength in the front-row.

Also in the pack was Wayne Springall, a second-row man from Manly. When approached to join the club I was asked was there any Manly players who would fit into the Illawarra mould. I strongly suggested Wayne 'Jack' Springall as a player who would do a wonderful job in the back-row. Jack was also one of the team's funny men and was always playing tricks on the other lads. Jack was well liked in the Wollongong region and as a plumber he took up doing work for the local business R. Jones Plumbing. Rod Jones and Jack got on like a house on fire and I reckon if it wasn't for Jack having a business in Sydney he would have possibly lived in the 'Gong permanently.

Lee Pomfret was a utility player from Canterbury. Lee's notoriety came about in a match against Wests Magpies when big Bob Cooper, with one punch, splattered Lee's nose all over his face. Lee was a consistent player who wouldn't let the team down in any game.

The team manager was Darcy Russell, who was also the sales manager at Wollongong's Dwyers Holden – an Opel type vehicle – dealership. He had an enormous rugby league pedigree, having played in the first team for the mighty Wests Magpies in the 1960s. Darcy was an outstanding full-back and knew the game, the players and the management. He was also a particularly good man manager in this fledgling club. Darcy's wife Judy, a former model, took the Illawarra cheer girls under her wing and they were a credit to the Illawarra club.

As the season came to an end I was named in the Australian train-on squad for the upcoming 1982 Kangaroo tour, but once again I missed out on selection. The selectors plumped for a second-row man from Easts – Ian Schubert – who was apparently given the chance to play one match at full-back and on the strength of that game was awarded a seat on the plane as a full-back when for the past two seasons he had only played in the forwards. Politics, as happens in most sport selections, was again prominent. In many respects, though, it was a blessing. I was able to go away, take a well earned rest and prepare for the second season syndrome that the club would undoubtedly face.

The board were busy trying to strengthen the squad and managed to lure the Kiwi international prop Mark Broadhurst to the Steelers on my advice. Mark and I were good friends after our season together at Manly in 1981. He had a big blue with Manly, after playing first grade most of the season, he got dropped to second grade two rounds before the end of the regular season. He didn't get back into the first grade and when Manly made the Grand Final he was not even named as one of the reserves. He told Manly if they did not release him from the last year of his contract he would sit it out in New Zealand. We got him and I felt him signing was a massive fillip for the club. As we went into our second season I was confident we would do better.

Sadly this was not quite the case in 1983 because we lost the first six games of the regular season. Everyone at the club was getting worried and not without reason. When we did start winning games we did so by the narrowest of margins, beating St George 25–24 and Cronulla 13–12. There were, however, bigger problems for both the club and the country really, and that was the recession that was gripping the place. There was something like 20 per cent unemployment in the Illawarra region and it kicked back on the club. At one time 10 of the squad were unemployed and relying on their footy money to put food on the table. The Leagues clubs that supported the Steelers were also feeling the pinch and four of the eight actually ceased their funding so the $20,000 each that had been promised at the start of the season was down from $160,000 to $80,000. Players with options on their contracts, including me, were told they would not be taken up and they should look for new clubs at the end of the season.

On the paddock I was getting into trouble again, once more with Parramatta and Ray Price at Belmore Oval. Price came in to make a tackle on me and hung on as I got up to play the ball. As Price would do in my opinion, he hung on for an extended time. When I did get him off I was accused of walking on him to get clear and play the ball. The ref Kevin Roberts saw nothing untoward and allowed play to go on. The touch judge from the far side came onto the field to report on the incident. I found this amazing because he was further away than the ref. He reported that I had stomped on Ray Price's head and on his report the ref said he had no choice but to march me to the dressing sheds. Price, in fairness, had to leave the field but not because of anything I had done. I was pretty gutted as it was the third time I had been marched and on this occasion I knew that I had done nothing wrong.

Having been to the judiciary twice before and copped four match bans I was not prepared to go again and not fight it, so I engaged a barrister who watched the video and planned a defence at the meeting in Sydney on the Monday. I thought I had better go fully armed because I was going to plead not guilty to the stomping charge. My barrister got the hearing put back to Thursday so that he could call witnesses in my defence. Our argument was that the ref who was watching the action saw nothing to call a penalty for, but listened to a touch judge further away than himself. To his credit, Ray Price came and gave evidence on my behalf and after a few minutes the judiciary decided there was no case to answer. They could not resist having a dig however, saying that they were giving me the benefit of the doubt. I found it difficult to see where the doubt came from, but I had got off. Had I not gone with a barrister I wonder what the outcome would have been, a four to eight week ban I suspect.

To end a pretty good week we won yet another close match, beating North Sydney 12–11. With the scores locked at 11–11 and time running out we got possession and drove into the Bears' half. They were so intent on stopping me trying for a field goal that it allowed our prop Mark Broadhurst to send over a wobbly one to win the game for us. They say that a week is a long time in politics and sport, and so it proved for just a week later the proverbial hit the fan. The newspapers revealed that I had signed a contract to play for Hull KR in England.

Through Alan Fitzgibbon, Hull KR and Colin Hutton made contact and everything progressed from there until I had to apply for a transfer. Hull KR actually applied to the Rugby Football League in Great Britain to register me as a player pending the lifting of the transfer ban between Australia and Great Britain. The club had already signed Mark Broadhurst, but as a Kiwi he was ok. The Australian Rugby League were getting a bit heavy handed about the whole thing and Hull KR were told to keep their hands off me. It was the ARL chairman, Ken Arthurson, who said that negotiations would not be tolerated until the International Board meeting in New Zealand after the Grand Final. A little later Arko announced that the Australians would oppose the lifting of the transfer ban. He came up with the correct, but daft, argument that Australians could go to England and no transfer fees were involved, but if an Australian club wanted to sign an English player they had to pay a transfer fee. It was a frivolous argument because when players in England signed for a club did so for life, unlike in Australia where fixed term contracts were the norm.

Once more I had to go to law and my solicitor served a letter on the ARL demanding a clearance to play in England and giving them seven days to respond. My argument was that I had fulfilled the terms of my contract with the Steelers and was a free agent, able to do what I wanted. The ARL refused to give me a clearance and we ended up in court. My barrister contended that the ARL were restricting me from plying my trade as a professional footballer. The Steelers had given me a letter of clearance saying that I had fulfilled all my obligations to them. At the first sitting, the Chief Judge, Justice Helsham, said he could not make an order sought by my barrister to refrain the ARL from continuing to refuse to grant clearance for me to play in England because he required more time to consider the complaint. At a hearing the following week he refused to allow the ARL an adjournment because the English season had already started.

I thought we had a very good chance and went to court on the Monday confident in our case. However, my confidence was misplaced because Justice Helsham refused to order the ARL to give me clearance even though I was not attached to any club. The reason given was that it was outside his jurisdiction as the League was not a corporate entity and he couldn't tell them what to do. It was hugely disappointing to me and our legal team who had worked hard to find the correct reasoning to provide clear judgement options for the justice to act.

Shortly afterwards, the International Board made a decision to allow players to transfer and the door was now open to everyone. I was extremely proud to be the first Australian player to go to England, quickly followed by Steve Martin from Manly and many others. And so it was that I would take my family across 12,000 miles to The Old Dart to once again play on the green pitches of England in the cold and damp. Let the "dreamtime" begin...

9.   Hull KR and the Steelers

I suppose I could have stayed in the Sydney comp. There were a number of clubs that offered me a contract, but I fancied a chance to go and play back in England. It was almost 10 years since I had gone over to Leigh and my memories of that time were now dim but favourable. I signed with Hull KR because of the respect I had for Colin Hutton, their chairman. I say signed for Hull KR, but that was not strictly true because in all the time I played for the club I never had a written contract. Everything was done by word of mouth and a handshake between Colin Hutton and me. There were very few, if any, people in Sydney you could work with in that manner back then or today for that matter. Colin Hutton told me that he had the makings of a champion side, wanted a champion player, and he brought me over to England.

This opportunity to play in England was the start of a major love affair with the country. The people and families we met and became close friends with across the breadth of England's north were wonderful. The time spent in the north of England still remains a joy to our family. There will be more on some of these fine folk as we travel through this next period in the life of a gypsy considering the number of opportunities presented to me in my career.

We arrived in Hull in early October. The transfer ban between the two countries was lifted pretty soon after the 'hung' decision in the Sydney court. Upon arriving at Manchester Airport with the children all wrung out from the 26 hour flight, having vomited most of the way over, it was terrific to be on terra firma. Due to the late approval to fly I had to arrange for my work permit to be brought across to Manchester Airport from Hull when I arrived. The customs and immigration people were wonderful and understood our plight after a long flight with young children. Though the officer I spoke to asked me where it was we were to be living to which I replied, "Thorngumbald". He quickly said, "Sorry lad but there is no such place!" You could imagine the look on our faces when we were told this, but as he smiled I nodded and said "Well if there is no such place we might be back tomorrow on a plane back home" to which he had a laugh. We waited patiently for the permit to arrive in the very capable hands of Ron Turner, the Hull KR club secretary. Ron was a big, big man with a welcoming disposition.

He told me that another person from the club, Max Gold, a director and local solicitor would help transport us across the Pennines to Hull. I suggested my Illawarra colleague, Mark Simpson, travel with Ron in his car with the luggage and we would travel with Max. We had a good laugh when we arrived at Craven Park, Hull KR's ground, to look around and meet the chairman, Colin Hutton who was waiting for us on arrival. Mark told us it was cool driving in the car across the Pennines with the window down, as he needed the fresh air, if only to keep him awake after the long flight.

When we left Craven Park to be driven to our new home in Hull, we drove down Zetland Road and passed the Zetland Arms Hotel which became a bit of a place to be for the overseas lads. We went through some older areas with structures built during the war years. Fortunately, the club had arranged for us a lovely semi-detached house in the wonderful eastern village of Thorngumbald. We arrived at Standage Road and went inside to begin our eight month stay in England. We were looking forward to a successful time and a period when the family could continue to build our family relationships that are so important in society. After settling into the house I took time out for a kip before heading out to training later on.

Meeting Roger Millward was one of the exciting moments of my career because I had played against this diminutive half-back when Roger was at Cronulla and marvelled at his ability and toughness. While I slept Linda took a short walk to the local shops, which were only 400 yards away. Just around the corner a young girl stopped Linda and asked if she was from the new Australian family in her street. Of course it would have been easy for a bright lass to recognise a foreign face in a small village. The youngster was Suzanne Gale and her introduction to Linda was "If you need a babysitter I am available and live directly across the road". You could imagine Linda's astonishment at this young girl's approach and the relief to know the locals were friendly and welcoming. It certainly made our start a positive one.

In fact, we were extremely lucky to get to know the Gales – Roger, Angie, Suzanne and Mandy who remain close friends and I should say are 'our family from England. Mark Simpson had lived and played in Wollongong for the Collegians club before joining the Illawarra Steelers as an up-and-coming half-back and was keen as mustard to try and make his mark on the English game. He was here on a trial basis. A solidly built half who took the game to the line and tackled strongly, Mark was also an Australian junior water ski champion. Later on he missed his girlfriend Sue so much and was so homesick we were worried about him. Fortunately, Sue arrived for a short holiday and Mark was a different person, no fidgety ways, not grumpy and loved going out with the players with his girlfriend Sue on his arm.

Mark also made one of the most unusual debuts for Rovers. He entered the game at about the 25 minute mark, promptly got stuck in making the tackles and passing the ball to the backs in fine fashion. An incident in the 35th minute meant Mark was to be remembered for this game. At this point the much loved Cumbrian Paul Hogan, Rovers' second-row man, had lost his contact lens from his left eye and was frantically looking for it on the pitch with the physio, Geoff Plummer, assisting. Well, play went on minus Hogan, Rovers were defending and naturally being forced back towards the halfway line with one defender missing from the line. Mark, after making a tackle, ran backwards to get back onside and Hogan and Plummer were bent over on all fours searching diligently in the thick grass that is typical of English pitches. As Mark made his way back, he was oblivious to the bent-over Plummer, duly tripped over him and came a terrible cropper. The spectators cheered loudly and roared with laughter. It was evident that Mark was as embarrassed as well he might ever have been and from there until half-time was unable to compose himself. The coach, Roger Millward, made a call and brought Mark off the pitch to allow him time to gather himself. It was one of the funniest things I have ever witnessed on a rugby league pitch. We remind him of this event almost every time we meet.

After arriving in Hull history repeated itself because I once again had the opportunity to play against 'home' opposition. At Leigh in 1973 I had played against the Australian Kangaroos. At Hull KR we were pencilled in to play the state champions Queensland. The game was refereed by Robin Whitfield and would result in an English career-long difference of opinion on decisions made in the heat of a game between him and me. The Queenslanders were over in England on a three match tour starting at Craven Park. Colin Hutton was a very good friend of Artie Beetson from the year Artie spent playing for Rovers. Queensland were looking for a game and Colin duly obliged because it would mean a world class game in Hull which the Hull KR supporters would enjoy immensely. It was also a chance for Artie to return to where he was an adored former player.

The attendance was big which was to be expected when the likes of Wally Lewis, Gene Miles and Colin Scott were set to play. No one expected the type of game that eventually took place that day. Everyone, myself included, expected Queensland to take over where the Australian touring side the previous season had left off. The Hull KR supporters were expecting Queensland to play a scintillating brand of footy that would blow the English teams off the pitch. Nothing could have been further from the truth because that was the last thing they did. They resorted to the type of footy played in Sydney in the 1970s, but even more brutally if that were possible. I am not sure if the ref Whitfield had been pre-warned to be lenient and make allowances for the type of footy played down under at the time, but one thing was for sure, I thought that he offered the Hull KR players no protection whatsoever in the first half of a brutal game. The Queenslanders had free rein to do as they pleased and boy they did.

After 30 minutes we had lost three players to injuries. Prop Roy Holdstock was carried off on a stretcher with a severe dead leg, and was quickly followed by the hooker David Watkinson with a bad injury. A little later we lost our stand-off Steve Harley with a broken wrist. It was only due to the fact that it had been agreed both sides could use four substitutes that we were able to keep 13 players on the paddock. Queensland had gone into a 6–0 lead thanks to a penalty and try by the great Wally Lewis, but as a result of penalties for foul play George Fairbairn had pulled the score back to 6–4, giving us a chance as half-time approached. As the half was coming to an end, an incident occurred that changed the whole face of the game.

Our Kiwi prop Mark Broadhurst decided that if the referee was not going to control the fouls, he would make some players think twice about continuing with dirty play. The Queensland hooker, Shane Bernardin, had been repeatedly niggling players, Broadhurst in particular, in the tackle. In the 36th minute he tackled Broadhurst again and continued the niggling. Broadhurst, who had been a boxer back home, decided enough was enough, and after playing the ball let fly with a beautiful short left hook. Bernardin was spark out before he even hit the ground. The response was magical, the whole crowd erupted cheering and applauding the punch. The look on Broadhurst's face was such that not one Queensland forward made a move. I think he would have taken the lot of them on at that moment with the same result. There was no doubt it was a sending off offence, but so much had gone on before that the referee was reluctant to do it. I think the crowd would have come onto the pitch and lynched him there and then if he had. I believe he decided that discretion was the better part of valour and penalised Broadhurst. After that, the Queenslanders knew that retribution would be swift. Broadhurst let it be known he would be dispensing it not the referee. They were never the same afterwards.

In the second half we began to play some footy and put Queensland under all sorts of pressure. They could not handle it as we took the lead from a kick through which our wingman won the race to score. That gave us an 8–6 lead we defended until the end. Even the great Wally Lewis began to feel the heat and made a number of wrong decisions. He even declined a shot at goal that would have levelled the score, kicking the ball into touch, then kicking himself when he realised what he had done. It was that game that brought home to me just how important the crowd was to an English team. The grounds there have the supporters closer to the action than they are back home. In Sydney they would be a good 10 metres or more between the touchline and the nearest supporters. In England on some grounds it was less than two metres. You felt the crowd was on top of you when you were playing. The other thing was the English supporters were much more vocal than the Australians in a very patriotic manner. Funny how clear the insults hurled at you were easy to hear while you seemed to struggle to pick up the plaudits.

The other big difference I found was the dressing rooms. In Sydney when you went into the dressing rooms at half-time whether the weather was warm or cold the first thing you got was bucket of iced water and a flannel to cool yourself off with a cold cup of water. In England the first thing you got was a cup of tea. Tea in a china cup no less. It was very strange for me to see players lining up for a cuppa. I remember the first time walking off the pitch and being asked if I wanted a cuppa. Hell no, I asked for the bucket of water and a flannel to which our kit man, Jack Ounsworth, obligingly placed in front of me. The Poms thought I was mad because it was a cool day and they didn't want a cold bucket of water to cool down at half-time. Anyway, it worked. I had cooled off, the English players had warmed up and it was time to return to the field.

Roger Millward had played in numerous tests between Great Britain and Australia where feuds were common. He advised us that with just one fit substitute to make sure we played them down their end, kept up the tackling effort and prophesied that the game would go to the wire. He said that it was Queensland's first game in England so Rovers had the best chance to beat them. Rovers were a rock on this game day and I firmly believe it was the making of the team to be able to tough it out in some matches in 1983–84.

With the Queensland game out of the way we were able to get down to the everyday business of league footy. I found that the priority was winning the League Championship. Being league champions was what mattered, the Premiership at the end of the season was a bonus. Steve Hartley's injury meant we needed a stand–off and Millward asked me if I fancied the job. Colin Hutton had told Roger about my ability to play stand–off from when he saw me play in Sydney. It was a position I really began to enjoy; playing pivot seemed to suit my style of play in the English game. It had been some years since I had played stand–off. As a junior player it was the position I most enjoyed because you were always in the thick of the game calling the plays, setting the pace and direction so it was easy to slip into the role.

Certainly the partnership I formed with Kiwi scrum-half Gordon Smith proved very successful. We went on a six game winning run which only ended for me when in the sixth game against Whitehaven I damaged ankle ligaments after only five minutes at Craven Park. I jumped with excitement when Mike Smith scored for Rovers and came down awkwardly. I was out of action for a month or so with the ankle in plaster or in pot as the English would say.

When I came back to the game after about four weeks, winter was beginning to settle in and the cold at training was biting. Icy drizzle hit you in the face from a horizontal line off the Humber River that was about one mile from the Holderness Road ground.

As November came around the club director, Max Gold, asked if I would like to bring my family along to his house near Manchester, a couple of hours drive from Thorngumbald, to celebrate Guy Fawkes Night on 5 November. I agreed it would be great for the Dorahy family to enjoy a bit of English culture and the English version of cracker night. Everything was good until Max said come out into his dark back garden to light the bonfire which was a load of grass clippings and a few tree branches.

Max's two girls and our three children were all outside with us when Max said "Oh, I won't be a minute. I will just go and get some fuel to light the bonfire with." I motioned all the children to go the back door and wait until they were asked to come out to the bonfire. When Max returned with the petrol he poured it all over the bonfire and the fumes could be smelt from a distance. Max had forgotten to bring the matches to light the fire so once again retreated to the house to fetch them. At this point I decided this was getting serious and I retreated towards the fence about seven metres from the bonfire. The fence was about two metres high and I wondered if it was low enough or should I get back to the house with the children. Well, Max came back with the matches and as he struck the first one nothing happened, but with the second match it no sooner sparked and 'boo-om' the fumes caught alight and I could see it spreading towards me and the fence. I turned and jumped onto the top of the fence in sheer fright. As I sat on the fence I looked back towards where the fire was coming from and saw it almost touch my backside. I was relieved I had pushed the children back to the house because had they still been within five metres of the fire they would have copped the full brunt of the fumes lighting and it could have been disastrous.

In the end we had a lovely night. The children thoroughly enjoyed the fireworks and the bonfire that kept us all warm before heading inside for some wonderful Jewish food and wine before jumping in our car and heading back to Thorngumbald on the other side of Hull.

It was around this time that Linda first ventured out after a match because we didn't believe it was fair to overextend our use of the childminding efforts from Suzanne Gale, our neighbour from across the road. Besides Suzanne was just 15 years old and looking to complete her GCE exams at school. Jackie Smith encouraged Linda most to seek additional childminding time from the Gale's and we were pleased when Suzanne's mum Angie and dad Roger agreed to Linda's request when she went home after the football match to take over from Suzanne. We did say we would be home by 8.30pm as Suzanne had school the next day. Roger and Angie were okay if we were a little late, but to be mindful of Suzanne requiring her sleep. We ventured out with the players and their wives and partners and as the English do they first go back to their club premises for the obligatory function then head out on the town usually going from pub to pub have one or two drinks and moving on. There are plenty of pubs in an English town and many were happy to accommodate the players calling in. In fact I think it helps keep the players sober because they are not drinking between pubs and get into the pints after arrival at each establishment.

On this occasion the players were going to the Hull KR captain's pub, the White Horse Inn, just over the bridge towards town off Holderness Road. We arrived about 7pm at a typical English pub, small, one bar and lots of drinkers and when the Hull KR team it seemed the pub was going to burst. Linda and I were in a round with Mike and Jackie Smith, George and Debbie Fairbairn, Mark and Ann Broadhurst, and Linda's brother Scott who was visiting at the time. Little did we realise at the time, but we were in for a long night. It was customary that when you join a round, the round remains constant and it didn't matter who was buying, the drinks kept coming. The time crept passed 8.30pm. Linda did the right thing and called Suzanne's mum Angie who agreed to our staying later, but requested we be in by 10pm so Suzanne could get to bed. Linda did not have a watch on her arm this night and was asking Jackie Smith what the time was to which Jackie would say "oh about 9.30pm" then the next occasion "oh about 9.45pm" when in fact the time had gone that quickly that neither Linda or I realised until the mine host rang the bell and announced "last orders". It was 11pm! Linda was aghast that we had let the time run on so long and just as this occurred the pub phone rang and a request for Linda to come to the phone. It was Roger Gale and he was not a happy man, justifiably. A good time was had by all, we had drunk enough alcohol to drown and in the days of no random breath testing we jumped into the car and drove home from town to Thorngumbald.

While driving home Linda and Scott both said it was up to me to speak to Roger, they were going straight up to bed. Upon arriving home Roger came to the door and said "And what time do you think this is? You agreed to be home earlier and our Suzanne has school tomorrow! This will be the last time Suzanne does sitting for you!" We were devastated that we had taken the liberty of pushing the limit of the Gale's goodwill, were forever apologetic and most grateful for their forgiving nature. We never did it again and made sure we knew the time when we were out with our new friends from Hull. It took a few weeks for us to go out again and only after Angie and Roger, over dinner one evening at their home, did they say to us that although they were not happy with the last outing we had, they were more than happy to allow Suzanne to do some more childminding as long as we were not going to stretch the time out. Of course we obligingly agreed.

In December 1983 the James Cook High School team, coached by Brian Smith, who was taking over the coaching role at the Steelers, were visiting England. They were playing several games against teams across the north of England including one in Hull. While in Hull Brian arranged to meet with me to talk over playing for him at Illawarra Steelers in 1984. I said I would think it over because this was my first season in England and would give him an answer shortly.

I remember one game against Whitehaven in January 1984 for no other reason than it was probably the coldest playing experience I have ever had to that time. The team arrived in Whitehaven on the Saturday evening for dinner at the hotel we were staying in. There was a cold wind blowing, but the weather was okay. Upon awakening on Sunday morning and looking out the hotel window, the ground was white with snow. I had wondered how it would be playing on snow-covered grounds and was about to find out later that day. By the time we arrived at the Recreation Ground in Whitehaven there was a force 10 gale blowing across the ground from the Irish Sea. At kick off time it had increased to storm force 11 and a driving icy rain was blowing in my face. Within a couple of minutes of kicking off the pitch had turned into a morass of mud. The game should never have been played, but it was and luckily we came home with a 22–10 win and consolidated our position in the top four of the Championship ladder. The road back to Hull is a very long ride in the coach down the M6 from Cumbria and across the M62 into Hull, but the time was spent singing, drinking beer and playing cards. I was never a great card player, so as usual got hammered when involved in a game. We got into Hull around 11pm that night and Linda met me at Craven Park for a lift home.

Another cold moment came when Hull KR played Bradford at Odsal Stadium. It made me wonder why I had made the decision to play in England when it was as cold as this.

At Odsal the dressing rooms were situated at the top of the ground. It was an old quarry converted into a rugby league ground with a motorcycle track on the perimeter that encroached onto the corners of the in-goal areas. To ensure the players' safety the club would place grass down before each home game on all four corners. It was an amazing thing to see when Bradford would deliberately kick towards the corners to provide the chance for the ball to bounce back into the field of play or into the in-goal area for a try scoring opportunity. The Bradford players would work hard to get to any kick to the corner, but would come in two waves – one to win the ball as it bounced or could be caught on the full and the second wave to catch the ball if it bounced well over the heads of the first line of players.

By the time the team walked the long track down to the pitch through the spectators – which wouldn't be allowed today – my feet were absolutely frozen and didn't warm up all match. Mark Broadhurst wore plastic bags on his feet which he reckoned kept his feet dry and warmer. It was also my first match against a young black player called Ellery Hanley. The 'pearl' as he was later known was a very tough opponent, skilful and terribly strong. Ellery bumped me off just once when I went into make a tackle on him, but not again in this match. Unfortunately we lost 20–0.

However, we had taken over the top spot from Bradford and for the first time in a season or two I was in a position to win some meaningful silverware. I was concerned about past disappointments with both Manly and Wests and whether they would haunt me in England. For that reason I wanted no distractions back in Sydney, so agreed a contract to play with the Steelers in Illawarra for the 1984 season. I didn't believe I was finished with top flight Australian rugby so was happy to finalise the deal with Bob Millward. I could then concentrate on playing for Rovers and try to help Rovers win the Championship. Colin Hutton was happy for me to go back home for the off season and we agreed verbally that I would return to play for him the following season, 1984–85. Once again it was all done on a handshake and I was pleased to come back. He had told me he had a champion side and we were playing like one as the business end of the season was approaching.

The one disappointment in that first season in Hull came in the Challenge Cup. Like all Aussies I had watched the final on numerous occasions at home on television from Wembley Stadium. I was keen to see if I could play there. In the quarter-final we went to Widnes and sadly came unstuck, losing 21–10. In one of those queer quirks of football we had to play them once more on the following Wednesday in the league, again at Widnes. This time we came away with the two

96

points, winning 17–8. While I was happy with the two points I remember thinking they were still in the Challenge Cup and we were not. As the season came to a climax we clinched the title with a couple of games to go. We did it at Leigh, where I had first played in 1973. After 10 years of disappointment in the Aussie game, in my first full season in England I had a Championship winner's medal. What made it all the sweeter for our fans was that in the end we pipped our arch rivals Hull FC to the title by just one point. It was with plenty of pride that on Good Friday 1984 the derby game was played at Craven Park. The Hull team made a guard of honour as the Robins took the field, applauding a fine effort by their local rivals. Well done Hull FC.

Having won the Championship, we set out to do what had not been done before, namely to win the Premiership play-offs as well. Having finished in top spot we played St Helens at Craven Park and managed to win 21–16 in a hard, close game. We had fully expected a close encounter as had our fans and that we would meet Hull in the final for a local derby final. Sadly, Castleford had other ideas and turned them over 22–12 to get to the final at Leeds the following weekend. I was in an English Premiership Final.

In the final, Roger Millward pulled off a master stroke. He decided to play three prop forwards in the pack from the start. His thinking was to sacrifice speed to enable his big forwards to wear down the Castleford pack. I have to be honest, at half-time everyone, but him, had concluded the plan had not worked because Castleford were winning 8–0 and looked good value for their lead. In the second half Roger made changes and I started to have more influence on the game. I made a break and put Gary Prohm in for a try to get us back in the game. Another try by Mike Smith gave us the lead and I finished off by scoring a final try to give us an 18–10 win. As the game was coming to an end I heard the crowd roar and wondered what was going on. One of our players told me that the announcer had just told the crowd that I had been won the Harry Sunderland Trophy for man-of-the-match. I had won two major trophies in my first season in England and was the first Australian to win this award. What a season and club to be involved in. The club had done what no one had done before and won the double: Championship and Premiership. Colin Hutton, who had brought me to Hull KR saying he had a champion side, really did and no one deserved it more than him. I am glad I took the opportunity to come back to England and join Hull Kingston Rovers.

97

Scoring against Featherstone at Craven Park in January 1984.
I scored two tries and kicked five goals in a 34–0 win.

At home in 1983 at Standage Road with Cara, aged 22 months,
and a badly sprained ankle.

Applauded onto the pitch by the Hull FC players at Craven Park after Hull KR had won the Championship in 1983–84 (Courtesy *Hull Daily Mail*)

Hull KR with the Championship trophy (Courtesy *Hull Daily Mail*)

Some of the players I particularly remember from Hull KR were:
- George Fairbairn – full-back, a dour Scottish lad with strong defence, bustling attack and a dry sense of humour. George had represented Scotland at rugby union and made the big switch to league at Wigan before signing for Rovers to become one their best ever full-backs
- Mike Smith – centre, a local lad who was always at the top of his game. 'Smudge' was another strong player equally adept at centre, stand-off or loose-forward. Represented his country and became a very good friend from our time there. Married a beautiful lady named Jackie Smith – yep Smith to Smith didn't have to change much
- David Hall – a ball playing loose-forward who really didn't get the chance to achieve as much on the representative scene as with Malcolm Reilly and Steve Norton in front of him
- Len Casey – a front-row man who never took a backward step. Was the captain of the club and was always strong on and off the pitch
- David Watkinson – hooker, a dour hard west Yorkshireman from Leeds who was as tough as teak and gave the team its much needed edge from the ruck.
- John Millington – front-row, a big blonde bombshell of a man. Funny as a comic, but would carry the ball forward all day
- Chris Burton – back-row, another Leeds lad who was all elbows and knees. The opposition must have hated playing against Burto as he was a tough one to bring down and was quick for a big man.
- Andy Kelly – back-row, came from Wakefield on a record deal. Kel was a big lovable lad who became very good friends over the years at Rovers. Good wide running forward.
- Gary Prohm - Kiwi centre, loose-forward with a work ethic second to none.
- Mark Broadhurst – Kiwi front-row, tough as nails. Mark also had a marvellous work ethic but also a terrific ability to offload the ball in seemingly difficult positions that set up many a score.
- Gordon Smith – Kiwi half who also worked hard on the pitch driving his team from the half-back position.

My first season at Rovers was a wonderful experience in football, which will always be cherished. The success of the team was a real bonus on top of meeting so many people who are still very close friends.

Following our win in the Premiership and with the season completed, the family and I jumped into a car from David Borrill's Jaguar garage in Beverley and drove up to Scotland for a quick holiday. In the small Triumph were Linda, Dane, Jason, Cara, Linda's mum Ida and Linda's nan Rita. We visited the castle on the hill, Edinburgh Castle and ventured up to the hallowed golf course of St Andrew's GC and had a walk around both tourist sites. We bought some souvenirs from St Andrew's such as golf club covers, tees, balls and caps.

I got on the plane a very happy man the following week with the family to go back to play for the Steelers in the 1984 season feeling fresh and ready to go again. I could never understand why players became "jaded and mentally tired". It must be because they were unhappy with their lot in life and didn't enjoy all aspects of the game, their club or their personal life. For me to play 12 months of the year was a bonus and one I wanted to make a success.

On my return to Wollongong Showground – now the WIN Stadium – out of the tannoy came blaring the tune to *Welcome Back Kotter* and the fans were singing "Welcome back, Joe". As it worked out I stayed home for the 1984–85 English season and Australian 1985 season as well because a business we owned and operated had run into difficulties when the manager decided to take a portion of the profits without approval. In a cash business it is important to be there most of the time. I never ran my own business again until we purchased a family-run hotel in Gloucester, NSW some years later.

I had been approached by Andy Kelly, the big young Hull KR back-rower, who had asked if there would be an opportunity to play with the Steelers if he could arrange clearance to come to Australia. I pointed out to the Steelers that Hull KR had paid a lot of money, around $250,000, to bring him to Hull KR from Wakefield Trinity. The Steelers signed him on a short-term contract after Colin Hutton agreed to let him play in Australia. Andy was soon on the plane with the family and me. He was like a cat on a hot tin roof: anxious, nervous and excited all at once when we arrived after the 24 hour flight.

We landed in Sydney to be met by a throng of the media keen on meeting the new big unit. Andy was very impressed that he received this attention as a relative unknown. He was a bit miffed when I started speaking to people in Sydney, and took me aside to ask me to slow down because he now couldn't understand me.

I said welcome to the reverse of going to England because gee it was sometimes really difficult to understand the lads when they got excited talking to each other in a group with their strong English dialects. Especially when having a drink at the pub after a match, it was difficult to understand the Pommie lads with their Hull, Leeds and Wakefield accents as well as George Fairbairn's Scottish accent. Still, Andy handled it pretty well and soon caught up with the Australian accent once he began training that afternoon.

I was going into my third straight season without a break and really should have been exhausted, but I think winning the League and Premiership rejuvenated me and removed any feelings of tiredness I may have had. My form continued with the Steelers much as it had ended with Hull KR. I remember one match against Eastern Suburbs at the old Sportsground next to the Sydney Cricket Ground when Illawarra had kicked a ball through and there was a rush of players trying to get to it. Brian Smith made a mention of it at training the next Tuesday evening when he said something like "Gee if you players would only try as hard as Joe has in this moment we would have more ball and make more of the opportunities that present themselves". Basically, in competing for the ball I had made sure I got in front of the Easts player by nudging him aside. Just normal practice on the pitch in my opinion, but it was great to receive the accolade.

One change that I was quickly made aware of was that the authorities had introduced a $1,000 fine for any player or club official who criticised any of the match officials, particularly the referee, to the media. I quickly found out why. The Steelers travelled up to Penrith and early in the game Penrith Panthers put up a bomb. I was under it waiting to collect the ball when a Penrith player dragged me to the floor. In the melee that ensued Penrith scored under the posts and we were 6–0 down. Everyone in the ground saw the incident, including every journalist and radio commentator, but sadly the one person who did not was the ref. Late in the game, Greg Mackay crossed for a try that would have brought us back to 15–14 with the conversion attempt to come. Again, we thought that the only person in the ground who saw Mackay bounce the ball in the act of scoring was the ref, Giles O'Donnell, a local guy from the Wollongong area who happened to be the same age as me and played against me as a junior player and he wiped out the score.

There were a great many people angry with the ref that afternoon. It seemed to me then, and I feel the same today, that the authorities have the wrong idea. Imposing fines to stop people criticising a referee is not the way to solve the problem. Train referees better and make them accountable by standing them down if they have a bad game or a series of bad games. It happens to players, so why should match officials not have to suffer the same fate? I went through the whole season in England without even a caution and yet when I got home once again I fell foul of the referee, or more accurately the touch judges.

I felt that I really needed to spend time ensuring that our fitness centre in Wollongong was operating successfully before considering leaving it for a second time. That meant staying in Australia rather than returning to Hull in September 1984.

I explained the situation to Colin Hutton over the phone and his reaction was typical of the man. He told me to get the business up and running and when I was ready there was a place waiting for me back in Hull. In hindsight, I had a summer to recuperate and spent the 1985 season playing for the Steelers, growing the client base of the gym and ensuring good management was in place so I could have another season at Hull KR.

It was good to be at home but towards the end of the 1985 season Brian Smith told me I had completed my days in Sydney football and should think about retiring or go back and play in England. Gee, I didn't think I was playing that bad and to top it off Brian Smith wanted to drop me to reserve grade about two-thirds the way through the comp. During a team selection meeting, which I believe became a little heated, Brian insisted he wanted to drop me, but the selection committee stood firm and ensured I stayed in firsts for another week because they believed I was playing as well as I had for years. I received word of this altercation in the selection room and understood why Brian Smith was a little uneasy around me. It was the week I needed if I was playing badly, because I came out and played the house down. Brian did not have the chance to consider dropping me again. He didn't come to me and explain his thoughts on my game. I thought he had strong ideas and wanted to make a name for himself. I thought he also got offside with a number of other high profile players in the club and though he stayed at the Steelers the team ended in last position on the ladder for three out of his four years there. I got the impression that Brian was someone who wanted his own identity at the forefront. I believe this was much of his downfall over the years and led to him seeking a coaching spot in England, which in many ways assisted him turn his thinking around. I thought it was all down hill after Fitzy's good set up.

The season went reasonably well with the Steelers, but once again I found myself on the wrong side of the match officials. When we played Souths I copped an early bath and once again it was on the report of a touch judge rather than the ref taking the initial action. I had taken the ball forward and passed it when my opposite number, the Souths stand-off Neil Baker kept on running at me. I saw him coming from the corner of my eye and realised that he was coming in to hit me with his arm raised, even though I had released the ball. I simply raised my arms to protect my head. Baker ran onto my arms and knocked me back. Again, the referee Mike Stone saw nothing wrong, but the touch judges ran on and said I had attacked Baker's head with my forearm. Stone walked me and the judiciary stood me down for five matches, it cost me around $4,000 in missed match fees. Strange how we cannot criticise match officials, but they can interpret any incident how they like without challenge. The slim chance we had of making the play-offs that year ended with that suspension.

I sat on the side line for five weeks and came back to play the last two games for the Steelers. I had been contemplating for a while quitting the Sydney comp. I had become a year round rugby player and, to be frank, I found the English game easier on the body and their style of play suited the way I liked to play. I was also a little disillusioned with the running of the game in Australia and the coach had a problem with my ability so I announced I was to retire at the end of the season from Australian rugby league. Unbeknown to me my team mate Rod 'Rocket' Reddy was also going to retire at the same time. The last game of that 1985 season was going to be my last game for the Steelers.

So it was on the 1 September 1985, 14 years to the day from when it all began I was to bow out or so it seemed. There was no fairy tale ending to my career, quite the opposite in fact. We were playing Parramatta and in the dying seconds of the game with the scores locked up at 16–16 poor Rod Reddy got pinged by the ref. Up stepped Mick Cronin and, cool as a cucumber, slotted over a penalty to take the game 18–16. I left the game a loser whereas on debut I had left it a winner. But in rugby league not everyone can be a winner on their first or last game. It was a very emotional day for me, not something I would normally associate with my career. I had mixed feeling as I boarded the aeroplane with my family to go back to Hull KR and my fourth season of footy without a real break.

Illawarra's tribute to John Dorahy

"The centenary of rugby league in Illawarra will be celebrated in 2011. The Centenary Committee was required to appoint an 'Ambassador' to use throughout our planning and be available to promote one of the 'Greatest nurseries in Rugby League'. This honour was awarded to John Dorahy, who ticked every box of the criteria. What a wonderful playing and coaching record he has established.

John was elevated to play first grade with the Illawarra Western Suburbs club at 17 years old back in 1971. He went on to represent Illawarra, Country, New South Wales and Australia – John is one of the 43 Illawarra internationals.

John Dorahy returned to his junior district to become the first captain of the Illawarra Steelers in the initial season of 1982. He played on with the Steelers until 1985, as captain, and was the club's top points scorer in four of his five seasons. After successful playing and coaching stints in England, John returned to coach his former Illawarra Wests first grade team. This was followed by advancing on to administration levels at Illawarra Wests – a position of director, which he still holds today. What a wonderful career and contribution to his junior district! Now complete by being named 'Centenary Ambassador'.

John will always be remembered for his great on-field ability as an attacking back, great competitor, uncanny kicking game, goalkicking freak and his cover-defence saved many games for all the clubs he served. Despite all that he achieved in Australia and England, I know he regards the 'home-coming' to be Illawarra's first captain and lead the Steelers in the 'Big League as one of his career highlights. The field goal that Joe landed from 45 metres out to defeat his former club Manly, 26–25, at the old Wollongong Showground in 1982 is still regarded as one of Illawarra's greatest victories.

When we assembled the initial Steelers team, John Dorahy was our priority signing. He had no manager and said: "It will be an honour, just pay me what you can afford." I can disclose that it was very little compared to what players are paid today and were paid back then.

The Dorahy family has always been associated with rugby league. John has been greatly supported by wife Linda and his twin sons Dane and Jason and daughter Cara. Illawarra Rugby League has benefited from their family contribution."

Bob Millward OAM

Training with Hull KR during the 1985–86 season
(Courtesy *Hull Daily Mail*)

10. So close at Wembley

It is always difficult going back to a club for a second season when you have had so much success in your first. That proved to be the case at Hull KR and I suffered one of the greatest disappointments of my whole career during that season. On my return Roger Millward put me straight into the team at stand-off. I slotted into the team as if I had never been away. Colin Hutton, true to his word, had no hesitation in bringing me back over to Hull and I wanted to repay that trust. It felt good to be back.

In my first stint at the club we had won the Championship and Premiership due to the consistent manner the team had played week in week out. On my return that consistency was missing, but what had been acquired was the ability to perform well when the chips were down. In England, unlike back home, there were a number of competitions that were available the club entered. There was not just the league, but also the Yorkshire Cup, John Player (later Regal) Trophy and the big one, the Challenge Cup. We seemed to be better suited to the cup comps than the grind of the league in 1985–86 and had mixed fortunes in them.

The fans wanted you to win everything, as all fans do, but our fans appeared to have a soft spot for the Yorkshire Cup. All the ties could be looked on as a derby game and they liked the bragging rights that came from beating a fellow Yorkshire club. The club had not won the Yorkshire Cup for over a decade. When we started on the cup trail, hopes were high and the first round draw was as high as it gets. There are many local derbies in the English game, Saints and Wigan, Warrington and Widnes, Leeds and Bradford, but for the Hull KR fans there was only one that really mattered, Hull FC versus Hull KR. In footy in Hull you either supported the eastern side of the city (Hull KR) or the west (Hull FC) and the first round draw paired the two clubs together. The game was to be played at Craven Park. A real derby.

I had played in derby games on both sides of the world, but that cup tie was different. It was my second game back and the pressure was on. Even though I normally did not get nerves before a game, this one generated an atmosphere it was impossible not to be affected by. On the day 10,115 crammed into the ground and the noise when we took the field was deafening. It turned out to be a blood and guts game with both sides giving their all. For most of the game we were behind in a tight, low-scoring affair. With just seven minutes to go, Phil Hogan scored to level the scores at 10–10. As I placed the ball for the conversion one half of the ground was silent. The black and white half were screaming and shouting in an attempt to put me off. As the ball sailed through the posts the black and white half fell silent while the red and white half went crazy. We won 12–10. Our fans went home happy and with the city bragging rights. The players enjoyed a drink that night.

We had an easier time in the second round. Bramley were the visitors and were easily seen off 30–6 to set up a semi-final match with Bradford, again at home. We won 11–5 to take us into the first final of the season. I had been in midweek finals back home, but this was different somehow. It was part of the regular season, not a made for television tournament. We met Castleford in the final at Headingley; it would not be the last time we would play them in a cup final. On the day Gavin Miller had a blinder and with two tries took the man-of-the-match award. We managed to squeeze home 22–18 that afternoon and I was able to add a cup winner's medal to my other two winner's medals with the club. There are no short cuts in a final; the hard work done in lead-up games is put to the test very quickly. Hull KR had a number of finals under their belts from the previous year or two and were primed for this one.

With one cup comp out of the way, another came up fast on the rails; The John Player Trophy. We got a reasonable easy run in the comp beating Halifax, Oldham and York on the way to a semi-final with St Helens, once again at Headingley. We managed to beat Saints 22–4 and would meet Wigan in the final in the New Year. The problem was that having the cup success had a down side because we were building up a backlog of fixtures. When we played semi-finals in the cup we had to drop a league fixture and we would face a lot of games in a short space of time at the end of the season. In the final it was a game we should have won, but sadly were on the wrong end of an 11–8 scoreline. Late on in the game we had Chris Burton sent off and with him went any chance we had of getting the better of Wigan. So it was two finals, one won one lost.

We did not have time to lick our wounds before the Challenge Cup draw was made. Incredibly the draw paired us once again with the black and white half of Hull. Once more we were the lucky club as we got the home draw. If the Yorkshire Cup comp had whipped the fans into a frenzy, the Challenge Cup draw was even more frantic.

However, problems were mounting back home. The manager that I had put into the gym in Wollongong informed me that he needed to move back to Rockhampton. That left me needing to find a replacement, which was a little difficult when I was in Hull. The only way round the problem was for Linda to return home and manage the gym until I finished the season and could get back home. So Linda flew out with Cara from Manchester on the day before playing Hull so she could manage our gym and I stayed on in Hull with Dane and Jason. The other problem was that my form over in England was attracting the attention of clubs back home and I was being approached to sign by various Sydney clubs.

When I left the Steelers it had been my intention to not play the Sydney comp again. There was only one thing, or rather one person that would make me change that decision, Warren Ryan! He had been appointed as the coach of Canterbury and made it known he would like me to play the season with them. The joy I felt at the chance of playing for Ryan, some 14 years since he had given me my first grade debut, was tempered by a call from home telling me that my former Western Suburbs team mate John Donnelly had died. He had been surfing up at Byron Bay and suffered an epileptic fit, causing a heart attack, while in the surf and drowned. He was just 31 years old.

In Hull, all eyes were on the first round Challenge Cup game and once again we came out on top, 22–6. I kicked five goals. As Linda was flying home I knew there was only one way I would have her back in Hull and that was to make the Wembley Final. Big ask, but I knew we had a chance if we played well. Our reward was a second round tie with York. We travelled up to York and came back with a 34–6 win and place in the last eight. It began to sink in that I was just two wins away from playing a final at Wembley Stadium. I had watched enough finals back home on the television in the early hours of the morning and now I had a chance of playing at the great stadium. Just two games. The draw once more was kind and we played Leigh at Hull. A 25–10 win meant that the club had at least emulated the efforts of the previous season and got to the semi-final. Then they had lost at that stage and so no one at the club was taking anything for granted. I was just hoping that the draw would be good to us just one more time. It wasn't. We were to face Leeds in Leeds, but as it was the semi-final and was to be played at a neutral venue, the game was played at Elland Road the home of Leeds United football club.

There were 23,866 fans inside Elland Road on that Saturday afternoon and the game was a typical cup tie. We were struggling in the game after just a quarter of an hour when Chris Burton, our second-row, had to go off with a broken arm. We were always playing catch up after that. Things got even worse just after half-time. The ref, Robin Whitfield, sent our half-back, Paul Harkin, off for a trip on Tony Currie. We were losing and down to 12 men. I was struggling, having caught a bang to the cheek which was fractured, but we kept that one quiet. That tackle by Cliff Lyons the Leeds stand-off was not penalised so I had to grin and bear the pain that comes from a fractured cheekbone. In spite of all the adversity, the boys stuck to the job and we slowly clawed our way back as the second half went on. In the end we managed to score a try and convert to bring us level with Leeds at 24–24 when the final hooter went.

On reflection, I think we were the happier of the two teams as we walked off. We knew we had played a get out of gaol card while Leeds facing 12 men and had been well in front so thought they had been robbed. The only problem was that I was in a situation similar to the one I faced at Manly. I had a fractured cheek bone and we had a replay against Leeds on the following Thursday, again at Elland Road. There was no way I could have it operated on as this would have meant missing the replay. We managed to keep the injury secret and I decided with Roger Millward to play, and have an operation immediately after the replay. When we returned to Leeds there were 32,485 crammed into the place. If the first game had been a thriller, the replay was even better.

Incredibly at half-time there was no score from either side, the nearest thing was when I tried a drop-goal just to give us a fillip and take a one point lead, sadly it crashed back into play off the upright. Paul Harkin who had been sent off in the first game was having a stormer, determined to make up for Saturday's efforts. Just before half-time we lost centre Gary Prohm with a damaged rib cartilage, but that seemed to inspire the pack and in the second half they really took control of the game. Early in the half Harkin dropped a goal and we were on our way, eventually we ran out 17–0 winners, Leeds really had been robbed. The following day I had the operation on the cheekbone and hoped I would be fit for the final. One thing I did right after the semi-final was go into the hallway near the changing rooms and ring home to tell Linda that she would need to come back along with Cara and whoever else in the family could make it because I hoped to be walking out onto the Wembley turf come May. That was the deal – for her to fly back if we made Wembley.

While I was injured I began to get offers to play the Australian season back home and one in particular attracted my interest, it was the club where I had started my career. The Illawarra Western Suburbs Red Devils offered me a player-coaching spot for the 1986 season and I was delighted. Hull KR were, however, a bit sceptical. They wanted to see the contract and, more importantly, the insurance policy Wests were taking out on me. Colin Hutton was not going to risk losing me because the club could not get me medical treatment should I require it. I must say that I recovered from the operation much quicker than expected and was only out for around 10 days. Though I was confident my healing powers were up to it as they were back in 1981 when fracturing my cheek bone in a match against Parramatta. What it did mean was that I was able to enjoy the build up and hullabaloo that accompanied getting to Wembley.

The build up to Wembley was insane. Everyone wanted to buy you a drink at the local pubs and wherever you went everyone was in fantastic spirits. East Hull was becoming a sea of red and white as the match day got closer. I would leave the lads, Dane and Jason, at the Zetland Arms Hotel with Marjorie Hutton who would get them to work around the pub to lessen their boredom. Of course, Colin was almost always at Craven Park ensuring the Rovers club was heading in the right direction, which it was.

There was a time lag of a month between the semi-final and the trip to Wembley. This provided the time to prepare mentally for the match. But in that time Hull KR had to play 10 matches over a 32 day period. This exhausted most of the players because the Craven Park pitch had become a quagmire of mud and sand.

I remember one match when I was rested by Roger Millward and was sitting in the stand in earshot of the radio commentators. I overheard David Doyle-Davidson, a former Hull KR player and doyen of Hull radio rugby, comment that the pitch was in no shape to be playing quality rugby and that the players had to be very fit to cope with the demands placed on them from a successful season.

111

Hull KR 1985–86 (Courtesy *Hull Daily Mail*)

With Dane and Jason at Wembley the day before the Final.

112

At season's end the Premiership was played for by the top eight teams. We had to face Wigan the week before the Wembley match. The match was played at Wigan's Central Park and boy were they waiting for us.

The match started at a furious pace with Wigan trying to run Hull KR out of energy as quickly as possible. However, we stuck to our game plan and got at Wigan as much as they put it to us. We were fit after playing over 40 matches in the 1985–86 season though injuries did dent the team.

Earlier in my career I learnt about having patience and biding your time when someone has cracked you a good one, as I thought one of the Wigan youngsters had done to me in the John Player Trophy final.

Now, he took a ball on the right side of the pitch and started running to his left across the back of the ruck away from the terrace end of Central Park. Little did he realise he was running towards me, not initially anyway. As he saw me coming into make the tackle, he stepped off his right foot away from me and almost ran backwards towards the try line, but straightened up to continue running sideways to the left. I saw my chance and followed him like a bloodhound to my right and kept him within easy distance for a tackle. As he decided it was time to step off his left foot I was now a bit hot under the collar, and was waiting for this moment. I hit him with one of the best tackles this side of the Mersey, with my arm bouncing off his ball-carrying arm. It collided with his chin. He went down hard and as he woke was spitting blood. I walked away from the tackle and left him to it. The referee said the tackle was fair and didn't notice anything untoward. Phew, if only the referee knew what league players did when timing and opportunity is right. And it still occurs in the modern game even though the television can highlight some of them explicitly. Though Hull KR lost the match I was happy with my retribution on his cockiness.

The four weeks went very quickly. Linda and Cara had arrived back in England to be at Wembley with me. We enjoyed the week leading into Wembley with Linda buying new clothes to suit the occasion. Finally, we were on our way down the M1 to London. The coach was driven by Trevor, who had driven us all season to our away games. The four hour coach trip to our hotel in West London was a pleasant and exciting trip with most of the lads playing cards and some, like me, just mulling over the position we were in. I reflected on how lucky we were. I was really feeling terrific about life and my first Challenge Cup Final. It is one of those quirks of life when not everyone has the opportunity to be blessed to play on the hallowed turf of Wembley Stadium. Like in Sydney, only a few rugby league players who get the chance to play in a Grand Final. The lasses were in a second coach and until after the match were staying at a separate hotel away from the lads. Probably a good thing because I am sure some the girls would have been more nervous than the lads and caused some raised blood pressure, which was not wanted in the build up. We arrived at our digs for the few days before the big match and trained enthusiastically. Roger Millward had to bring us back into line so we didn't over do it, we were that keen.

On the Friday prior to the match both teams made the customary visit to Wembley Stadium for a walk around and to accustom ourselves to the monstrous and cavernous stadium. Exciting, definitely – this is the Holy Grail of rugby league. To play at Wembley was like a dream come true for each of the players, but for me was extra special as an ordinary Aussie guy who had watched the final so often on television in the late hours of the night. This was a special time because the family visited England to be with us. My father, Kevin and uncle Bill Beedles, who was originally from Bebington in Lancashire, but had moved to Australia and married my aunt Marie, had travelled from Australia to watch me play in one of the most prestigious matches to be played in rugby league. Uncle Bill had been a great admirer of my playing days and it was magic to have both him and my father here in England to watch. Unfortunately, my mum was not able to fly due to an ear problem which was later to be found to be a tumour. Also travelling from Australia were Linda's parents who assisted with the child-minding activities while we were caught up in the moment. In fact Linda was able to sneak her parents onto Wembley on the Friday as part of the ladies' contingent from Rovers, which was, of course, special for them.

While at the ground our gear man, Jack Ounsworth who had been such an obliging person snuck in some sand and a couple of balls for me to have some practice kicking goals. Both Jack and his wife Pat became close friends over the time we spent at Hull KR. You wouldn't believe it though. I took a shot at goal on the right hand side of the posts about two metres in from touch down to the right of the Royal Box some 25 metres back. I say you wouldn't believe it – on match day with just two minutes to go I have the chance to line up a kick at goal after John Lydiat scored in the corner only inches from the corner post.

To say I felt déjà vu was incredible. I had practised this kick the day before from much the same spot, but with a little more difficulty. I felt confident I could land the kick to put Hull KR in front. Unfortunately, it was not to be and the kick went sliding to the left of the upright. Castleford snuck home winners on the back of a well controlled game by them. Malcolm Reilly had prepared Cas very well, but I am sure the hectic schedule for Rovers in the lead up was a factor in why we were not quite as sharp as during the rest of the season. Some players were carrying injuries, which in normal circumstances wouldn't bother them but the big stage of a Wembley final is different.

The journey to Wembley Stadium from the hotel had been interesting for a couple of reasons. The coach was escorted by four police motorcyclists and as we neared the stadium the number of people waiting along route at all the pubs to watch and wave as the coach passed was amazing. It certainly increased the adrenalin.

We had arrived at Wembley Stadium in good time and had the chance to walk around the ground prior to kick off. As we walked out into the stadium we were met by about 20,000 supporters from both sides who cheered or booed the team depending on who they supported. The next time we would walk out was an amazing feeling. We lined up opposite the Cas lads from the chairman, coach, captain and then in team position numbers. As we entered the stadium the noise was so loud it was unreal with almost 90,000 supporters there. The two teams walked across the pitch to the centre where we lined up like soldiers waiting to meet the guest of honour. The national anthem was played by the band and sung by everyone inside the stadium including me, because it was an anthem I had sung a thousand times in my school years before Australia changed over to their own anthem. I enjoyed the moment.

At the end of the season we went to Scotland again, this time with Ida and Don in a larger car, once again supplied by David Borrill. During our time in Edinburgh we visited a local restaurant for lunch of haggis and pizza, but not much haggis was eaten. When we had finished lunch Linda decided to go to the toilet at the back of the restaurant.

A presentation by Colin Hutton and Max Gold during my time with Hull KR
(Photo: Brian Teal)

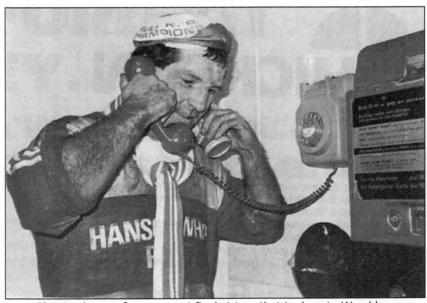

Phoning home after our semi-final victory that took us to Wembley.

She seemed to be gone for some time. Cara jumped at the chance to go and fetch mum then promptly came running back crying out in her four year old voice "Mummy's stuck, mummy's stuck". I sought permission to go into the ladies and see what the commotion was and sure enough Linda couldn't open the toilet door. It was stuck solid and wouldn't budge. It was very difficult to open because it was a floor-to-ceiling door. The latch was broken and Linda couldn't turn the knob. Eventually we freed her and walked outside laughing. We kidded Linda that we could have walked off and left her to it none the wiser. Poor little Cara was distraught and didn't like going into toilets for a wee while after this event.

Another new experience in England had been the snow. During the winter our good friends the Gale family had us out on the snow in nearby Beverley at the west wood. Roger had ingeniously built a snow bicycle without peddles and we tried it out on the common in Beverley, not far from the famous racecourse. Roger had attached a couple of cut down skis onto the forks of the bike and made a snow bike. We all had a go – Roger, Dane, Jason and me with lots of fun, plenty of laughs as the big falls happened to each of us.

Roger and Angie were a wonderful loving and welcoming family who were keen to assist the Dorahys in assimilating into village life in East Yorkshire. Roger would ask if we wanted to do some sightseeing around Yorkshire. We readily agreed and Roger would hook up a CB radio in our car and have one in his so that as we came upon a significant vista or point of interest he could speak on the CB radio. A typical comment was "Hey look to your left, there is the farm house used in the television show *Emmerdale Farm*". There were many moments like this and the funnier side was he would always want to end by saying "over or over and out" in his English accent. This made us laugh so much it would hurt our stomachs. Seriously, the Gales showed us much of East Yorkshire right up to Whitby where Captain Cook sailed his Endeavour from to discover Australia in 1770.

Following our wonderful time away it was time to drive back to Hull pack up and travel to Australia to coach the Western Suburbs Red Devils in the Illawarra RL competition one of the best RL comps in NSW. This was to be my first attempt at head coach with a club steeped in history and great pride. I was looking forward to it with great anticipation except for the fact it was by now almost halfway through the competition due to the late return home. We made the

117

finals and because I was injured in the last game and not able to play we lacked some direction on the park during the semi-final and were knocked out.

Keith Henniker was the club secretary and was a long time player, coach, manager and club employee of Wests. Keith came up with catch lines when Wests competed through 1969 to 1973 grand finals such as "Wests to Shine in 6-9", "Wests to go in 7-0". Keith was a Wests stalwart and loved his Red Devils.

11. Red Devils and a Rovers return

To some extent the great disappointment I felt due to the Wembley loss was mitigated by the fact I was going home and also back in time. I was returning to the club that had launched my career and was delighted to be doing so. All I wanted to do was to coach, play and give something back to the club where I had started – Western Suburbs 'Red Devils' in Wollongong. I had agreed to take on the job of player-coach and must confess the coaching side of the game was having an increasing effect on my thinking as I was arriving at my senior years as a rugby league player. Little did I know when I returned home I was also returning to a row with the Aussie rugby league authorities once again.

I got back to Wollongong the day before Wests were due to play and within 24 hours of arriving I was running out for the Red Devils, almost 15 years since I did so for the first time in the top grade. I had played only three games for the club when the proverbial hit the fan once more and the game's officialdom flexed its muscles against me, not for the first time. While I had been in Hull the Australian authorities had once again altered the rules. It seems they had grown alarmed at the large number of Australian players who were opting to play the off season in England. The players could make a great deal more money doing so than they could earn during an Australian season. The problem was that the season in Australia started before the English season had ended and so the Aussies in England were not getting back home for the start of the season in Sydney or would have to leave the club and return before end of March.

The first I heard about it was when Bob Millward rang and told me of the problem. He had been told by Ken Arthurson, the ARL chairman, that I was not eligible to play because I did not have a clearance from them. Arthurson was quoted at the time saying: "No player can turn out for any club unless he has a clearance from the ARL and Dorahy doesn't have one. Dorahy and his club now face the prospect of disciplinary action which could include fines and other penalties."

Of course, this only pertained to the NSWRL Competition and as Wests Illawarra was in the Country Rugby League Divisional competition it did not apply to me, so was not relevant.

That was all very well apart from one small detail, that being I had received clearance to play before I left Hull. I was in the Hull KR club office when Colin Hutton rang the board requesting a clearance for me. When the chairman put the phone down he told me clearance had been granted and I was OK to go and play back home. When the ARL and NSWRL effectively banned me from playing, the first thing I did was ring Colin Hutton and he again confirmed that I had been cleared to play. I immediately got onto the authorities and said that they had given me clearance and that Colin Hutton was willing to confirm this. Once again, in typical ARL fashion, the moment I claimed I was cleared to play, they decided that an inquiry would need to be made both in Sydney and in England, but in the meantime I was unable to turn out for Wests.

The reason the whole matter came to light was simply because of action by the Canterbury club. They were the reigning premiers and their secretary Peter Moore had rung me up. They had just lost their full-back Mick Potter with a knee injury and then lost his back up Phil Sigsworth. They had even lost reserve grader Matthew Callinan so were struggling in the full-back spot. Their coach, Warren Ryan, was keen to bring me in and I was just as keen to link up with him again. I played for many coaches in my career, but the one I consider to be the best was Ryan. He was by far and away the top coach I played for. Once again I felt that the ARL action was a restraint of trade and it also discriminated against Australians because British players were not subject to the ban.

I felt it was a case of having to go to the law once again, but decided that I would seek a meeting with Arko. However, prior to doing so Arko told the newspapers "If he feels he'd like to take legal action then that's his prerogative."

Then the ARL secretary got involved and said that "Dorahy had returned from England after the deadline and was not eligible to play with any club."

I still felt that I was in a strong position, but then got shot down by Peter Moore who said that the club would not support me in going to court. He even went so far as to say I should "think more of the orderly conduct of Sydney Rugby League rather than his own career". I thought that was a bit rich as they had approached me, not the other way round. On reflection I feel Moore did not want a confrontation with Arko and the ARL.

Artie Beetson got it exactly right when he wrote in his column in *The Telegraph* on 19 June 1986: "It's high time the Australian Rugby

League stopped discriminating against Australian players. That's right-the ARL is crucifying its own players by farcically enforcing its 31 March deadline for footballers spending the off-season in England.

It's ridiculous that any Englishman or New Zealander can jump on a plane and straight into a Sydney club any time before the June 30 transfer deadline..."

One thing I did discover in this whole affair is that the authorities have a long and unforgiving memory toward anyone who doesn't toe the line. Another thing is that I felt that the ARL were quite prepared to interpret their own rules in whatever way they wanted usually to suit their own ends. The reason I say that is quite simple. I was banned from signing for Canterbury and the reason was that I had failed to return to Sydney before the 31 March deadline. On that date I was playing in the Challenge Cup semi-final replay against Leeds. Playing for Leeds that day were Cliff Lyons and Tony Currie so they also failed to get back home in time. Canterbury, when they could not sign me, turned to another player to solve their injury crisis, that player was Tony Currie. How can it be that I was unable to play but Currie was? The rules were the same for both of us, supposedly. The same people ruled on the Currie signing, where was Arko or the secretary, Bob Abbott, and, more importantly, where was Peter Moore? Was he thinking of the orderly conduct of Sydney rugby league? I think not. The whole affair left a sour taste in the mouth I can tell you.

For my part, I went back to playing and coaching Wests Red Devils and enjoyed the experience immensely. My form was such that the Steelers began making inquires about me staying in Australia and playing the 1987 season with them. It was never a possibility, particularly after the run in with the ARL. Also, I thought that Brian Smith had not been a fan of players with high profiles and in 1985 had told me that he did not see me playing first team in 1986 or beyond, and that I should look to retire.

I had shaken hands on a deal with Colin Hutton to return to Hull and was not about to renege on it. As I said earlier in all my time at Hull KR I never had a written contract and everything was done on a handshake. Besides if I was at the backend of my career I wasn't feeling it but enjoying every moment of it. Hutton was one of the most honourable men I ever met in the game and I felt that his like were certainly in short supply within rugby league. I ended the season with

Wests Illawarra and before I left had my say about the ARL and that I thought was its loose interpretation of its rules in an interview with the *Illawarra Mercury*. Hull was also a place where the family enjoyed warm hospitality and the football promoted open attacking rugby that the supporters loved to watch and definitely suited my style.

It was to be my last season with Hull KR and sadly it was not as successful as the first two seasons had been. That is usually the case in the game. It was difficult back then for any one team to monopolise the game. Wigan in the early 1990s were able to do so simply because they were full-time professionals and trained every day. Teams now have a salary cap and that is evening up clubs in England, although some are still dominating in a manner we do not see in Australia.

We played well, but in the big games that season we seemed to come up short and so eventually won nothing. For my own part I was playing as well as I ever did. I was playing mainly at stand-off this season and while I had lost the edge of speed that counts against the best, it did not seem to hinder me when I played in that position as it was all about setting up my supports and the back line with early ball to allow the likes of Mike Smith and George Fairbairn to strut their stuff.

"Everyone remembers the last minute conversion that John missed in that Wembley final, but there was an incident which I felt was far more important. Just as half-time was approaching, Gary Phrom scored to the left of the posts. It was a trade mark of Gary's that whenever he scored he always dived toward the posts once he was over the try line in order to make the conversion a little easier. On scoring that try he actually dived away from the posts. I remember saying to my wife 'this is an important kick'. Sadly, John put it wide. No one remembers that.

There was one incident that epitomises John as a footballer and it also happened in a game against Castleford, the Premiership Final. John made a break and had Gary Phrom in support. As he approached the full-back, he dummied. Well, it was not really a dummy as such as the ball never moved, he simply nodded his head and the full-back turned to tackle Phrom. That was John, he made things look so simple on a rugby field."
Colin Hutton

"John was well named as 'Joe Cool', because that was how he played the game, he was a great footballer. He was a smashing bloke and was so disciplined on the field it was unbelievable. I only ever saw that

discipline drop once. When we played Castleford he gave away a penalty which cost us, but on the whole he always kept his cool.

When he came to Hull I think he enjoyed greatly what he had around him, good players, a good club and good people. Certainly he and his family joined in the atmosphere that was at the club then. I remember the game against Queensland, they were billing themselves as the World Champions and Artie Beetson who had played at Hull KR was keen to come back to play us with the Queensland side he was coaching. I remember Broady (Mark Broadhurst) smacking the Aussie hooker who had been niggling all the game. I swear to this day that I actually saw the referee burst out laughing when he did. That was one hell of a game, a hard tough uncompromising game that was.

In the Premiership Final against Castleford, I started the game with three props and played Smith at stand-off in the first half. Even when we were losing 8–0 at half-time, I knew we would win the game. I knew Cas and knew that the longer the game went on and we were still in with a chance of winning we would beat them. It is a measure of the man that after the game John came up to me and said 'Well coached mate' I knew that the planning was right for that game and in the end we ran away from Cas.

Wembley was a different story. I actually think that had John kicked that goal at the end it would have been an injustice to Castleford because I felt they were the better team on the day. It is funny to recall that on the Friday we went down to Wembley and I was talking to John who asked what would happen if he had to kick from the touch line because there was not a great deal of room between the touchline and the perimeter fence. I told him 'You will need to get your timing right'. The last kick at goal he had was from the very spot we were standing on when we had that conversation.

I had watched John play in Australia and when the chairman went there I told him if he could get John he would be great for the club. He was a great footballer with excellent hands and good speed, his defence was second to none. There was nobody better at reading and understanding a game, and I am delighted to have the opportunity to be able to give my opinion, a great man and a great footballer."
Roger Millward

The time was fast approaching, however, when I would have to hang up the boots and get a proper job. I wondered if that was the time to do so or if I had one last season of top grade football in me? That was a decision I had to make as the season ended in Hull. Out of the blue I got an offer to play the season with the North Sydney Bears under the Frank Stanton's coaching. After a great deal of soul searching I felt that I should give it a go one last time in the top flight in Sydney. I got on a plane and headed home. After training with the Bears I was selected to play against, of all clubs, Western Suburbs.

I felt in good shape because the demands of the English game and the style of play was nowhere near as demanding as the game in Sydney. That first four weeks back in first grade for the Bears was physically demanding, but because of a few rule changes and the tightening up of the play-the-ball area I found the game had opened up a little more than when I last played. I also put in a lot of extra training sessions in my fitness centre in Wollongong.

Certainly the press felt that I was adding a little to the Bears rather than hindering them so I was pleased with that. In June I turned out for Norths in what was my 200th first grade appearance in Australian Rugby League. It was a milestone I was immensely proud of and something many players never experience. North Sydney made a presentation to me that was totally unexpected and certainly valued immensely, especially as I was new at the club. It was a different feeling to when Western Suburbs ignored my 100 appearances for the club. I guess all the speculation about leaving versus staying had an effect, but in the scheme of things even if Wests had made the honourable gesture at that time it would not have changed my mind about leaving to join Manly.

I suppose Norths were very happy with their investment because even though I was now 33 years old they were talking about me playing on in the 1988 season. When you have always enjoyed simply playing footy, when the time comes and it dawns on you that you cannot go on forever, it seems you enjoy every game even more. It could be because deep down you may think it could be your last. I was determined to enjoy every game for Norths and not worry about next season.

A little while after arriving home from England we sold our fitness centre and I had to find employment because there were very few full-time professional players in Australia, unlike today. It was either employment or no rugby league for Joe Cool. This was to be my first real job working for someone other than myself or a family company. I began work for the Ryobi power tool company as the area manager for south east NSW. I was enjoying it thoroughly, achieving excellent results with the boss suggesting if I keep up the good work I would be looking at quick promotion plans.

However, my job was not suitable for playing top tier rugby league because I was away from home travelling every fourth week and so Frank Stanton asked to talk to me about my work situation. He told me that if I was to be away one week per month travelling around NSW then he would continue to find it difficult to pick me as first team full-back on the weeks I was not training with the team. Naturally I was disappointed and said "Sorry Frank, but I need to work unless the club will employ me full-time". There was never a chance of this, but Frank had an option. I met Frank before training, which changed my employment path forever.

He offered me the chance to work at the Universal Australia Company (UAC) at which he was the national sales manager. UAC was a Japanese poker machine company based at Alexandria in Sydney and needed a sales executive for the inner west of Sydney, my old stomping ground. In these years it became the norm to see a number of current and former rugby league players employed by the poker machine companies. Some of the rugby league fraternity included Johnny Raper, Gavin Miller, David Trewhella, Russell Gartner, Warren Jowett, Ray Brown, Bryan Milthorpe and many others who were and are still working in the gaming industry. Frank suggested I speak to Jim Henry, CEO at Norths Leagues Club and president of the Club Managers' Association who would outline to me the benefits of working in this industry.

I met with Henry, who was a dour Scotsman with a strong accent and loved a hint of scotch on the rocks occasionally. Jim told me that work in this industry was hard, as it is in any business, but if you have commitment and build the relationships you can succeed. But it was the following comment that had me move across to the gaming industry: "It allows you to meet new people and have lunch and a drink with them, play golf with your clients and do some business at the same time while providing you the flexibility to attend training whenever Frank calls it." I was hooked and so began a successful career in the gaming industry. I thoroughly enjoyed the 1987 season and got good reports from the media who said I was playing like I was still in my early 20s.

It was then that fate and history took a hand in my career once again. I had played very well in the early part of the 1988 season and with injuries came certain opportunities. It was time for the City Origin versus Country Origin match in Sydney. When the phone rang I thought it was just another family member ringing up for a chat. In many ways it was, because on the phone was Warren Ryan.

He had been appointed to coach the Country Origin side and after 16 years, when I had first played in the Country set-up as a 17-year-old with him I was excited. He told me that the original choice at full-back, Garry Jack, had fallen foul of the judiciary and been suspended. I was going to play full-back for him in the Country side and he was going to try to beat the City boys. This was something we as players together had not managed to do all those years back. In life you get special opportunities and this was one chance at repaying my best ever coach, enjoying the fruits of having played well in a club side and be recognised by rep selectors.

It was strange taking the field in the City versus Country game and thinking back to when I had last played for and with Ryan. This time when the City side ran out they did not look awesome, they looked just like the Country side and beatable as well. It was a game that would rid the demons from the 1980 City versus Country match when I was injured badly enough to damage my rep chances for some time.

I enjoyed every minute of the game. Quite frankly it did not last anywhere near long enough and not because we lost by two points. I was able to chime into the line from full-back anywhere and anytime I liked. It was just like the old days in the Wests side. The other oldie in the team, John Ferguson, crossed for a try and I managed to kick seven goals from seven attempts to keep us in the hunt right to the end. I was a little miffed that a 'try' by me was not awarded in the first half because Country were right on top and I am sure we could have achieved a different result had it been awarded. I felt my performance justified the faith Ryan had in me and was delighted when I walked off the paddock that evening. I have always been interested in rep football, but I suppose it is true to say that the selectors have not always been interested in me. However, it was a lovely way to go out of representative and first grade football if that was to be the case. A number of the journalists were suggesting that I would be selected as the NSW State of Origin full-back, but as usual I was passed over again. No worries though, I was just happy to have played in a team that competed and introduced a young stand-off to rep football in Laurie Daley.

One of the benefits of having a family early in life is that you get to grow with them in a close way, as our twin sons would testify. Dane and Jason both loved their footie. When we came to Norths I was asked by them if they might have a chance at being ball boys for Norths because they were now old enough to be good at it. I duly enquired and the twins were ecstatic to be informed by Norths' secretary, Bob Saunders, that he wanted them to be involved. They took to it like ducks to water and on occasions assisted in slowing the opposition down at penalties by getting the ball to the spot in a fashion for which the touch judges often admonished them. The twins displaying professional skills before their time.

It was now 1989 and I was coming to the end of my first grade career in Sydney, but was attracting the same reviews and comments from the press as I had when I came into first grade. The funny thing was that now when I tried something it was described as guile rather than a mistake when it did not come off. I suppose age does have some compensations. The club still wanted to sign me for the following season and because I had no other offers on the table I was considering it, though the money was not great. My young family were growing up fast and I wondered if it was time for footy to take a backseat to family. I also knew that it was really time to hang up my boots and see if I could continue in footy, but as a coach.

1989 was a solid year and the football was still tough with Norths again competing and being in the hunt early in the season, but flagging as it went on. It was a shame because Frank Stanton had great qualities as a coach and had instilled into the Norths club a new edge, one that provided the opportunity for them to reach their first final series for many years in 1990, unfortunately after I had left.

At the back end of the 1989 season it was announced I was to go to Halifax as player-coach. One of the young up-and-coming players, David Fairleigh, who was just 18 years old, approached me to see if he could come to England and play with me at Halifax. David was unhappy at Norths with the second team coach Steve Martin, who was to be the first team coach in 1990.

David, his father and I sat down for a long talk about the positives and negatives of playing in England at his age. At just 18 years old he had the world at his feet with the abilities he had shown in rugby league in 1989. I strongly suggested he speak to the Norths coaching staff about how the club saw his potential. I also strongly suggested that for a player of his ability it is better to play in Australia and make it there before trying to ply his trade in England. Common sense happened in the end when he decided to stay at home, played for the Bears for many years, made rep teams and became a Norths legend.

It was interesting though when Steve Martin phoned me just after Fairleigh and I had our meeting to absolutely grill me about trying to pinch Fairleigh from the Bears. Of course, I pulled him up quickly and told him the complete story of how I was approached and made the strong suggestion that Fairleigh stay in Australia at Norths to achieve his real potential. I am sure Fairleigh would have been a star in England, but he decided to stay with Norths.

I received a bad thigh injury playing at North Sydney Oval with just six rounds to go in the season. I had torn the right leg quadriceps muscle badly which meant me having two weeks off. I then injured it again in training before the penultimate round, so missed the last two games and didn't get the chance to say a proper farewell to the Norths faithful by playing out my time with them. That was sad because I thoroughly enjoyed my stay at Norths for the last three seasons. I had found another new lease of life in football, received the chance to work in the club industry in gaming, and as in any team game made a number of new friends.

The most disappointing thing to see from the future of Norths was when they had to join forces with the Manly club after the Super League war. It should never have occurred and meant the demise of a foundation club in rugby league. Today they are hoping to re-enter the NRL by relocating to the Central Coast. Best wishes I hope it happens.

I became aware that Hull were looking for a new coach and because the family and I knew Hull and had enjoyed our time in the city, I made inquiries. From that I put together a CV and applied for the job. Sadly, I was not successful and Hull decided to go with Brian Smith who had left the Steelers where his success as a coach was limited, at best, but he benefited by going to England to coach. With hindsight, I think it was a good decision if a safe one. He had a track record of coaching in first grade while I had only coached country first team football. It was then that I got an offer out of left field that was too good to refuse.

Chris Anderson contacted me to say Halifax were looking for a player-coach. After making inquiries and speaking to Chris, I sent off a CV. After the Hull rejection I did not hold out much hope, feeling they also would go for a proven coach. They must have talked to both Colin

Hutton and Chris Anderson and liked what they saw in the CV, because they offered me a three year contract to move over to Halifax, initially as player-coach.

The first year was as player-coach and the final two as coach. It was the coaching role that was the main attraction for me at that time in my career. I spoke to Chris Anderson for some advice because he was Halifax's player-coach from 1986 to 1988. I received excellent tuition from him regarding the club set-up, what pitfalls to look for and good advice on who to have as my assistant coach. Chris also let me know the idiosyncrasies of the chairman, David Brook and his board.

After much soul searching I accepted Halifax's offer and enquired if there was any money available to bring players over with me. In the end I took Brian Hetherington, who had played centre with me at the Steelers. I also managed to persuade Lindsay Johnson, the prop who had played with me at Hull KR, to come as well. My injury at the end of my time with Norths meant I left the ARL in a sad way after 15 years in first grade, sitting in the stands watching, but then we cannot always have what we want. I was disappointed on the one hand, but excited at taking up a new challenge in England. Little did I know then that I was walking into a minefield at Halifax.

On arriving, my family and I were provided a beautiful home, or so we thought, at Ainley Top between Halifax and Huddersfield, just off the M62 motorway and near the Hilton Hotel. To say we walked into a tip would be an understatement, though it was made good after a week of heavy cleaning. The house was filthy and there was bedding all over the place in the garage where some players had stayed.

I was not staying there with my family. We put our bags into the car and were provided with lodgings at a hotel in Halifax until we could clean the house. We were impressed with the Halifax people, especially Dee Brook, the chairman's wife and Margo Thornber, the club doctor's wife, who came in and assisted Linda in cleaning the house from top to bottom. Both Dee and Margo were gobsmacked that the house could be left for someone else to clean in such a state.

It was a blessing to have a chance to stay in town because we had time to get accustomed to it and its people. Compared to East Yorkshire, gee the West Yorkshire people have strong accents, some we couldn't understand however hard we tried. Being the midst of it was another lesson of life.

Early days, but great people and a beautiful area...

Action from our Regal Trophy semi-final against St Helens at Central Park.
(Courtesy *Halifax Courier*)

Making my point – coaching at Halifax in 1989. (Courtesy *Halifax Courier*)

12. Problems at Halifax

The first thing I did once I accepted the job was to ensure I spoke to Chris Anderson again. He had left the club a little over a year before and was still aware of what was happening at the club. He was in constant contact with David Brook, the Halifax chairman, so he had a good understanding of the ins-and-outs of the club.

Chris gave me two very sound pieces of advice: to make sure I had a legally binding contract and when I got to the club to ensure I appointed my own assistant coach.

I was happy to say that David Brook came up with the formalised contract and so the first piece of advice was not needed. I received a signed contract that could be used should non-payment occur and I mulled over the assistant coach advice as I travelled over to West Yorkshire. I arrived just six days before we were to play our first game of the new season.

Living and working in the Pennines at Halifax was a wonderful experience for the whole family. The scenery was absolutely beautiful in the hills and valleys. Our lads attended their first grammar school at Rishworth. Dane and Jason were thus introduced to rugby union. They thoroughly enjoyed union as well as playing rugby league at weekends for Siddal ARLC. They joined Siddal because it was Mick Scott's club and wasn't far from Ainley Top on the way into Halifax.

When I got to Thrum Hall I found a club which really was down in the dumps. They had been relegated from the First Division at the end of the previous season and had parted company with coach Ross Strudwick and Graham Eadie before the end of the season. The club had also parted with a good number of top flight players to balance the finances at the club or so I thought. All of this meant that many of the players retained by Halifax were so demotivated it seemed a sad place to come to and work. But having secured what I considered my first top flight coaching position, I was more motivated than the proverbial bull looking at a red rag.

Having coached Wests Illawarra Red Devils in 1986 and coming direct from North Sydney who were under the astute and disciplined coaching of Frank Stanton, I set about applying similar principles at Halifax as I had used in Wollongong and learnt from Frank and my previous coaches over the years.

131

I was introduced to the team at my first training session. I could feel curious eyes looking at me wondering what sort of coach I was and whether I was a disciplinarian like Strudwick or more like Chris 'let's have a good time while working hard' Anderson. I emphasised that to achieve the goals we would set it was the team that mattered; we needed to stay strong as a group and be there for each other all the time. If the team played well, we would win and if we won, we would all get winning pay. We would also be close to silverware and share some good times together.

It is worth noting here the English players loved the weekly payment method and would fight tooth-and-nail for the extra cash each week. The difference between the Australian payment system and the English one is that in Sydney we agreed a sum of money, signed a contract for payment, went out and played all the season and then at the end of the season we collected our contracted payment by cheque and that was it. England was different. At the start of the season, the club and the players agreed the match fees to be played for. There would be a sum agreed for each match that was won, a lesser sum for a draw at home, a win payment for an away draw and a much smaller sum for a loss. We played at the weekend then the following Thursday night at training the players collected their wage packet. If a player was not selected to play at the weekend he did not receive any wages at training. It was as simple as that.

There was however the added complication that most clubs employed a some what *ad hoc* bonus scheme. With English rugby league running at least four different competitions during the season, if a club was involved in a big game, for example a cup tie or a big derby match then they would offer an extra incentive for winning the game, in some cases as high as £2,000 per man.

In these early days I needed substantial help in making the team selection because I was unaware of some players' abilities, not having played in England for three seasons. David Brook gave me lots of advice and tips on how to run the team, as most chairmen do in England. Much of it was sound, but there was one initiative with which I ended up being very unhappy. Brook had invited Alan Hardisty, the former Castleford and Great Britain stand-off, to be on the coaching and backroom staff, essentially to be my assistant. Initially I thought gee, with a former player of Alan's stature this could be a good option, but things didn't work out with Hardisty.

132

I was fortunate to have another former player around, Jack Scrobie, and he gave me an honest opinion of a player's skill and advantage to the team and who to look out for around the club. He was also the stats man who provided me with excellent feedback at half-time and after the match. Jack Scrobie was a good man, as Aussies say a 'fairdinkum bloke' and I could trust his advice and comments every day because he would tell it how it was, not what he thought I wanted to hear, which I was happy with. Besides, he was a former player and his experience was valuable.

I made it clear to the players when I took my first training session that the team would be selected on the form they showed both in training and the game. There would be no favourites as to who was guaranteed selection and that included me. It would be the needs of the team on form and who we were playing in the next match that would dictate selection.

I quickly learned there was one major difference between coaching at Wests and coaching at Halifax. That was the expectations of the supporters. In England there is only one division the supporters and the club want to be in and that's the First Division. They made it very clear what they wanted and that was first and foremost promotion back to the First Division, anything extra was simply going to be a bonus for them.

In the early season games we had anywhere between 6,000 and 8,000 supporters in the ground, that was higher than most First Division clubs were attracting and much better than the 1988–89 season under Strudwick. It was just extra pressure for me as a coach though I didn't concern myself with the thought or the stress. I just took the Joe Cool approach and went about making the team competitive. While I did not feel out of my depth I realised a little extra input would not go amiss, so I spoke regularly on the phone to former coaches and their advice was invaluable.

As is the case with most new coaches at senior level, it takes a little time to gain the confidence of the players and get into place what your plans are, but being a player-coach made it a wee bit simpler. Well, I believed it did because it was partly my responsibility being on the pitch with the team to force a win from each match.

Six days after my arrival we went out to play the first game of the season when Rochdale Hornets were the visitors. As the teams took the field there were 6,671 supporters in the ground. The atmosphere was electric as is usually the case at any English game. The players were nervous and it showed in the first 40 minutes. When we got in the dressing rooms Halifax were leading 10–6 with the forwards struggling to hold the Rochdale six. We improved in the second half after we provided the direction the team must take in the second half and eventually ran out comfortable winners 36–12. It was amazing the effect that win had on the players; after a poor run and relegation they had forgotten what it was like to win a game.

It was after this match that I met one of the Directors called Peter Greenway who became a good friend during the 1989–90 season. Peter was a big man who did a power of good for the club at that time. The win was also a big boost to the supporters and the town. Everyone was saying they felt a change was in the air. The following weekend we had a home game against Oldham and went in as underdogs. The win the week before had whetted the fans' appetites and 8,612 watched us turn Oldham over 22–12. As is the case at any club the supporters love a winner. The Halifax people were looking for a return to the success of the Anderson era and were prepared to come along and support us.

Halifax still had a good nucleus of top players from their recent 'golden era' – Colin Whitfield, Brendan Hill, Wilf George, Les Holliday, Mick Scott and Seamus McCallion and with these guys we could build a future. With the inclusion of some Australian experience in Lindsay Johnson and Brian Hetherington, I believed Halifax could at least be very competitive and push for honours.

Sometimes coaching can seem easy and just two weeks into the season I was happy with how things were going. There was just one fly in the ointment as far as I was concerned. Remembering Chris Anderson's advice, on arriving at the club I had told David Brook that I wanted to appoint my own assistant coach. Alan Hardisty, as outlined above, was already in place and coaching the reserves. My request to bring in my own choice as my assistant did not go down too well with Brook or the board who I felt were loathe to upset Hardisty. Eventually they said I should 'see how it goes' in the early season and come back to the issue later on. I was not happy, but accepted the decision and moved on.

By this time I had formed an excellent rapport with Mick Scott, a local lad who made good at Wigan during their Cup wins, but moved back to Halifax when Chris Anderson was coach. I asked that Mick be the second team coach and also be available to play for the first team. This was agreed as Scotty was still a quality player and could provide the necessary experience, toughness and guile required in any team and current experience to pass on to the lads in the second team.

Our third game was a Yorkshire cup tie against Dewsbury at Crown Flatt, a ground like Halifax's Thrum Hall noted for its awkward slope. Once again we came up with a great win. Suddenly morale was sky high and the doom and gloom of the previous season was forgotten. Sadly, that win was the beginning of what was to be a downward spiral for the team and the club. The second round of the Yorkshire cup paired us with Hull at Thrum Hall. Hull were a First Division side and because we were not expected to win the board offered a large bonus if we did. I honestly think they did not believe they would have to pay out, but the team proved them wrong.

I was excited about playing Hull because I would be up against Brian Smith, my former coach at the Illawarra Steelers and the person who had told me to retire in 1985. Of course, this made the match against Hull all the more exciting and I was looking forward to putting one over on him. There was little contact between Smith and me before, during or after the match and that was how I liked it. We won 13–2 after we had totally outplayed the First Division outfit.

I wouldn't have liked to have been one of the Hull players at their next training session because I am sure Brian Smith gave them 'the rounds of the kitchen'. After the game David Brook had a face of mixed emotions. On the one hand he was delighted with the win, but on the other thinking where the bloody hell was Halifax going to find the extra money?

The two players I had invited from Australia to beef up the team in problematic positions, Brian Hetherington at centre and Lindsay Johnson at prop had proven their worth very early on. They had helped instil a competitive edge in tight games and this shone out in the Hull match. Brian formed a great partnership with Colin Whitfield and Lindsay was a stalwart in the front-row alongside farmer Dick Fairbank and big Roy Dickinson, the former Leeds and England prop.

The semi-final draw put us against Bradford Northern, another First Division outfit, again at Thrum Hall in an evening match. By the time the match was to start there were 9,454 crammed into the place. Bradford seemed to struggle in the first half and went in only 6–4 up. My half-time talk was about confidence and playing as strongly in the second half as we had in the first, but importantly not to stop trying until the final hooter. I felt we could win the game, the players responded to the pep talk and yet we found ourselves 16–4 down.

Unlike the previous season when I am told the team would have capitulated, they dug deep. We managed to pull the game around and got away with a 16–16 draw against a formidable first division outfit. There was a chance for us to win in the final minutes with drop-goals being the order of the last 10 minutes as we camped in the Bradford 30 metre area. The team used the slope of the pitch well, making Bradford chase the ball uphill and then we would run them down the slope to wear them down sooner than they would like – something Chris Anderson had told me to ensure I used to our advantage.

This draw was to be the beginning of payment problems. The board had to find yet another bonus payment and unfortunately it was slow arriving. When we trained on the Thursday the bonus was not in the player's wages and they were not happy. This was especially tough because we had to visit Bradford for the return match. It was explained that there was a cashflow problem and it would be resolved shortly. If there is one thing that will affect morale at a club, particularly an English club, it is when the players do not get their weekly pay packet that they play hard to earn, and so it proved to be. Ten days later we went over to Bradford's Odsal Stadium for the replay and got stuffed 26-4. It was likely Bradford thought they would march over Halifax at Thrum Hall better than Hull had found, but the Fax team made another First Division team work their butts off to achieve a win.

There was an interesting moment during this match. It occurred late in the first half with Halifax attacking the Bradford end. A kick went up and Bradford spilled the ball for a scrum to be set about 20 metres on the far side from the dressing rooms. Big Karl Fairbank, the brother of our prop Dick, knocked Lindsay Johnson to the ground after Lindsay had blocked his path to the kicker. Fairbank then decided to try and belt the daylights out of Lindsay. He was on all fours and trying to cover up because he knew what was coming from Fairbank. I was closest to the two players, ran to them, wound up my right arm and let swing with a strong uppercut to Fairbank's nose. My punch had him reel back, breaking his snout and he landed on top of Johnson. Lindsay pushed him off and at much the same time Fairbank woke and asked "Who did that?"

I was already some 10 metres away and being a 'non-fighter' I was terrified Fairbank would jump up and belt the crap out of me. And what use would that be? Interestingly, the officials never saw anything of the incident and so there was no report, nothing to worry about. I think they thought I had pushed Fairbank over and kept running. But the truth of the matter was I cacked myself thinking he would clobber me. But as Fairbank jogged back to the scrum to take his place in the front-row he did say as he passed me "What did you do that for?" I don't know who told him, but I did notice the big man try and stay in close proximity to me for a chance to smash me in the tackle or off the ball. Fortunately, this didn't happen because I could still have been in hospital. At training the next Tuesday Dick, Karl's older brother, told me that Karl was not happy I had broken his nose for the first time... not that Karl was the best looking man in the village. I know what it is like to have your nose broken and sympathised with his pain and discomfort.

I only broke my nose twice, both times in England some years before, when playing for Hull KR. Once was against Featherstone at Post Office Road. The other was against Oldham at Craven Park. I am unsure of what happened so will say no more. The worst event following a broken nose is when you are training and as I did once, only I was too smart to do it again, I ran into a training mate. Boy, did that hurt, possibly more than the original break

Back to the situation at Halifax. The players were discontented and all the good work at the start of the season began to evaporate. At the same time other forces came into play. My relationship with Alan Hardisty was not going well. I thought that he was making waves by whispering in players' ears that they should be playing in the first team. Then we lost a couple of crucial league games because the players were becoming more disillusioned with the lack of payments being on time. Matters came to a head when we played Fulham in the first round of the Regal Trophy, which was the new name of the John Player Trophy. Fulham were coached by my Halifax predecessor, Ross Strudwick.

I believed that Hardisty was no longer loyal to me and what I was trying to do. On the morning of the game I confronted David Brook at breakfast and told him what I thought. I also told him that we would beat Fulham, but win or lose Hardisty was out. Brook spluttered and muttered, saying he would have to consult the board. From his reaction I believed I was under pressure and had we lost I would have been sacked, even though Halifax had done better than expected so far despite the lack of financial stability and loss of players. Thankfully the players got the 'cup fever' again and we won easily 32–18 on what seemed to be an open playing field in west London somewhere – I thought I was back playing at Figtree Oval No.2 field as a junior player.

The board met that week and Hardisty was out. Immediately I brought in and confirmed Mick Scott as assistant coach at the club. This was a great decision because Scotty also owned a local pub, where the players often adjourned back to for a drink to relax and relive the game or the week's highlights. More importantly, Mick was as true as the sun rises in the east and I could count on him to back me up as long as I was straight. I was comfortable with that.

For the first time in my football life I had a feeling of pressure, but I was safe for a while at least. I made it known to the board that if we were to push for promotion we needed to strengthen the team. I was quickly made aware that there was no money available to sign players, and any new players would have to be signed on loan. Halifax brought in two players on loan, Kevin Dick, a half-back from Leeds and Gary Atkins, a stand-off from Castleford. These signings came only after we had put in a dreadful performance on 26 November at Carlisle, losing 30–20. I knew Kevin because I had played against him at Leeds when I was at Hull KR. Dick was an older player, clever with the ball and with a good kicking game, but slower than what was needed in the middle. Atkins was a relatively unknown outside Castleford, but also a fair player in the Second Division. That said, both players were not the standard required to ensure promotion to the First Division, but they were all that Halifax could afford. Brookie and his fellow directors believed they were great buys.

It was around this time that Halifax endured some bad weather. The pitch froze over and life for the Aussies was tough. One memory from then was one morning when Dane and Jason were racing to be ready in time to walk down to the bus stop on the road into Halifax. Dane took off and told Jason "hurry or you'll be late". Jason followed a few minutes later. The distance wasn't far, only a two minute walk. On this day the weather was very windy and Jason was passing the Hilton Hotel at the bottom of the road when a strong gust of wind picked him up, tossed him onto the road on his knees. Jason made his way back to the house with torn trousers, bloody knees and a sad face his mother began to patch him up. Dane soon followed, shouting at Jason for being so late. Dane had stopped the bus for so long that the driver had told Dane he could wait no longer. Dane jumped off and stormed back home to find Jason because he was worried about him. When he saw Jason and heard his woes he laughed so hard I thought he was going to wet himself – he didn't. Jason got patched up and Linda and I drove them to school. We had to go across to the other side of Halifax and through some terrible snowy roads. It was a lesson in driving in the Pennines and a funny story when told by Dane and Jason.

Meanwhile, Halifax were becoming a team with two faces. If the good one turned up we playing well, if the other turned up we were awful. The trick was making sure the right one turned up more often than the bad one which we did most of the time. The Regal Trophy second round paired us with Salford, another First Division outfit. Once again the board fell into the same trap. They thought we could not win and promised a hefty bonus. The players responded accordingly with a sterling effort. After a shaky first half we really turned things round and eventually won 20–6. The board did not know whether to laugh or cry. David Brook was looking a doomed man with heavy financial woes. In the next round we played Featherstone, another First Division side, and again upset the odds by winning 23–10 at Thrum Hall. However, in the league we were slow to start and by now were languishing in eighth spot and seemingly out of promotion contention. The top three teams were promoted. The fans' feelings were mixed; happy with cup success, but angry at our promotion prospects.

There was some good news for us early in January when it was announced that the club had been voted the Stones Bitter Championship Second Division team of the month for December. It did nothing to ease the club's financial situation and the players were still not getting paid at times. This was proving difficult for me as coach because players were coming to me for assistance. Mick Scott and I managed to keep the lid on the situation because of our success in the Regal Trophy. We were now in the semi-final as we had been in the Yorkshire Cup earlier in the season. We received a tough task as we had to travel over to Wigan's Central Park to face St Helens and their coach Alex Murphy. The norm in Cup games is using a neutral ground for the semi-finals. As we went into the game the Saints were coming off a three month long 12 match unbeaten streak. Once more no one gave us a chance, the board offered the big bonus and again the players came up trumps.

We put our league form on the back burner and set about winning a semi-final. In a very tough and physical match we walked off the field on the right side of a 10–9 score line. Murphy's face was a picture as I passed him walking up the tunnel after the final whistle.

"Everyone who knows me knows that I am a bad loser, I hate to lose, but that day John and his lads turned us over. The game in truth was a formality for Saints, but Halifax came and did the basics right. They tackled well and remained focussed for the full 80 minutes. You know in a game you do the basics week in and week out that is what Halifax did and we didn't. By the end we would not have scored had we played all night. John was not one to panic or start flapping around, he just got the very best out of his players that day. He knew that you could not make super stars out of players who were not super stars, but what he could do was make them better players simply by improving the skills they had.

After the game I was not very happy, but I shook John's hand and wished him all the best for the final. Mind you, I had to grin and bear it at the time. I had a number of bad experiences with Halifax while at Saints. Not only did John turn us over by one point in that semi-final but we also lost at Wembley to them again by just one point [when Chris Anderson was Halifax coach]."
Alex Murphy

Again, having won the semi-final, the board did not know whether to laugh or cry. We were through to the final, the club's first in that competition since the 1971–72 season, but money had to be found to pay the players the bonus they had earned. Then the board had to consider paying for all the trappings that come with being in a final. There were suits, tracksuits, and so on to be considered. Before the final we had three bread and butter league games to play. We won two, but the week before the final the players did not turn up and Ryedale-York beat us 18–14. It was not the ideal preparation for a final, but we had to get on with the job. When we faced Wigan at Headingley the board had decided to give the players a £2,000 bonus for winning.

In the final we faced Wigan and what I thought was a poor refereeing display. Though we never really envisaged beating a top class team such as Wigan, we believed we could put on a good show.

I felt that the referee seemed afraid to take action against Wigan for the indiscretions that in other games would lead to penalties and or even dismissals. It seemed like Halifax were expected to lose, and make mistakes that a First Division team wouldn't, which would inevitably mean penalties and easy scores for the opposition.

We lost the penalty count 11–4 with I thought some dubious decisions at best. All four Wigan penalties were for foul play. I felt that they should have been penalised for offside. On three occasions the Wigan captain, Dean Bell was guilty of a high tackle and each time the referee simply awarded a penalty, but took no other action against him. So often a high profile player gains an advantage that lesser players are not afforded. We lost 24–12, but I believe that it could have been so different if we had received a fair shout from the officials.

Halifax played well and deserved better treatment from the officials. Lindsay Johnson was having a tremendous game and Wigan were struggling to cope with him. One of his breaks set Wilf George off on a run and as he was being tackled into touch he passed inside to Richard Milner who scored. The touch judge, however, put his flag up claiming George was in touch when he passed the ball. As the match was being televised the commentators could look at a replay and it showed clearly that the touch judge had been wrong with George's pass being made at least a half-metre inside the line. Thus the try should have been awarded. Unfortunately, unlike today, we did not have the benefit of video referees to adjudicate on such incidents.

After the game the ref copped a good deal of flak for his performance from the media, particularly for the leniency he had shown toward the Wigan players – and I felt rightly so. The ironic thing was that John Monie, Wigan's coach, blamed Halifax for the rough house tactics when I thought his players were responsible. This was Monie's first major final in England and with the expectations of winning high against a Second Division club with an inexperienced coach, it was noteworthy that Halifax had put on a tremendous show to run the best First Division team closer than many critics expected. The press had expected a thrashing of at least 30 points and much to their disappointment Halifax did a good job.

Another interesting flashpoint occurred in the first half of the match when we were attacking from inside our half. John Lyons, our scrum-half, put a long kick into space with the ball rolling into the short in-goal area, which is the norm at Headingley and all English rugby league grounds. The Wigan players seemed to be slow getting to the ball and Brian Hetherington and I raced forward to put Joe Lydon, the Wigan full-back, under immense pressure. Joe and I reached the ball at the same time. I tried to dive onto the ball, but Joe just got his foot to it, and kicked it over the dead-in-goal line. Joe fell on top of me and in his rush to stand up stood on my chest. There was some pushing and shoving between Brian and Joe before I had a chance to get to my feet and give him a tongue lashing.

The referee intervened and settled the commotion but he just told me to move away, spoke to Joe and told him not to do it again. I thought the 50–50 decisions did not go our way.

We were now at the end of January with just a few months to the end of the season. The financial situation at the club seemed to go into further decline following the Final and the players' spirits were low. One director left and another was brought in to assist with the finances. Discipline on the field was not good with eight players sent off during the season and that did not help our league situation with quality players sidelined. And for the record, no it was not a case of bringing the Wests Magpies' game plan to the club.

Prop forward Brendan Hill, who was a favourite with the fans, asked for a transfer. He felt that I had a down on him and was being made a scapegoat for our poor league form. In reality big Brendan was a good player on his day, but I felt struggled with the grind of staying in top form week-in week-out. In fact he was one of our best ball-playing forwards when on song, I felt he simply was not playing well and that was why I dropped him. In March, club captain Tony Anderson was transfer listed simply because the club needed cash to stay afloat. The reported mis-management of the club over the previous years was coming home to roost and the present playing staff and I were having to suffer. Players found that their sponsored club cars were suddenly repossessed because of non-payment by the club. Players also had to wait for their wages and as April came were not getting paid at all.

It was a very sad situation. While it was going on the fans were asking why we were not challenging for promotion back into the big time. Rumours were rife in the town about the financial situation the club was in. Tony Anderson was transferred to Oldham without my approval, but I understood the position. Tony did not want to leave, but the reported £70,000 transfer fee was needed by the board for the club to stay afloat.

In March the *Halifax Courier* had published a 10 point questionnaire addressed to David Brook about the club's financial plight. Brook chose not to respond.

The questions asked included:

- Why the board was transfer listing players who were crucial for the club's promotion bid?
- Was the sale of Tony Anderson brought about by one particular creditor?
- Would Les Holliday be sold if a firm bid was received for him?
- Why has the board not revealed the club's true financial situation?
- Why have there been no accounts and financial statements for the last two seasons?
- After the present crisis, can the board tackle future crises?
- Do the club's debts put it in danger of being wound up?
- What is the extent of the club's debts
- Will you see through this present crisis and confirm your allegiance to the club?

The players were coming under increasing pressure, matches were being lost, morale was low, wages were not being paid and some players were simply turning up to training whenever they felt like it because they had to earn additional money elsewhere to survive. It was a situation that could not go on and I decided I had to take action on behalf of the players.

I reluctantly gave an interview to the paper and said exactly what was happening at the club. I told of players receiving cheques on a Thursday and taking them to the bank on Friday, those cheques 'bounced' on the Monday. I said "How can you motivate players, if you went to work and the boss asked you to put in extra hours, then hands you a cheque at the end of the week and it bounces. It is very disappointing that it should end this way. Players have been sold and I had no control over that, when in truth we should have been bringing players in."

I really did believe that in the early part of the season I had managed to turn the club around, but the financial situation had kicked all the challenge out of the players and I found myself struggling to continue the motivation.

You can imagine Brook's reaction when he read the interview. He said he was "absolutely shattered" by my outburst. He said that he

143

intended to rebut much of what I had said, and even threatened to take legal advice. Then he did what he had done all season, said he would take time to consider his reaction to this, and my future with the club. He told the press that he had set up a lunch date with me for the following week to discuss the matters. We never had that lunch.

In spite of all the board wrangling we managed to secure fifth spot on the ladder. Promotion had gone, but we were still in the Second Division Premiership and the chance of a final at Old Trafford.

Sadly, the players saw this as an opportunity to claw back the wages they were owed. Some of them wrote a letter to the board which they all signed. They said that if the unpaid wages were not paid, they were not prepared to play at the weekend in the play-off game against Ryedale-York. In typical fashion Brook was unavailable for comment, while the club vice-chairman Stan Ackroyd said he was unaware of any letter from the players. I realised afterwards that speaking to the chairman first about the player discontent would have been smarter, but it had happened and we had to move on.

He became well aware of the letter the following day because the reserve grade team was due to play their last match of the season against Castleford at home. We could not raise a team because the players had agreed among themselves not to play. The players had met before training on the Tuesday before the play-off and the second team match, and decided that if the board did not meet their demands then they would not play on the Thursday evening for the second team. Mick Scott and I tried to persuade the players to turn out, but they would not move. In the end Mick and I were the only professionals to play alongside a bunch of local amateur players we roped in to play a Castleford team with several first team players. When fans turned up to watch the game, the ground was locked and we kicked off the game 40 minutes late. It was lucky we did because we were waiting on several of the local lads to arrive for the game. Not surprisingly, we got flogged. However, it did was focus the board's mind that the players were serious.

An interesting point about this second team game was the referee. A young Stuart Cummings was the match official. He was making his way in the game and I did not think was sympathetic to a bunch of amateurs playing against a strong Castleford team. We got caned in the penalty department because the lads couldn't keep the pace and were regularly caught offside or going high in the tackle.

In the heat of the match I reacted with a verbal barrage to the referee requesting a fair go and a penalty. Stuart's response was to send me off for "continued questioning". As it was the final three minutes I was not concerned, but was very disappointed to be sent off in my final match playing for Halifax and my last rugby league match in a competition. I had played injured that night and was not able to play in the match against Ryedale-York. I am not sure if I could have stopped the loss anyway but it would have been nice to finish my playing career in a proper manner.

We managed to persuade the players to turn out against York, but as was to be expected their hearts were not in the fight and we crashed out. No opportunity for a match at Old Trafford and no happy fans looking forward to another final. It was a sad way to end the season for everyone.

With all the boardroom antics and financial troubles I was not prepared to sit and wait to see if I had a job the next season, so made plans. The next weekend we left for Sydney and realised that the chances of me being back in Halifax the following season were at best slim to non-existent, so set about finding a job, I still had to pay the bills and certainly wasn't paid the sort of money Brookie was sprouting about otherwise I would have still been there. While at home I was an easy target for Brook in an attempt to defend himself. It became known that the club debts were around £800,000. Brook claimed that one reason was the financial demands I had placed on the club.

He gave the impression that the club were paying me £92,000 ($200,000), which was nonsense. I accept that he did provide an excellent bonus structure, because he didn't believe Halifax could win the number of matches we did, especially in the cup games.

In the end an administrator was appointed to run the club. While I still had two years to run on my contract and was entitled to be paid for that period, it was obvious that no money would be forthcoming. I cut my losses and said to the administrator and the club that in the best interests of the club and the game I would not be making any claims on them.

For the first time in my adult life I was not involved in footy. It was a strange feeling and something I was keen to address, the problem was how, where and with whom?

Was rugby league a dead horse for Joe Cool? As a player definitely. I was now 35 years old, not getting any quicker and the injuries seemed to be coming on more often and lingering longer. It was a good time to call an end to my playing days. And as most professional players come to know, there is a right time to put the shirt back on the hook and give the young ones a go. It is just something you get a gut feel for and know without being told.

"I would have to say that when John came to Halifax, he was the best coach they had had in a long time. He was technically much better even than Chris Anderson. Chris was a player's man really, whereas John really thought about the game and the technical aspects of it. When he came, the club was in trouble financially due to the way that the chairman had been throwing cash at it previously. We had a good number of Aussies at the club who were costing a fortune. Then Ross Strudwick came along as coach and I have to say now, looking back, he was perhaps too far ahead of his time back then. Some of the things he wanted the players to do, sliding defence and such like, are normal now, but were unheard of back then. He tried to change too many things at the club too quickly. The result was we got relegated. Once that happened many of the top earners left the club and in the lower division it was left to John to turn things round.

I think the chairman, David Brook, was coming to the end of his reign. But the players looked up to and believed in John. He had done it in this country, he understood the problems of training in the mud and the freezing cold, not having the right training facilities. More importantly, the players knew he had done it on the field.

In the first few months of that season, John turned the club around and we were playing well. We should have got to the final of the Yorkshire Cup. John missed a kick that would have won the game for us, but we only managed a draw and then lost the replay against Bradford. Then the problems started with the money, players were getting paid, but they were not getting the full wages that they should have got. In spite of that, John managed to raise the team and we got to the Regal Trophy Final where we got beaten by Wigan. Mind you, we did turn St Helens over at Wigan in the semi-final. That day ordinary players played as a team for 80 minutes. We did everything right and the team spirit that ran through the team was tremendous. The trouble was the success on the field was causing money troubles off it, and in the end the players had had enough and at the end of the season went on strike.

The trouble began well before then. From the players' point of view they had bills to pay like everyone else and they were not able to do that simply because they were not getting paid. In the end they had had enough and went on strike. The chairman left soon after the end of the season, but I have to say some of the things that were said

about John once he had gone home were disgraceful. He was an easy target really as someone to blame for the problems at the club which really were not his fault."
Mick Scott

Looking back, there were some wonderful characters at Halifax. Mick Scott was a player, assistant-coach and landlord of the Punchbowl Hotel where many a night was had enjoying a drink and talk well after 'last orders'. Many a match was played out several times over a drink or three and the AWP fruit machine copped a workout. Mick is a terrific man and one who, with his family, we count as lifelong friends.

Les Holliday was a likeable lad with excellent ball skills and terrific left foot kicking game both in general play and as a goalkicker. He would quietly take the mick out of anyone. Another member of the pack was Dick Fairbank, a prop forward and local farmer. Dick was a tough uncompromising forward with a farmer's tale to tell. He would turn up to training on his tractor in the middle of winter with little more than a training shirt to keep him warm. Roy Dickinson was a big former Leeds and England prop with a wicked sense of humour. He was a tough, uncompromising defender with good ball skills.

Wilf George was a tall speedy right winger of Caribbean descent. I felt that he could have achieved more if he had a little more go in him. He had the largest hamstrings in the world. Eddie Riddlesden was another Caribbean winger with a huge 'ants nest' style dreadlock haircut. Eddie was a strong player. In the centre was Colin Whitfield, who was also a goalkicker. Colin had a real Lancashire wit and caught out plenty of lads with his tricks.

Seamus McCallion was an Irishman who played hooker and was the team barometer. If all was well, Seamus played out of his skin. If it wasn't then the ball didn't seem to get to right place as quickly.

'The Doc' was Stephen Thornber. He was a real doctor with a cool attitude and was professional at his tasks. He drank at The Murgatroyd pub, which we promptly named the 'library' because it had a very quiet bar with a low ceiling, no open windows or air conditioning and was full of cigar and cigarette smoke that made the London fog seem like a mist. The three Aussies and a few other players enjoyed a drink at the library on a Thursday on the way home from training.

However, if you made too much noise as Aussies sometimes did, their fellow patrons would all look up from their drinking with friends or playing dominoes to stare at you, pleading for quiet.

The Aussies at Halifax included Lindsay Johnson, his wife Michelle and two kids. LJ had a real country Australia look on life having originated in Gunnedah in country NSW. It was about doing the job and having fun at the same time within the rules of the club and life. We would enjoy a late drink back at the Golden Fleece pub between Elland and Ainley Top after several matches.

Lindsay now owns and manages a motel in Tamworth in north west country NSW, about a seven hour drive from Sydney. It is the home of country music in Australia. Everyone is welcome and the best time to visit Tamworth is for the Country Music week in late January.

The third Aussie was Brian Hetherington, with his wife and two girls. Brian was the straight man and I guess with two girls had to be refined to a point. Brian was a great signing by Halifax and provided a real competitive structure to the backline. He now lives in Figtree, about a one hour drive south of Sydney, just around the corner from our family and is a teacher at a local high school.

Allison, the Aussie physio, came to club on a hunch that Halifax were looking for a good physio. She was on a working holiday in England and decided to stop over in Halifax. Sorry Allison, but her claim to fame was on Australia Day, 26 January 1990, when the Aussies spent an evening at the Hetheringtons' home in Huddersfield having a BBQ, Aussie sweets and some drinks. Allison promised to make and bring a Pavlova sweet. However, when the time came to eat it there was a big surprise. It was a gooey mess, couldn't be eaten with a fork, but had to be eaten with a spoon. Not much Pavlova was eaten that night. There was great amusement. We promised not to tell anyone or to invite Allison to functions that required sweets to be brought along. She is now a physio in Dee Why, near Manly and I hope the Pavlova has improved.

13. Home and away

In moving back to Australia in May 1990, Linda and I had to readjust to life without professional rugby league in our daily lives. Upon our return to Figtree I was quickly on the phone to contact Frank Stanton to seek possible employment back with Universal Australia in the gaming industry. At the same time I quickly told Frank that I was not available to play rugby league as I had decided to retire. Frank was happy about this because it meant my focus would be on work and I would not be distracted by football.

Fortunately for me there was an opportunity available to manage the South East NSW region. This covered from Southern Sydney to the Victorian border and out to Canberra in the ACT. This was the region from which Frank plucked me from the Ryobi sales role while I was playing at Norths in 1987. I was delighted that Frank would allow me to work for him again. The option to work from home was a bonus. From end to end it was a seven hour drive with no stops. I soon organised a schedule and made the most of the opportunity driving up and down the south coast of NSW.

For visitors to Australia the coast of NSW is one of the most beautiful drives in the country. Beaches that just ask you to stop and swim at, hills and valleys like around Halifax, towns that have a friendly atmosphere inviting people to stay a day or two longer. The farms on the drive tempt you to open the windows to get a feel for the clean air and smell of country life. And for golfers, bring the clubs because the courses on the coast are to die for. Just ask my dad, Kevin. He hit his first hole in one at the Gerringong Golf course on 15 April 2010 at the buoyant age of 84 years. My hero! My favourite courses are Kiama, Nowra, Catalina Country club, Narooma, Tura Beach and Merimbula where the hospitality is superb.

I set about my new role with some relish. To ensure I had a chance to move into management roles in the future I felt I needed to further my accountancy studies that I had taken when I left school. I took an Advanced Certificate in human resources at the local TAFE College in Wollongong. Life was getting back to normal Linda was enjoying being in her home, the children were settling into school and I was thoroughly entrenched in work and study.

It is an interesting point of life when you think about the opportunities that life itself brings to individuals and families alike. Here we were having travelled the globe in the pursuit of sport that provided my family an opportunity to live in a different culture and the time to envelop ourselves in their daily life. It was so invigorating you do not realise until you stop, that what you have is sometimes more beneficial than you realise. Sometimes the things you let go of can be on the one hand the best thing you do and then again mean you have to make major adjustments that sometimes hurt the balance of life within your family and create new meaning. The old saying 'To gain something you must always give up something' was ringing true.

This period was one of those moments where the choice to come home from England changed us forever. The family settled into the everyday life in Wollongong. Cara took up dance and thoroughly loved it becoming a little star in the process and one of Doug's leading lights at Wollongong's Dance World. Dane and Jason were playing rugby union for the local Waratah club and going so well they were chosen to represent the Illawarra District. Linda was enjoying getting back to some form of normality of life. At last we were able to buy a dog, a King Charles Cavalier, which we called Miles as we felt we travelled miles and miles around the world before we could settle and have our family dog. So all in all, life was good.

Our neighbours, the Creighton family: Milton, Jan and four girls—Janelle, Nicole, Elizabeth and Penny—were happy to have the Dorahys back in Figtree. And the Dorahys were very happy to be home enjoying their friendship. Penny especially was happy because she now had the two boys to develop the already strong friendship from the previous nine years living there. Jan and Milton were down-to-earth solid people that anyone would love to have as neighbours and friends. Always ready to lend a hand, happy to call around for the occasional drink, Milton was the commensurate handyman able to steer me in the right direction to find a solution for any problem around the house.

One of the most interesting things about this time in our lives was how the constant coming and going had changed how we communicated with our close friends. The more we were away, the less we blended back into their lives or the life as we knew it. Of course, life changes everything and lives change everyday for everyone. I remember going down to the local pub at Figtree. When I walked in it was though time had stood still. I knew most of the people in the pub and they were all sitting in the same spots and talking to the same people as when I had left years before. In talking to them life hadn't changed too much and they still enjoyed going to the pub everyday to catch up with mates.

I had spare time for the first time in my life and enjoyed spending this with Linda and our children. There was always the caravan to go to for the weekends situated at Nowra Ski Park. The ski park was a haven away from the rush of weekly work and with the children now older, we would get out on the water and ski way up the Shoalhaven River and spend the day in a serene environment of river, farm land, trees and quiet moments when no other ski boats were about. The three kids learnt to ski on the Shoalhaven River and today are proficient barefoot skiers. However, they still can't get me to do a deepwater barefoot start.

In mid-1991 I came into contact with David Waite who I had played with in my early years at Wests Illawarra Red Devils. From a casual conversation David asked if I was interested in a coaching role with him as he was taking over from Alan McMahon at the Newcastle Knights as first team and club coach. I mulled it over first for a couple of weeks before getting back in touch with him and agreeing to talk about what was involved.

In September I drove to Newcastle a few times and met the coaching team—David Waite, Alan Bell, Robert Finch (second team), Peter Sharp (under–21s) and Robert Tew (under–19s) at Alan Bell's home in the Hunter Valley to discuss the forthcoming season. We met twice more at David's place in the southern suburbs of Newcastle and Robert Finch's place in Valentine after which I agreed to move to Newcastle and became David's assistant coach at the Newcastle Knights. After making this decision I drove to Newcastle a number of times to look at property and talk over the setup of the Knights for the 1992 season before training began in November 1991. I then began driving to and from training, a six hour round trip that had me home just before midnight. I was fortunate that Frank Stanton was amiable about me moving to Newcastle and provided the option to move for work as well.

Linda and I looked and looked around Newcastle and settled on Belmont North, or Jewels as it is now known. We were again lucky to have great neighbours in the Coulins and an older couple, Norm and Joyce, were quiet older neighbours, who were always there, on the other side of the driveway. We came to know them when the family

151

drove to Belmont North to clean the house before moving in. It was during this visit to clean that we almost considered reversing all decisions and staying in Figtree. Linda and I were in the bar/rumpus room making a plan of attack to clean the house.

The kids were running around exploring every detail of the house and yard when the boys came down the stairs and out the back door to the rumpus room. Cara was following about 20 seconds behind. As she came into sight in the rumpus room, our worst nightmare happened. The boys had closed the double glass doors and Cara was flying across the floor her sight set on getting outside as soon as possible. You know when you see something happening and you try to say something to warn someone of trouble … Well, I had that moment. I was trying to shout to Cara—stop! But nothing came out of my mouth and by the time I could jump off the bar stool Cara had crashed through the glass door. Yes, crashed through. The doors were quite old, had very thin glass and didn't have any warning on the glass to indicate they were closed. Linda and I rushed across the floor to Cara who by now had sat down on the outside of the door and was bleeding all over her body. I stepped through the broken glass door carefully and picked her up. As I put my hands through and under her legs behind her right knee that had taken the brunt of the hit crashing through the glass, her knee suddenly burst open to the bone. "Oh s..t!" I said and put her down and shouted to the boys to get some towels, and told Linda to run next door and call an ambulance because our phone was not operating yet.

The ambulance arrived in good time and prepared Cara for the short ride to the hospital. Linda went with her and I drove behind. Fortunately, Cara was okay but very, very lucky to come away with just a split knee and many small cuts. I say lucky, Cara could have cut her leg off, or worse still had she sat down backwards onto the still upstanding jagged edges. It could have been devastating. So we didn't do any cleaning on that day and drove home wondering if this was not a sign to say we should stay in Wollongong.

Nevertheless, we eventually moved and settled in okay and were very happy to have the neighbours we had. As is always the case our kids had also made friends across and down the street so we soon had people calling in and greeting the Dorahys to Belmont North. It made a difference.

The football was getting serious now as we reached January 1992 with upcoming trials. As I mentioned earlier, I was fortunate to have Frank Stanton provide me the chance to work for Universal in Newcastle and was given a productive area to manage. My senior manager in Newcastle for Universal was a guy named Brian Ennis, father of the Canterbury and NSW player Michael Ennis. However, I left Universal when an opportunity came up to move across to Aristocrat in Newcastle to work under a former playing mate in Warren Jowett from Manly and my old country sales manager from Sydney in Don Mealey. Aristocrat was the largest poker machine manufacturer in Australia, so it was a good move. After meeting with Warren it was agreed that the additional role of coaching would assist business development and he was happy for me to combine the two roles. This move gave me the chance to meet with David Waite and Alan Bell during the day in preparation for the week or training sessions as my position at Aristocrat had a lot of business in Newcastle. My client base were all onside if I was called into the football club office for some extra work. As long as I informed the people and the boss, generally it was okay.

Newcastle was very different to other places we had lived. It was very different to Wollongong, although the children, as always, settled into the new surrounds easily wherever they had to live. Our neighbours, the Coulins, encouraged Dane and Jason into sailing at Belmont 16 foot Sailing Club on the Manly Junior craft. Linda and I spent many Saturdays watching the boat races from the club deck and enjoying a social drink with good people. Later, in 1992, Dane and Jason represented their school, St Mary's Catholic High School at Gateshead, in the State Sailing Championships on Pittwater in the northern reaches of Sydney. Pittwater is where the television series *Home and Away* is filmed, though the spot where Dane and Jason sailed was at the southern end of the bay.

My first concern at Newcastle came on a summer day not long after moving. We were invited to lunch at the Belmont Sailing Club. Enjoying lunch that day were the Finch, Tew and Sharp families. I was asked fairly early in the conversation how I knew David Waite and what my actual role was to be at the club. Interesting question, because I was sure all points were laid on the table during previous meetings of the coaching team.

I duly outlined how David and I had played together at Wests Illawarra from 1971 to 1973, and represented NSW Country before

David left to join Canterbury at the same time I left to join Wests Magpies in Sydney. I said my role at Newcastle was as David's assistant coach, and assisting the lower grades where necessary. At this point someone responded with: "I'm David's assistant and you're my assistant!" I was a little nonplussed by this reaction and soon left the lunch because I didn't want to get included in any messy upheaval after just arriving. I left the sailing club saying that I was here to assist all coaches, but my main role was to assist David's first team. I said I would seek his clarification of my role and convey back to these guys what was happening.

David soon put it all right, explaining the roles again and everyone got on and did their job with success for all. Newcastle began well under his direction and coaching team. During meetings David brought in a new play that he reckoned would revolutionise the way teams attacked. The play involved from one to three different attacking points across the pitch, with up to five different options depending on the team we were playing and the options available. It was a simple play and one I was already accustomed to because I employed the same type of play when coaching at Halifax. I had unveiled my new play against Wigan in the John Player Trophy Final. Though we didn't score from it in the final, it certainly opened up Wigan like a can opener. I must say in looking at all the options available and the players that were to execute this play, David was able to put some polish on how it was executed by Newcastle. Living in a one team town such as Newcastle did remind me a great deal of the English game, because the Newcastle Knights every other week were boarding a coach to take them to Sydney the day before a match to prepare. Not unlike how in England the team would assemble at the ground or a meeting point and board the coach before going to the match.

As the season unfolded it was obvious Newcastle had a terrific chance to make the play-offs and we did. Players and fans were excited to be in the 1992 final series and justifiably so. It was the experience that was needed at Newcastle and everyone learnt much from final series. Though we didn't fare as well in the finals as we wanted, it gave the club a strong feeling of wanting to return and compete in the finals again.

Just before the 1992 finals I had an approach to coach Featherstone Rovers. I took this seriously, but I did not want to let down David and the Newcastle players by jumping ship just prior to the finals, so reluctantly let the chance go. Another Australian coach was chosen, Steve Martin who had been coach at Norths Bears after Frank Stanton. Little was I to know from this that greater opportunities were to come about the next year.

During the season it had been obvious some of the coaching staff were jockeying to place themselves higher up the coaching team ladder and with David Waite considering possible changes it was a time bomb. During the summer of 1992 to 1993, Linda and I took the time to enjoy Lake Macquarie and all it offered. We invited David and his family down to the lake for a ride in our speed boat. Naturally David and I were forever talking about football and our darling wives would remind us it was supposed to be a break from the grind of the game. David told me that I was a big part of his plans and not to worry about the undermining nature of some at the club, we just had to work on having a winning team.

After a terrific summer the football started again in 1993. Work was going along fine with lots of poker machine sales over long lunches and presentations to boards.

1993 was to be a watershed year for the Dorahys because it was again evident that the coaching team at Newcastle was not 100 per cent united. So, around February 1993, I made a decision to consider life away from football and applied for a role at Bartter's Chickens at their Canberra farm and office. I was invited to fly down to Griffith for an interview and to meet the management team. I boarded the plane in Sydney, a small twin engine, 22 seats, one captain and no flight attendants. After sitting down the chap across the aisle from me introduced himself as Peter and asked where I was heading. Peter then proceeded to ask a number of other questions about my work life and family history, along with questions on my football career. The big question was "What do you intend to do if successful in being offered the job you are going to the interview for?" I replied that my intention was to leave the game, concentrate on work and the rewards it would bring. At this point Peter said he should tell me his surname. "I'm Peter Bartter and own the business to which you are heading for an interview." I was gobsmacked, but didn't let on how nervous I had just become. My hands became instantly sweaty. I had to compose myself and hoped I had not embarrassed myself with my answers so far.

After about an hour and half flying we landed. Peter was met by a chap named Geoff Frost who was one of his partners. We travelled out to the plant and went into the office before being shown around the facility. It was a huge poultry plant and its size surprised me. Following the interview, Geoff told me he should have an answer no later than the next day. I was given a lift back to Griffith airport. At 4.55pm, just as I was preparing for the return trip to Sydney, I was surprised to see Geoff walk into the departure lounge. He told me that Peter, Geoff and one other person had deliberated about the position after interviewing another person for the role. The outcome was that I had been successful and he offered me a new job as general manager at the Canberra office to look after the South East NSW region. I returned to Newcastle a happy man and then had to consider the next steps. Part of that was to drive from Newcastle to Canberra to inspect the poultry facility and the house which was part of the package. The other issue I had to face was to tell both my work and football employers that I was leaving Newcastle for Canberra.

It was in the week after agreeing to move to Canberra, a new job and lifestyle that I received a call from a good friend, Mick Scott. My former assistant coach at Halifax told me that John Monie was leaving his head coach position at Wigan at the end of the season to take up a role at Auckland, a new franchise in the ARL. Gee, was I now interested in staying in rugby league or was it ludicrous to think that John Dorahy, Joe Cool, would, if he applied, be able to land such a job? "Don't be daft" I quickly said to myself. Now I did have a brief flirtation with yes, no, yes, no and came up with why not?
I made a call to Maurice Lindsay, who I thought was still the chairman of Wigan. After getting onto Maurice he soon told me he was now the chief executive of the RFL and that a chap by the name of Jack Robinson was the new chairman. He was the man to contact about the position.

I called Robinson and we talked about all manner of football things. Most interestingly, it was not what Jack said or how he said it, I knew instinctively from this call that I would get the job if I applied and achieved an interview. Don't ask me how, I guess it was an inner perspective, a God thing that drove me to make the call, to be strong, apply and then see what happens. Jack Robinson received my application the following week and responded within a week to say that all applications would be considered. If successful in being short-listed, I would be required to fly to England for an interview. I received the next call within two weeks and quickly had to make arrangements to fly. I spoke to my employers at Aristocrat and Newcastle Knights, explaining that I required a week off to clear up some things at home and was obligingly given time off by both. I am sure they believed I had trouble at home and needed time to fix things up. You can imagine what Geoff Frost's reaction was like when I had to call him in Griffith to seek his agreement to my need to travel to England and search out this opportunity to secure the world's best rugby league coaching role. He wasn't happy, but understood and I am eternally grateful to him and Peter Bartter for their best wishes.

One of the players at Newcastle, David Boyd, had known of my uncertainty at the Knights because the players could feel the tension in the coaching team from the coaches in the lower grades. David also knew of my interest in leaving the Knights should a good opportunity be available. I told him in confidence that I was applying for a big job and if I returned from the interview with a smile then he would know I had secured another coaching position. Boydy was true to his word and didn't tell anyone about our conversation, though he was keen for me to take him with me wherever it happened to be.

Linda and I flew out on Sunday arriving in Manchester on Monday morning and hired a car. It gave us a chance look about the Wigan area for schools, housing options and catch up with some friends, though on the quiet.

The club put us in Tom Rathbone's hotel just outside the Wigan town centre. Tom was one of the club directors and putting us here helped to make this trip as clandestine as possible because Wigan didn't want anyone to know who was being interviewed. I met Jack Robinson on Monday afternoon at his furniture factory in Wigan where I was given a timetable for the interview process. Wednesday evening was the night, with two other candidates also up for interview. I was later given the names of the people who were interviewed – Australians Steve Martin, the current Featherstone coach and former Norths coach, and Steve Simms. I had planned the application and interview well and was confident going into it.

At the meeting were the four Wigan RL directors – chairman Jack Robinson with Tom Rathbone, Jack Hilton and John Martin (Martin Leatherbarrow). I was told that each of the directors had a copy of my excellent application and had read it with great interest. They wanted my slant on my career as a coach. I provided as much detail of my short career coaching to date as I could, and embellished it with my playing career in England and when I coached against Wigan in the John Player Trophy Final at Headingley in January 1990 when Second Division Halifax had competed very well against First Division Wigan. Because I had to rebuild a team from the Strudwick era and battle at a club with financial worries, the success of making a good go of this role at Halifax impressed the directors.

The meeting must have gone well because Jack Robinson spoke to me the next day and invited Linda and I to the Wigan match at Central Park on the Friday evening. He also suggested we take a good look around while the directors mulled over the presentations by each candidate and the interview process.

The next morning, the Friday, I was asked to meet Jack Robinson at his furniture factory at 11am where I was to be informed of the board's decision about who was to be Wigan's new coach. After a few polite words by both of us, Jack said in his strong Lancashire accent. "You did well at interview John, the board has made a decision and agreed with my recommendation that you be offered the job as coach of Wigan."

My first reaction was to almost jump at Jack and kiss him, but I thought better of it. I replied, "Thank you Jack, I am honoured to be offered the role as coach of Wigan and would like to accept the role, thank you. What do we do now?"

Jack was happy that I was chosen because he had found my methods exactly what was required to improve the Wigan team and continue the collection of silverware. He was impressed with my attitude and desire to play attractive rugby, while ensuring the defensive qualities were still there. We went into his office and sat down for about 40 minutes planning the next steps. Jack was most insistent that no news be provided to anyone about being selected, because he had to inform the other candidates. He didn't want the announcement to distract everyone concentrating on the end of the season. He felt it best so he and I could make plans.

I returned to the hotel to pick up Linda who was waiting to know how it went, wondering was it a day of sad reflection or being euphoric. I walked into the hotel room and straight away Linda knew from the expression on my face. We embraced and were very thankful and excitedly happy.

Linda and I trooped off to view several schools in the area and took a drive up to Kirkham, 45 minutes north of Wigan towards Blackpool because we were given a heads up by Tom Rathbone that it was quite a good school. At each school we spoke to the headmaster, were shown around the school and given some excellent background on each. But it was the drive up to Kirkham that was of most interest to us. We thought the Kirkham Grammar School was the perfect fit for our children. We had decided many years before that if we were to travel then we had to make sure the kid's education was uppermost in our thoughts, ensuring a high level of tuition.

The headmaster, Mr Stacey, was a wonderful advertisement for the college and the town. He provided an excellent picture of what we could expect at Kirkham, including a strong emphasis on academic excellence and discipline with sport not far behind. Mr Stacey had a good first XV rugby union team, but was very interested in a couple of Australian lads in Dane and Jason. It turned out that one of their teammates from the first XV, Alex Sanderson, went on to play for England and captain Sale Sharks before being forced to retire through injury aged 25. Cara would be able to attend the junior school across the road, so we didn't have to worry about going to different schools to drop them off and pick them up. This meant long days driving for Linda – the kids had to be in class by 8.50am and did not finish until 4pm. Linda and I were now happy to return to Wigan and prepare to attend the match that night.

Linda and I were given VIP treatment at Wigan's Central Park that night. We were offered a chaperone, were given sponsor's seats and were entertained by a sponsor, Ray Miller and his lovely wife Ann came along to assist with looking after Linda. If there was one good thing Wigan RLFC did for Linda and me, it was to be introduced to Ray and Ann Miller. We were to become very close friends over the season we were there, almost family you could say. Certainly, I counted on Ray for wonderful friendship throughout the good times and a shoulder to lean on during the tough times. Ray was the Norweb representative looking after the Wigan and Norweb sponsorship deal. It was his job to ensure Norweb received value from the sponsorship agreement. Ray and Ann were the perfect hosts on the Friday night during and after the match.

Wigan won. The after-match presentation took place in the upstairs lounge area of the club. At this presentation I saw a number of players I had played and coached against who were interested to know why I was attending the game. I simply said that we were just visiting, had

159

been given the chance to come along to the game and were provided with a couple of complimentary tickets. Joe Lydon came up and said hello, which I thought was good of him because the last time we had been up close and personal was in the John Player Trophy Final in 1990 when he had trodden on me. Joe was a great guy, a person who you could trust and rely on, both on and off the field.

Linda and I made the flight home on Saturday. We travelled business class and enjoyed a glass of champagne to celebrate the successful outcome of our trip. If only we knew what the future would bring...

Once home I was confronted by David Waite who asked why I wasn't at the match on the Sunday. He had expected me back to training on the Friday before the match. Having arrived that morning and having to travel back to Newcastle, I had no chance of making it to the game. I also thought better of upsetting the team preparation when coming back from a week off with the players wanting to ask a load of questions.

Likewise, my boss at Aristocrat wanted to know: "Had I been to Griffith last week?" The simple answer was "No". But Warren didn't accept this answer because he had grown up in Griffith and had many friends and family in the area so knew what happened several weeks before. He then asked, "Have you accepted a job at Bartter's Poultry?" I had to say yes and he was most disappointed that I hadn't discussed my future at Aristocrat with him. I countered by saying, "I felt Aristocrat would have sought a meeting with me if they had plans for me?" If I had realised I was in Aristocrat's plans it would have certainly changed the path I had gone down. My bosses and colleagues at Aristocrat had become close friends, whom I felt I could trust and rely on, so it was a hard decision to move on.

Anyway, I was definitely leaving Newcastle and the job at Aristocrat. I was sad Warren was upset and that we had not discussed my future with the company before this. By leaving Aristocrat, I hoped I was not cutting off any chance to come back. However, I was now looking at what I expected to be the best time of my life and couldn't worry too much.

I spoke to Jack Robinson several times in the next month to prepare for the role ahead. The first thing he wanted from me was to find a good centre for the club. I suggested two centres to speak to about going to England to play for Wigan and said it was out of left field, but I firmly believed both would make excellent rugby league players. Their names were Tim Horan and Jason Little.

Robinson asked "Who are they? And are they capable of playing at this level?" to which I answered unequivocally, "Yes, most definitely, without a doubt. Tim and Jason are the current Australian rugby union centre pairing and compliment each other well." He suggested I try to make contact, find if they were interested and arrange to meet them both to talk over the commercial agreements.

I soon made contact with both of them and arranged to travel to Brisbane where they were from and meet them separately. First I met Tim who I found to be a really good bloke, up front with no hidden agendas. He was my first choice because I believed that his football prowess and temperament were most suitable to rugby league and would make the transition easily. We spoke at length and, to cut a long story short, Tim agreed he was very interested in considering the option to play with Wigan and making the huge step to leave rugby union, which was still nominally amateur, for professional rugby league. It would be an easier transition playing in England rather than Australia, so he was very interested. I was elated and we soon found a common ground for commercial agreement with the next step to arrange for Jack Robinson to have a contract drawn up for signing. If I hadn't got Tim's agreement, I always had Jason Little to back up my plan. It wasn't that Jason was second to Tim, it was that Tim was available earlier in the day than Jason. I was going to be happy with either player.

I met with Jason Little in the afternoon and found him to be a wonderful guy with a shy disposition, but a strong liking for playing football at the highest level. In our talks it was evident that Jason was keen to take the plunge and try his hand at rugby league. I was in shock. I had spoken to the two most exciting centres in Australian rugby union and was receiving the same message. Jason agreed he would like to have a shot at playing league and if I was coaching and Wigan were interested, then let's get this up and running.

Initially, Jack suggested one of them arrive for the 1993–94 season and the other for the 1994–95 season. I spoke to Tim and Jason about this new hurdle and neither was concerned. In fact, when I had explained the situation both were very happy to know they would play together at the same club in the same code. So the player to go over first was to be Jason, but during my next call to Jack found there was another major hurdle to overcome. After telling him I had secured verbal agreement from Tim and Jason to make the huge decision to come across and play rugby league at Wigan, I was mystified by his reaction. Jack said that he might have a better centre option than Tim and Jason. I asked who and he said "Vaiaga Tuigamala," Inga the winger no less. I tried unsuccessfully to compare the attributes required of a centre in league and a winger coming across from union to adjust to the game and the position. Jack was more interested in Inga than a couple of Australian players, and so it was that Inga would be on his way to Wigan. Mind you, this was in the first half of 1993 and Inga wouldn't be available until January 1994 so half a season would pass before he could play.

I phoned Tim and Jason to apologise for the opportunity of playing league going sour at the last moment. They were OK about it and wished me all the best in my role. Similarly, I wished both of them a successful future.

It was around end of April that the news hit the wire in England that John Dorahy had secured the job as coach of Wigan. There were many phone calls from both English and Australian journalists seeking confirmation. I spoke to Jack and he said he didn't know how it got out, but said it was now fine to speak to journalists about the move. It was also time to speak to David Waite about this twist in my career as a coach. David was a bit mystified how I had been given such a job with minimal experience, especially at the highest level. I told him it was a credit to his assisting me, but importantly it was the early coaching of Warren Ryan that provided me with the ability and confidence to take a chance like this. Newcastle held a presentation for me at the Western Suburbs Leagues Club in New Lambton, Newcastle. At the end of the presentation, David spoke, congratulated me on my achievement and wished me and my family all the best. A new adventure was awaiting us in Wigan. Pre-season training started in June.

14. Wigan

John Monie, who was leaving for New Zealand, was great. He sat down with me, gave me an appraisal of every player in first and reserve grade, who he thought was up-and-coming and who may well have reached their shelf life. At that time Monie and the club had won every trophy available to them at first, reserve and under-18 grade. A hard act to follow. I also remember thinking that I am coming to a club where there are a number of senior players with whom I had issues in the past on the pitch. Both Shaun Edwards and Dean Bell had had spats with me over the years I had played against them, as well as Joe Lydon when I was at Halifax. This would have to be addressed when we started pre-season training.

When the announcement of my position had been made, it sent shock waves around the rugby league world. Reactions were mixed to say the least. Alex Murphy wrote that I should not take the job because I was on a hiding to nothing. If I did not win everything then I would be branded a failure. If I won everything, then it was only what had been expected anyway. Some reporters wrote that Wigan were going for the cheap option and it was a sign of the growing financial pressure the club was under after the years of success under Maurice Lindsay.

At every opportunity I stressed that I wanted to take the club to the next level. I did not want to change things, simply make the players better. I put my cards on the table with both the board and the press that I wanted the team to play like a Sydney team. That was not to decry what had gone before and the trophies that had been won but I wanted to take players up to a higher level. I also said I thought I already had the players capable of achieving that.

When Wigan had offered me the job we had sat down and agreed the terms and length of the contract. In the end the financial arrangements were acceptable to the club and me. It was what the length of the contract should be and we agreed on a three year deal. I was not going to move from Australia unless a three year deal was in place. Jack agreed and understood where I was coming from because I had lived and worked in England previously. Linda and I had agreed that if we moved to Wigan we would buy a house at some stage, but when we went to the bank for a loan we hit a snag. The bank wanted a copy of the contract to be sure that it was for three years because they were not prepared to loan us money based on such a tenuous period of time as one year. I explained the situation to Jack Robinson who arranged for the documentation providing the relevant information to be given to the bank, which they duly received. I mention this now because it became very important at the back end of the season and all the intrigue and political factors that arose.

When I arrived Wigan had arranged for the customary media show. The obvious questions were asked:

What do you expect from a club such as Wigan?

Having played against many of the Wigan players do you expect to have any issues with anyone?

The competition between St Helens and Wigan is strong, how do you see it?

Will you make any major changes to the team make up?

Will you be bringing in any familiar names you have coached or played with at other clubs?

How many trophies do you expect to win?

My reaction to each question was a simple answer. "Wigan is a very proud and successful club that has built a strong following with its supporters. One that demands the success from its team and club. We will be doing our best to continue the fine work done by John Monie and earlier coaches before me."

The most poignant answer I provided was, "I have been asked to do three things, beat St Helens, win the Championship and definitely win the Challenge Cup at Wembley. If I can get the team to achieve each of these it will have been a successful year."

One of the journalists there on the day was a chap by the name of Neil Barker from the local newspaper. Neil and I formed a very solid and friendly relationship because I found him to be an honest person who did not print what is not to be printed. Not like some journos over the years. When I was leaving Wigan, Neil presented me with a Ping golf putter which I still use today. It was a generous and noble gesture to mark our time putting stories together. Neil made it easy to become a true friend. I hope to see him travel to Australia for the game of golf I owe him and to give him some good Australian hospitality in return for his many good deeds and understanding of different situations during the season. We played Royal Birkdale, Royal Lytham and other local courses and had a great deal of fun.

When I started in Wigan it quickly became apparent that there were issues that needed to be overcome. No one likes change and so any little thing I did was scrutinised, analysed and moaned and groaned about. I remembered the advice Chris Anderson had given me when I went to Halifax: employ your own assistant coach. I was told by Jack Robinson that would not be possible. Graeme West was the assistant coach. He had recently retired as a player and was a living legend at the place. It was either West or no one, so I went along with the guy who was in place. I suspected that West was upset that he had not got the job because he had applied for it. I quickly saw that while he was working alongside me, I thought there was a lot going on behind the scenes.

Not wanting to commit sporting suicide by pushing him out, I simply got on with doing the best job I could. I also seemed to get on the wrong side of Shaun Edwards who felt that he and Dean Bell had called the shots with Monie and they should have that same role with me. That was something that I was not prepared to accept and needed to assert my presence. In fact, Shaun stayed away for a time, saying he was still on holiday. Little did he know that it was no concern of mine, because we had great options to replace him.

I also took a long hard look, not at the first team players, but rather the reserves. They had won their league championship and cup for the previous two seasons and I was keen to see which of them were ready to step up to the first team. When I had arrived, all the talk was about a young kid called Andy Farrell, and he lived up to the praise he was given. But there was a blond haired kid playing at loose-forward called Mick Cassidy who I felt could also make a good hooker. There was a young, big second-rower named Barrie-Jon Mather who had great hands and good speed. I thought he could make it as a centre. Those three, all aged under 20, had been the mainstay of the reserves' pack that had been so successful. There was also Jason Robinson, who was now an established first team player, and Paul Atcheson, a promising full-back. I was delighted with what I saw because I knew I had players who would push the first teamers to perform well in order to keep their shirts.

At the first training sessions I had the trainers do several tests to gauge the players in fitness, speed, strength and agility. It was an interesting group of exercises and was taken well by all. We found some levels and I was keen to impress that for Wigan to achieve the opportunity to play against the Australian competition winners then we would need to improve our levels of fitness, agility and strength. With these results would come some extra pace from many of the players, but not all. We then began to implement a range of new calls for the plays used by all teams. This met with much questioning and Dean Bell asked why we needed to change what had worked for a number of seasons under John Monie. I replied "Did you have to learn new play calls under John Monie?" Bell's reply was "Yes." I said, "Thanks, now let's get on with this because it is a whole new ball game and how we work together will provide the results."

As the season approached I realised just how much pressure was on me from the supporters' expectations. Wigan demanded success, having experienced it for the previous six seasons. There was more pressure than any other club I had been involved in, including Manly. The traditional opener to the season at Central Park was a sevens comp. Eight clubs, including Wigan, competed for the trophy and even though it was supposed to be somewhat light hearted, that was not the case when I named my squad. All eyes were on me and we were expected to bring home the trophy. Luckily we did, but only after playing our 'Get out of jail' card in the very last seconds of the final against Leeds when the two youngsters, Farrell and Mather, combined to snatch victory from the jaws of defeat. The Wigan supporters all went home happy, as did the press. The first trophy of the season was in the bag. I wish that the rest of the season had gone as smoothly, but it didn't.

As the season began properly we were winning games, but were not playing as well or as openly as I had hoped. The problems I had forecast with Shaun Edwards quickly materialised and he roped in his mate Martin Offiah as well. We had drawn Whitehaven in the Regal Trophy. A dispute with them developed. I knew whatever I did I would be damned, but decided to discipline both players. Edwards I dropped to the bench for the Whitehaven game and Offiah I made play in the reserve grade game. Edwards cried off, saying he was suffering from the flu.

I also discovered early on at Wigan that there were a number of factions inside and outside the club. Jack Robinson was not as popular with the supporters as Maurice Lindsay had been. There had been some decisions before my time over players which had not pleased all the fans, and there were some who wanted Jack out.

In October 1993, I was invited by Dave Whelan to accompany him and several of his clients and business managers to attend the World Cup Football qualifier in Rotterdam between Holland and England. I sought Jack Robinson's approval about going. Jack agreed because the match was to be played on the Wednesday evening and I would be back for training on Thursday.

Dave Whelan had me picked up and driven to the local airport in Blackpool where we boarded his own twin engine plane. The seats faced each other with a table in the middle. Luxurious is the word that comes to mind.

The plane taxied down the runway and took off east towards Hull. We landed near Hull to pick up three other chaps then took off into the skies over England's north east and headed out across the North Sea towards Holland. I took my passport because I was travelling out of England and into a foreign country. However, it could have stayed at home. It was not checked in Blackpool and similarly was not looked at in Rotterdam on arrival.

During the flight over the North Sea Dave Whelan spoke to me and said that if he had been chairman of Wigan then I would not have got the coaching job at the club. I asked why not? Dave said that I did not have a high enough profile to be coach of Wigan. He said that John Monie had been a successful coach in Australia, what had I done? I carefully chose my words and said that if he was a rugby league follower he would know that I had a long history of playing in Australia at the highest level and had played and coached in England with great success. I said that the player-coach role I had at Halifax would itself have qualified me to be Wigan's coach. Also, my role as assistant coach at an Australian club also warranted the chance to coach at the highest level. I agreed that I was a greenhorn when it came to the head coach position of a First Division club, but was well prepared for the job.

We arrived in Rotterdam and headed for the coach that Dave Whelan's man in Holland had arranged. It was a 40 foot first class coach complete with soft leather seating, and a fully stocked bar that any night club would have been proud of.

We had to wait another two hours for the other lads to arrive from England. Dave even had some of his favourite Premier Cru white wine stocked and chilled ready for serving on arrival. When the others arrived we set off for the Rotterdam Stadium, some 40 minutes away and when we arrived there were thousands of Dutch people walking into the huge stadium. We alighted and watched the match. Holland won 2–0.

I simply tried to get on with my job of winning rugby matches. It was then that I made two errors of judgement that would come back to haunt me later in the season.

The first was to result in Wigan losing by their biggest margin for many years. At that time in England, clubs played far more games than they did in Australia or today in England. The fixture list was crowded with league and cup games and that season there was the added problem of the New Zealand tourists who were over to play a test series. Wigan had four players selected for the second test match on the Saturday, 30 October. Also, on the Thursday of that week we had another four in the Great Britain under-21 team that played the Kiwis in Workington. The problem was what to do about the game at Castleford that was due to be played on the Sunday, the day after the test? If we postponed the match, it would add to the backlog of fixtures we would inevitably face at the end of the season.

In the end it was my decision that we would go ahead and play the Castleford game. My thinking was it was still winnable and I could ask some of the players to back up from the test the previous day. Having made the decision, it could not be changed. Out of the eight players who had played in rep matches, six could not play. The result was a 46–0 thrashing by Castleford. The fans were less than happy, as were the board. I got castigated by the press and that whipped up the fans' fury even more. It was a lesson I learnt very quickly.

The second error of judgement I made was in the Regal Trophy Final at Leeds on 22 January, also against Castleford. The club had won through to the Final and because most of the squad had played in numerous finals in the recent past, I decided that to try to reduce the tension for the players we would treat it as any other game. Consequently, I decided that the players did not need to travel over to Central Park and then all travel to Leeds together. We arranged to pick up various players along the M62 motorway as we would on a league game involving a trip to Yorkshire. The results of my decision were worse than the Castleford league game earlier. In the final Castleford tore us apart and we were thumped 33–2. We missed 38 tackles and were never at the races. People thought the players were not up for the game because of my low key approach to it. Again, it was a lesson I learned very quickly and was determined never to repeat my mistake. The fans also felt short changed by the performance and the two matches against Castleford were not forgotten as the season wore on.

As we prepared for the Regal Trophy Final, I had spoken to the players about how to approach the match given this was my first final at Wigan and all the players had played in one or two before. I respected their judgement and with Dean Bell's agreement as captain we had a meeting to work out what the game preparation would be. The team was chosen and was ready to travel to Headingley.

In the lead up to this match some journalist decided to ask a clairvoyant from Blackpool to predict the winner and score. Her prediction was the score would include 33 points, but could be the total points, one team's points or the difference between the two teams. What she couldn't predict or wasn't prepared to give up was who would win. The amazing thing was the score ended up Castleford 33 Wigan 2.

Those two results were like manna from heaven for the people who were sitting on the sidelines looking for opportunities to turn the screws on Jack Robinson. When I took the job the board set only three parameters for me, to win the Championship, the Challenge Cup and to beat St Helens home and away. So in my eyes we were still on target for the board's objectives.

Then we lost our skipper Dean Bell to injury. That loss was eventually to lead to him and me disagreeing. He became, from my point of view, another part of the political problems that were besetting the club. Earlier I had sat down with Robinson to try and highlight areas where we could strengthen the team. We knew that Bell was leaving at the end of the season and would need to be replaced.

For the present, however, we had a problem that with Bell injured I had a hole that needed filling. Gary Connelly had joined the club in the summer and was playing well at centre on one side of the paddock. I decided to pull Barrie-Jon Mather out of the pack and run him at centre to replace the injured Bell. He proved to be a great success and over the next few weeks the threequarter line of Robinson, Mather, Connelly and Offiah gelled into a formidable unit, much to Bell's disappointment.

I was feeling pretty smug because I had pulled a rabbit out of the hat and got a top class replacement for Bell that had cost the club nothing.

During the ensuing weeks the pressure was immense as the team lurched from win to loss to win just staying in the race for the championship. When Wakefield visited Wigan's Central Park in February, we played terribly to fall to a team keen to win and inspired by a young Henry Paul. The referee was my good friend, Robin Whitfield. I thought he allowed so much lying on by Wakefield I considered arranging for blankets and pillows to be issued at half-time. It is well documented that in the after match press interviews I criticised Robin. I was not impressed with his fitness level. It saddened me to say this because over the years I was a fan of how Robin refereed, even though he and I had some good on field disagreements from time to time.

Jack Robinson pulled me aside and suggested I take it easy on the referees because we had a tough battle ahead to again be crowned champions. I agreed, apologised to all involved and focussed on the job at hand. This incident allowed the gremlins within the club to continue clawing away at me. My foes in the club were gaining support on the terraces. And when that happens it is difficult for anybody.

In the meantime, Mather grabbed the opportunity given to him with both hands and soon the press were talking of him getting a Great Britain spot in the forthcoming test against France, either at second-row or centre. For my part I was delighted with the way we were beginning to play. Sometimes we had lapses and lost games we really should not have, but on the whole we were playing the way I wanted and were getting closer to being like a Sydney side.

Then Bell was fit once more and wanted a spot in the team. He told me that he was an established player and the club captain. He said he wanted to end his career at the club on a high, and go out as the captain, playing and not sitting on the bench. He also felt that he should not have to play his way back into the team through the reserves. While I could see where he was coming from, I felt the team had more options in the backs with Mather and Connelly at centre and they added things Bell did not. I also knew that he had played a number of games at loose-forward and told him I would use him in that role as well as at centre.

Cutting a long story short, I thought he spat the dummy out big style with me and the board. Our critics claimed it was a case of the team was still underachieving and yet the skipper could not get back into the side.

Meeting Charles Duke, the Apollo 16 astronaut, who was staying with our friends the Stricklands.

The effect of all this was that Jack came under pressure to do something to assist Bell, who was a favourite with the fans even though he was leaving at the end of the season. Sadly, I believe that Jack felt he had to act and needed a scapegoat to cover his back. That scapegoat was me.

I was placed under pressure to find a spot in the coaching area for Bell. I was also still having problems with Graeme West, who felt that he and his reserve grade side were not getting a fair shout. I felt that he was still disappointed at not being appointed first team coach and because the team was playing well it weakened his position.

Jack insisted that Bell be given some recognition and eventually he decided to make him an assistant coach charged with handling the motivation of players. I have no idea what that was supposed to be about, but the press had a field day. They cut Jack Robinson and his arguments about Bell to pieces, while at the same time stating the obvious that they saw this move as one that weakened my position with the players. That was a simple fact. I had to accept the appointment and get on with my job. I determined to stick to my selection policy and tried not to alter the team overmuch. We were at that time in the season when the Challenge Cup came into play. Wigan had won the cup for the last six seasons and the fans had already booked their tickets and accommodation down in London so sure were they that we would be there again.

They must have had heart attacks when we went to Hull to play them in one of the early rounds. When we arrived at the ground there was a hurricane blowing off the North Sea straight down the field. We discussed what we should do in the dressing room and decided that we would play into the teeth of the wind in the first half. The plan was to hold Hull and then exploit the wind to our advantage in the second half. However, the reality was different in that first half we missed 18 tackles and let in 22 points. We managed to get Mather across the line just on half-time to go in 22–6 down. That try, however, gave all the players a lift and the feeling was that we could not play as badly in the second half. For my part I turned the air blue. I let some of the players hear some home truths and said we would not get to Wembley if we continued to miss tackles as we had in the first 40 minutes.

In the second half the team turned it around, the wind had not dropped at all and we used it well. On one occasion Andy Farrell was called on to take a goal line drop-out, he hoofed the ball down field, it bounced once and shot dead at the other end of the field. Hull could not get out of their half and we managed to scrape home 23–22, but I left with more grey hair than when I went in.

Hull had Royce Simmons as coach. Royce had won competitions with the Penrith Panthers and knew how to get his teams up for big games and this was one of those big games, especially for them. Maybe Wigan had gone into the game feeling over-confident.

In the stands that day, having travelled in the coach with the team, was Inga Tuigamala, who was watching the team for the first time. Jack Robinson apologised to Inga at half-time because he couldn't see Wigan coming back from this position. Inga told the chairman that God didn't bring him here to Wigan not to go to Wembley. Inga began praying silently for God's intervention, helped the Wigan lads realise their potential on the day and win a game they were more than capable of doing.

Speaking of 'Inga the winger', when he arrived the media world was abuzz with how he would make the transition to rugby league from rugby union. I was not concerned about his ability because I had watched several videos of him playing and saw the huge potential. My intention for Inga was to make sure he was ready when he made his debut. I did not want to throw him to the wolves by putting him under pressure to perform in a game that was almost foreign to him. So I spoke to Inga about the plan. He was concerned about a 'return on investment' for Wigan, which they would want as soon as possible. The chairman was a little taken aback about my approach, but I guaranteed Jack that when Inga did make his debut he would play better than if we were to play him in the first week of his contract.

Inga had to wait patiently for five weeks before getting the chance to play. He had been through the ringer at training, learning his new trade well. We arranged for additional training sessions and kept players behind to assist with his learning curve. In the lead up to the Widnes match at Naughton Park, we had an injury to Martin Offiah. I felt Inga was almost ready, but took the challenge to him and asked if he felt he was. Inga, who reckoned he was as ready as he could be, agreed. News of his impending debut was purposely kept from the media, and when he was named in the team that night, I am sure the Widnes coach and team had kittens. It is well documented that Inga had a great debut, scoring a try and making several huge tackles that cracked the opposition. Both Inga and I were happy after the match, as were the directors, and the many Wigan supporters there. I was lambasted by the media for keeping the secret, but hey, if that was all I had to worry about then I was cool about that.

Inga's next match was at home. Everyone wanted a sight of the big man and rightly so. Inga made one mistake in his second match that earned the ire of one of the experienced players. After a score, the team was all set for the ensuing kick off with Inga standing just in front of the try line. As things would have it, the ball was kicked towards him and he allowed it sail over his head to go across the dead in goal line. He was not fully aware of the rules. Everyone but him knew that he had to try to catch the ball. Inga thought we had a quarter line drop-out. His experienced colleague absolutely blew his top off and pointed to me in stands to get Inga off the field. I spoke to him at half-time and Inga continued to improve with every game.

We reached the semi-finals of the Challenge Cup, and were drawn to play our nemesis that season, Castleford. The game was scheduled for Headingley and would be a repeat of the Regal Trophy Final earlier in the season. As the game came up we were not playing well, the team was having one of those blips all teams go through, but it was something the press, fans and our critics were keen to exploit. On game day no one gave us a chance.

The players had other ideas, knowing they were not performing as they could. We trained well all week. Everyone was very quiet and working hard. They were hurting because everyone was talking about the 46–0 defeat in the league and the 33–2 destruction in the Regal Trophy. They were going to set the record straight. They certainly did because we took the game by the scruff of the neck right from the start, stifled the life out of Castleford and won 20–6. I was delighted because we played like a Sydney side and played the way I wanted them to play. The pack was outstanding, both with the ball and in defence. We left Headingley with a place at Wembley and silenced a great many of our critics, but not for long.

I was delighted to be going back to Wembley after an eight year lapse. When I last left the Wembley pitch I was devastated and I was determined not to feel like that on this visit.

The political problems were steadily building up off the field. It was obvious Robinson was coming under more pressure and it was showing. The confusion over the coaching position was not helping and as the run in to the end of the season was on us we were not a certainty to retain the title. We lost two games at Hull and Sheffield to put ourselves under more pressure and the last league game at Oldham had become a must win situation for us. It was one of those pressure games which during the season we had either lost or performed as we could and won easily. I was hoping it would be the latter case as the team took the field at Watersheddings.

I need not have worried as once the chips were down the players responded as I hoped they would and we really played a game that delighted me and ended up putting 50 points past Oldham to clinch the League Championship. As far as I was concerned the first of the two objectives I had set myself was done, we were champions. The second one was coming up the following weekend as we were to meet Leeds at Wembley in the Challenge Cup Final.

It was after the match against Oldham that I was interviewed by the Sky reporter and asked what I had to say to all the doubters. My response was, "They can go suck." Not very nice, but an Australian expression which means 'tough, who cares, do what you like, we won'. The print media made a big thing of it, but the damage had already been done to me within the club.

It was now the lead up to the Challenge Cup at Wembley. After training, on the Tuesday evening I had a visit from Jack Robinson to our home in Standish Lower Ground on the outskirts of Wigan. Jack was different to any other time we had spoken. I invited Jack into our front room lounge room where he outlined the position he found himself in over me. Jack told me that due to the pressures of the season and those on him, he was there to tell me he was unable to keep me at the club after this season. This was a shock, but more was to come. The reason was given that the players had lost confidence in me as a coach. I asked for the names of the players who were unhappy. Jack said we should speak to Dean Bell.

Now I suspected where this had started. Bell had been making his way back into the team from injury and couldn't see a place for himself due to how well Barrie-John Mather was going and with Phil Clarke at loose-forward. Anyway, we met before training and had it out. Bell said several players were not happy. I asked for him to name them or to have them in a meeting and thrash this out because there is no way this is true. Dean Bell was suggested to assist me as coach, but interestingly, following this meeting Dean told the chairman that he was not interested in this issue anymore, because it wasn't right and I should have a chance to complete my job.

At least I knew what was happening in the club. It is interesting to note here that my philosophy on life as taught from a young age was always treat others as you want them to treat you.

As a coach I do not and should not hold grudges. With Wembley beckoning the best team for the day had to be chosen. This time I chose it on merit and without the help of anyone other than advice from close confidantes, not including any players. The biggest sticking point was who to be on the bench. I had picked Inga on the wing so Jason Robinson was out and not happy. I chose Sam Panapa over Joe Lydon as the back sub, so Joe annoyed that he missed out. It was not easy, but my gut feeling said he was the best person for the job on the day. I admired Joe from my playing days and respected what he would bring to this game, but not for this final.

We travelled down to London on the Thursday with a short run in the afternoon to get the legs going. On Friday, as is customary, the teams go to Wembley to have a walk around and get a feel for the ground. It was gratifying to be there for a second time and hopefully rid the soul of past demons from my defeat with Hull KR in 1986.

It was Saturday and game day. All the preparations were done. It was a matter of individuals being ready. After an early brunch together, the coach set off for Wembley Stadium. The air was electric as the coach made its way through the throng of rugby league supporters from all parts of the country coming down to London for the weekend and a great game of football. The coach had a police escort because it was always bedlam getting to the ground in the heavy traffic. We arrived among hundreds of Wigan supporters wanting a last glimpse of the players before they headed into battle.

The players got off the coach, spoke to people they knew, and headed into the dressing room. These were big rooms compared to the small rugby league dressing rooms in the north of England. Time approached for the game, last talks were given and the players went through their rituals as they got ready for the game. Ring, ring, ring went the warning bell for two minutes. The players lined up with some having their last toilet stop before having to join the line. Both teams walked out of the dressing rooms and were placed into strict line ups before the timekeepers down the tunnel gave the nod to begin the long walk out to the centre of the Wembley pitch.

As you walk into the sunshine, the crowd sees the teams walking out and up goes the roar. At that moment the most amazing thing occurred. It was physical. The voluminous sound that reached the tunnel of players and staff came over us like a wave in the sea. It literally brushed our bodies and the hairs on our heads and neck stood up. That feeling of exhilaration and nervous excitement you feel when walking onto the pitch at Wembley is never forgotten. I could do it every week and never lose the want to return and enjoy the sensation or the moment. I had promised myself that I would return to Wembley one day as either a player or coach. I didn't once think I wouldn't. Here we were, back at the Holy Grail of rugby league in England. I was walking onto the pitch, second in line with my heart in my mouth expecting the opposite feeling to my last visit in 1986.

Leeds were a strong formidable outfit who would be difficult to beat. Some players would shine, I thought, while others would wilt under the enormous pressure that comes with Wembley finals.

We got to the middle, were introduced to the guest of honour before the national anthem rung out around the ground from the pipe band. The players took to the pitch as their names are read out over the tannoy system before the referee, David Campbell, blew time on with a shrill of his whistle. By now I had taken my seat and did not give a thought to the goings on at the club in past two weeks. I was only focussed on how the team would perform for 40 minutes.

In these games often little is required from the coach. The players had done their homework, knew the plays backwards and how to combat anything Leeds would throw at us. All was going to plan. Leeds played as we expected, so at half-time the dressing room was calm with attention tuned into my talk. Our first try had been spectacular. Martin Offiah had exploded through a hole on the right side of the pitch and taken on Alan Tait, the Leeds full-back. Martin slowed Alan down by running towards him and then like lightening took off so fast that Alan was unable to keep pace with him, but could only limit his ability to go under the posts. It was rightly described as one of the greatest tries ever scored at Wembley. We were 12–0 up at the break.

Half-time went quickly, even though it was only 15 minutes and the players trooped out to do the final 40 minutes of battle. The game was going from end-to-end for much of the second half until a second long range effort from Offiah sealed our victory. The final hooter went and Wigan had won 26–16. The Challenge Cup was ours. What a feeling it was, something that I was most thankful to God for because after all the effort put into coaching Wigan to win was euphoric. My family were on hand to share in the glory and celebration.

The team walked up the stairs to receive the Cup and their medals. The Cup was lifted high above their heads. The players and supporters celebrated. The Cup was taken on the customary walk around Wembley Stadium for the fans to see up close. The backroom staff all joined in the celebration and walked alongside the players. I had a chance to hold the Cup and lift it to the supporters in the terrace end and received rapturous applause. Job done, I handed it back to the players and let them carry on enjoying the moment. At the Leeds supporters' end I was again given an opportunity to show the Cup and was pleasantly surprised to have Dane and Jason allowed onto the field to also enjoy the moment. What a thrill for them, they held the Challenge Cup on the Wembley pitch and were in a photo holding it aloft with their dad. A very proud moment for three guys who were father and sons, but also best mates. To share this was something to hold onto forever.

We returned to the hotel with our wives and partners to begin celebrating, but I was not ready for the 'bad taste' moment that occurred during the festivities.

Jack Robinson rose for his speech as chairman and stepped onto the stage area to deliver his praise and congratulations to the players and the training staff. But nowhere in the speech did he mention me, not once. The other curious and highly embarrassing thing was that Jack didn't invite the coach up to speak. I was sitting with Ray Miller and he apologised on behalf of all the people in the room who were surprised by Jack's failure to mention me and especially that I was not asked to speak. It wasn't that I wanted any praise because it was the players who won the match. I was happy that they received all the plaudits on the night, but it would have been wonderful to have the chance to thank the players, staff and directors for the opportunity to coach Wigan. I guess I seethed a bit that night, but kept it bottled up inside me, not showing any hurt outwardly to anyone at the celebration. I did not walk out of the dinner, as has sometimes been said.

On the Sunday morning we all had a late breakfast before the journey started up the M6 motorway back to Wigan and the big supporters' celebration on the team's return. Towards the end of the trip, just after leaving the motorway near the lovely village of Ashton-in-Makerfield, we changed from the coach to a double deck bus to drive us into the town through the streets filled with hundreds of supporters. While most of the people on the bus went upstairs to soak up the atmosphere, I went and sat with the three directors who were still downstairs. John Martin had left early to prepare the club for the homecoming celebrations. After sitting down and having a chat about the match and the after-match celebrations back at the hotel, I asked Jack directly why he had not invited me to speak. To be honest, I don't think I heard his answer all that well because it was superfluous to the moment, considering the total embarrassment he caused me. There was no 'Joe Cool' at this moment because I arced up and told Jack some home truths about his and the club's actions over the course of the year.

I then said words that I guess hurt Jack personally in front of his fellow directors and ultimately dealt my position a real blow. "Jack, last night you embarrassed me and my family and the many close friends attending the party when you didn't ask me to speak. I would like to say one thing about the whole sorry mess … [it was] cheap and nasty … That's all I have to say." Jack grabbed my arm as I went to get up and leave. I pulled away and walked off to go up top with the players.

Jack followed me up a little while later, probably after being cooled down by the two other directors, Tom Rathbone and Jack Hilton. Within a few minutes of Jack getting to the top deck of the bus, he and I met in the middle. I told him he shouldn't let fear hold him back. Fortunately, he and I turned and walked away from each other.

I will put on record here that Jack and I did not come to blows, nor was there pushing or shoving, as has been alleged on occasions. It was not my way of settling arguments or distrust.

Dean Bell's role had been an issue for me throughout the season. He was a fine player for Wigan and New Zealand, but I believe was not at his best in the 1993–94 season. I think that at times Dean was worried that he was not going to get back into the team because of other players keeping him out. I believe that he was used as a conduit in his outburst against me by forces inside and outside the club. Bell came to me in the week leading up to Wembley, apologised, and said that he wasn't the type of person to back stab his coach. All I can say is he was very lucky that I did not drop him for the Challenge Cup Final, because I would have liked to do. We had so many good quality players able to take his place in the 15 man squad. I believe he would not have been missed.

The rest of the day went off very well and the thousands that turned out at Central Park to welcome their team home was amazing. It was just like returning to Hull in 1986 after losing the final. Then I got the feeling you take from the diehard supporters who will not give up on their team. This time we had come home with the Cup.

I turned up for training on the Monday and was asked to attend the board meeting on the Tuesday evening. I had a feeling that it could be ugly so I asked John Fitzpatrick, a lawyer, to accompany me. When we arrived John was told he was not allowed to be involved in the meeting, which I found to be very much against my rights when facing a meeting like this. John waited for me across the road at the hotel and I went into the meeting.

The meeting didn't last long as Jack asked me to explain myself for the outburst against him on the bus on Sunday. I replied as best I could and asked what if the positions were reversed, what would he have done in my position? I also explained that with the pressures of the past couple of weeks and not being asked to speak at the celebration party, I was not happy and deeply apologised for my behaviour. I was asked to leave the meeting while they deliberated. After what seemed to be an interminable time, I was asked to come back into the meeting. I was told that my contract would be torn up because of the way in which I had spoken to the chairman and was sacked for gross misconduct.

However, I was offered the chance to complete the season as coach. I asked, "Does that mean I take the team to Australia to play the World Club Challenge?" A curt "No" was the reply. I suggested that the season didn't finish until the trip to Australia was over, but again was told "No". Jack said that if I didn't like it then I could finish tonight. I said that if I can't do the World Club Challenge I won't do the Premiership matches. I met John Fitzpatrick at the hotel and didn't stop to speak to the media, who were like bloodhounds looking for the scoop. I guess by the way I scampered across the road and away from them they knew the outcome.

Oops! I just blew the three Premiership matches by doing what I did. It was not pretty because I had just given up lots of money and my life as a coach. It had major ramifications on the rest of my coaching career. I was in talks with the Illawarra Steelers to return home and become their coach. When I returned to Wollongong to launch the Illawarra Steelers book I was expecting to be interviewed for the role. This event changed their minds dramatically.

I engaged John Fitzpatrick as my solicitor to ensure I received fair compensation for all the pain and embarrassment I felt I had suffered. Wigan had to compensate me for lost salary for the 1994–95 season. I find it hard to believe that Jack Robinson would or could argue that I only had a one year deal with the club when it was he who provided evidence to clarify my position with the bank at the beginning of my time at the club. The bank had refused to grant me a mortgage to buy a house on the basis of a one year contract. Jack had provided the documentation showing I had a three year deal. It was only then that the bank agreed to advance the money to me.

"Having covered the game for many years, I felt that as a player Dorahy was magnificent. He was a very good coach and I think he proved that during the time he was at Halifax. Many Aussie players such as Luke Swain and Adam Cashmire spoke highly of him. When he came to coach Wigan he was working with a chairman who was finding Maurice Lindsey, the former chairman, a very hard act to follow. The problem was that Jack Robinson was running a business as well as running Wigan RLFC and found that a difficult balancing act. Lindsay, on the other hand, had totally focused on Wigan.

John arrived at Wigan when they were without doubt head and shoulders above every club, unlike today. The players were possibly reluctant to change, whereas today they probably would change their approach. I know that one player, while openly saying he was enjoying the new drills Dorahy had introduced, was in the dressing room agitating against what the new coach was doing! With hindsight I would say back then the club was so parochial that perhaps they should have stuck with Graeme West as their coach. The other thing is that if that is what the players wanted and felt, why were they not asked who they would have wanted as a coach?

I always found John Dorahy very approachable. He was and is a man of very strong beliefs, beliefs very few within the game can match even today."

Neil Barker (Manchester Evening News)

My final days in Wigan town were spent catching up with friends made during the time we spent there, enjoying some hospitality and sharing stories of friendship and mateship.

Part of my bonus if we won the Challenge Cup was an all expenses paid trip to any holiday destination for me and the family. This was paid for by Norweb for the additional marketing opportunities found in making the Wembley final. We sat down and worked out the best holiday we could have to end this year. Our choice was to fly home via the USA, visit Florida and take in Disney World before heading off to Hawaii for a few days of sunshine and rest. A great time was had by all, and over a drink we thanked Wigan for providing us the chance to live our dream.

The plan on arrival was to beat St Helens, which we did, home and away; win the Challenge Cup at Wembley; and win the Championship. A success in anyone's book. I was happy with my efforts in coaching a team full of excellent players and bringing on several young players to first team level, who went onto become international players.

The final success was that I had told the players at the beginning of June 1993 that we would be playing football to compete with the Australian team we would play in the World Club Challenge in 1994. The team achieved a meritorious win after all the lead up work.

Satisfied – definitely.

Could have done better – definitely.

Missed my chances – definitely.

Sad – definitely not.

Leading out Wigan at Wembley.

Winning the Challenge Cup. (Photo courtesy *Rugby League Journal*)

Left: With Dane and Jason at Wembley
(Photo courtesy *Rugby League Journal*)

Below: Triumphant return from Wembley to
Central Park.

15. Perth Western Reds

After leaving Wigan, the family holiday in America made all the ups-and-downs of the past year seem to be a foggy memory. It was important to allow the children their day in paradise as we went to Disney World in Florida before moving onto Hawaii where sun, surf, and relaxation were the order of the day.

We were enjoying a lovely cold beer when up walks this guy and asks "What are you doing here lad?" It was none other than Steve Hampson, the former Wigan full-back, who was returning from a playing stint at Illawarra Steelers. For the next few days, Steve and I had plenty of beers and spoke of the good times both of us had at Wigan as well as taking a pot shot at some of the people who were only interested in their own good and not the club's overall benefit.

One night, sat under a Banyan tree, my daughter Cara left her removable teeth brace on the table for Linda and me to look after. Within 40 minutes Cara returned, asking for her brace to put back in her mouth. It was nowhere to be found, either on or under the table. It was agreed that one of the waiters had inadvertently swept it up with the crisp bags and other rubbish. I asked about rummaging through the rubbish to look for the brace and the manager allowed Steve and me to empty the six 44 gallon drums that were behind the bar. Sure enough, it was found in the very last drum. Thank goodness for that and I went off to wash it in boiling water and disinfectant. While Steve and I were fossicking through the drums Steve came up with a great comment: "I wonder what the Wigan press would say now: 'Two sacked people from Wigan rugby league rummaging through the bins to make ends meet.'" Good one Steve, and we laughed over our drinks for another couple of hours.

The Dorahys arrived home with dad looking for work while we moved back into our home in Newcastle. Cara was most upset at having to return to school at St Mary's Gateshead. It wasn't long before I was in contact with Gordon Allen at the new Perth franchise and the opportunity to move west happened. At this time Jason decided he had enough of travelling and chose to finish his secondary schooling at the well-known St Gregory's College at Campbelltown in south west Sydney. St Greg's was known for its rugby league tradition and the ability bring young players on. Dane came to Perth and began a carpentry apprenticeship. Cara attended a local Catholic secondary school in the northern Perth suburbs after we moved into Sorrento, near Hillarys, on the coast about a 20 minute drive north of Perth. Linda again settled into another move and looked after the kids needs better than anyone I know.

At the beginning of the 1990s the ARL had been coming under increasing pressure to expand the number of teams in the league. The feeling in the game was that the league needed to expand into new areas of the country that had not previously had a senior club. To that end, the authorities put out an invitation to any interested franchises to submit their applications to the ARL. It was intended to be a competition. All the clubs that applied would be considered, but the intention was that only the best one would be successful and gain entry to the senior Sydney comp. In the end four franchises applied: North Queensland Cowboys, South Queensland Crushers, New Zealand Warriors and Perth Pumas, later to become the Western Reds.

In Perth the driving force behind the Western Reds' bid was their chairman Laurie Puddy. He was a self-made millionaire, mad keen on footy and was determined to bring top class competition not just to Perth, but to Western Australia. He began to search for what he considered to be the best team to put together a franchise bid that would succeed. He appointed Gordon Allen, previously chief executive of Western Suburbs Magpies in Sydney to hold that post in the new club and together they put in place the systems necessary for a successful club.

The ARL intended to make a decision on which club would gain entry to the competition in 1993, with the aim that the new club would enter the comp for the 1995 season. It was a very short amount of time for any new club to get up and running, but Puddy and Allen set about the task with relish. Gordon Allen quickly realised that the first step was to ensure that the new club had a strong junior development programme that would ensure strong back up for the first team if the bid succeeded.

If Puddy and Allen had not got enough on their plate, the ARL did not make matters any easier by the way in which they handled the announcement of the expansion club. The pair of them had been summoned from Perth to Sydney by John Quayle to attend a meeting on the understanding that a decision was pending and would be announced to all the competing clubs by the end of the day. Puddy and Allen left the meeting at lunchtime and travelled to Doyle's fish restaurant to enjoy what they thought would be a nervous meal. They were in the taxi on the way to Doyle's when Puddy got a call telling him to get back to Phillip Street for a press announcement.

Lunch was placed on hold as the taxi raced back to Phillip Street where Ken Arthurson made the announcement on television that the decision had been made to admit all four clubs that had applied for a franchise. Whilst ecstatic at their success, both realised that their job had just been made four times harder. Now there were four new clubs each searching for suitable sponsors, each trying to build a corporate identity and, more importantly, trying to sign players who would bring success on the field. What was a bit of a publicity coup for the ARL was a logistical nightmare for the new clubs.

Puddy and Allen faced a million and one tasks if the club was to be ready for the 1995 season opener. Allen in particular needed to employ all of his considerable powers of persuasion if he was to put together a competitive team. To add to their burdens, the ARL also required all four franchisees to lodge a $500,000 guarantee as part of the conditions of entry. In addition, Perth was also required to meet all transport and accommodation costs for incoming teams. Originally, these were for one team per club only, but within three months this was changed to two teams based on the decision of the Premiership sub committee, because it was felt this would assist with the development of the code in the west.

So, instead of having to recruit around 20 players, that number doubled as did the cost of recruitment, player accommodation and all the other costs of running two teams.

The club's first major signing was Mark Geyer. Later, Puddy and Allen managed to prise Brad Mackay away from the great St George club. It was a signing that few expected and many wondered how the club had pulled it off. Not for the first time the persuasive powers of Puddy and Allen rocked the rugby world. Other signings followed, including Rodney Howe from Newcastle, John Grieve from Manly, Dale Fritz, Matt Fuller, Brett Docherty, Matt Rodwell, Jeff Doyle, Chris Ryan, Brett Goldspink, Mick Potter, David Boyd, James Grant, Tim Horan, Chris Warren, Keri Parata and Shaun Devine followed.

While all of this was going on, the club was also developing its junior side. That team made its first incursion into an East Coast competition in July 1994, when they took part in the National

Championships. The Perth boys reached the final, which was played as a preliminary game to the under-19 Australia versus Great Britain match. Two players from that team, Greg Fleming and James Goulding, went on to play first grade when the club entered the competition in 1995.

For my part, I had returned home to Wollongong and was once again looking for work. Having tasted success at Wigan, I was keen to stay in the game and was delighted when Gordon Allen phoned. He told me that his new club was looking for someone to become Western Australia development manager and football manager for the first grade team. He also said that if I was interested in the job they would like to invite me over to Perth for an interview. I told Gordon that I was and so arrangements were made.

When I arrived in Perth, Gordon and Laurie had arranged for us to meet at Cocos Restaurant in South Perth. First I visited the Reds offices and looked at the plans that the club had in place. It was a convivial meeting and dinner. Laurie Puddy was, and still is, a connoisseur of fine wines, especially those from Western Australia. We sampled more than a glass or two and topped it off with a few glasses of Frangelico, an almond and chocolate flavoured liqueur.

It was, however, first and foremost a business meeting and I was grilled about my ability to provide the management experience that the role required. Both must have been impressed with my credentials and what I had to say, because they offered me the job. I could hardly say no after such a perfect introduction to the delights of Perth and their plans for the new club. I told them I would like the job, but wanted to return home in order to discuss the matter with my wife and family.

I did have a number of questions and issues: how long the contract would be for and also what the remuneration was to be. I was happy with the answers and the following day, with a clearer head, I met Gordon and Laurie with Peter Mulholland, the Reds coach, to discuss my acceptance of what I had managed to enlarge from development manager to include football manager of the senior squad and coach to the Reds Juniors in the local first grade competition. I was very happy to be back in football once again, and felt that the club was very happy to have someone of my experience on board.

The club had drawn up a list of players they would like to sign from English clubs, and Laurie and Gordon flew over to talk to players and club officials. Their reception and response from clubs was cold to say the least. The club did manage to sign a number of players, but they were not the top quality ones they had set out to bag.

When I started working for the Reds in September 1994, I found that the local people and the state had backed the club to the hilt. The club's isolation worked in its favour because they were not scrambling for backers on the east coast as the two Queensland clubs were. The list of sponsors who were onboard was very impressive: Tooheys, Cash Converters, Channel 9 TV, Red Rooster, QBE, Ansett Airlines, Grace Removals, Houghton Motors, Tyrrells Wines and Canterbury Clothing were the major ones.

Such was the enthusiasm Tooheys had for the club that they commissioned a new beer which they named 'Tooheys Red' with a big red kangaroo emblazoned on the can. Such was the power of the marketing for the club that Canterbury, who were the kit suppliers, told the club that the new shirt was the second best seller it produced behind the maroon State of Origin jersey. That was praise indeed for the new outfit. There was no doubt that the Aussie Rules boys in the state were looking over their shoulder with apprehension at what was being achieved.

Sadly, the same could not be said of the clubs on the east coast. There was not one club that wanted the club in the competition or would have ever wanted to fly to Perth to play. Laurie Puddy was, and still is, of the opinion that the other clubs did their best to limit the growth of the club from the embryo that, he believes, could have grown to become of the best stories in the game's history. Then came the fiasco of the split in the sport around Super League and the 'war' that developed, along with its aftermath.

Puddy's observations quickly became reality when Gordon Allen tried to arrange trial matches for the new campaign. Not one eastern club wanted to play the Reds, and certainly not in Perth. The club was forced to go further afield to find competition. In my opinion, it was a disgraceful way to behave by the established clubs, particularly against a newly formed club that needed all the help it could get.

Gordon Allen arranged a short tour to South Africa to play three regional representative sides. When the club arrived, they found that in most cases local rugby union players had been brought in to bolster the side and ensure the games were competitive. The games certainly were competitive. Plenty of beltings were handed out; by that I mean physical, high tackles, cheap shots and so on. One of the games was played as a formal test match against the South African rugby league test side in front of around 5,000 supporters in Johannesburg. The tour was a triumph for Gordon Allen's organisational skill and the co-operation of the South African Rugby League officials.

The club had other problems to face as well as preparing for the new season. Initially, when the franchise was awarded to the Reds, it was announced that they would be a one team city, just first grade. Then, at a later date, the concept was dramatically changed when the ARL, under pressure from the east coast clubs, decided that the Reds would have to field two teams – a reserve grade alongside first grade. This meant that at very short notice the club was faced with a massive increase in its operating costs. This was exacerbated because those same clubs had pushed for the Reds club to pay airfares and accommodation for the visiting clubs. This was on top of the Reds having to pay their own airfares and accommodation when they travelled over to NSW and Queensland. The club was being forced to operate with one hand tied behind its back. One really had to question if the established clubs really wanted expansion or not, certainly they had made it clear they did not want Perth in the competition.

In spite of all these problems, once the season started all the hard work Puddy and Allen had put in seemed to have been worthwhile. The first match the club played, in front of a 24,392 crowd, was against one of the most widely recognised clubs in the game, St George. The game was played at the WACA and resulted in a massive win for the Reds. To get some idea how well and how quickly the people of Western Australia embraced the concept of a Perth rugby league club, playing in the NSWRL, one only had to look at the results of the club's membership drive. There were many rugby league 'ex-pats' in Perth along with many rugby union supporters who warmed to the club.

We set up a huge marquee in the middle of the WACA. The aim was to get people to sign up for the club and establish a fan base. The marquee held around 1,000 people, but filled up all too quickly with enthusiastic local sponsors who met the demand the supporters had for food and drink at that membership drive. The response to the event was far and away over the club's expectations.

In that first season the club made steady rather than spectacular progress. I quickly realised that we needed to get more quality players, even if only for a short time. With that in mind I sat down with Peter Mulholland to try to identify weaknesses we needed to address. Our conclusion was that we needed to bolster the centre position and that we would not be able to do that in Australia.

The result was a phone call to one of the players I had coached at Wigan, Barrie-Jon Mather, and the New Zealand centre Craig Innes who was with Leeds. Both were able to come on short term deals to play during the English close season. Both B-J and Craig were valuable acquisitions and they quickly established a rapport in the centres and the city. B-J was a particularly good buy because he was hungry for success and eager to show off his skills in Australia. As I had coached B-J and recommended him, Peter Mulholland was happy to have him on board.

I also made a scouting trip to New Zealand to look at the junior Kiwi trials just outside Hamilton where I identified two players, Toa Kohe-Love and David Kidwell. The Reds could only afford to bring one player over and after meeting with both of them and watching their trial form I decided Toa Kohe-Love was best suited to the jump across to Perth from his home city of Wellington.

I first became aware of moves towards the formation of Super League in October 1994. When Super League was formally announced in April 1995, John Ribot and his Super League dream changed everything simply by sending his people to Perth to sign up any players who were willing to switch allegiance. Sadly, those players who did not wish to switch also came under intense pressure. One of the interesting examples of the paranoia the events generated came when Ken Arthurson accused Laurie Puddy of plotting to take the Reds over to Super League. Nothing could have been further from Puddy's or Allen's minds, they were loyal to the ARL because that organisation had supported the Perth franchise.

It then became a case of damned if you do and damned if you don't for both Puddy and the club. John Quayle, the chief executive of the ARL said that the ARL could no longer support the Reds because they required all their funds to fight for their position back on the east coast and those clubs involved there. At a time when the ARL needed to support the outpost club, they simply retreated back into their entrenched Sydney stronghold. Super League was offering players vast sums simply to sign up with them. The knock-on effect of this was simple; in order to stop defections from the top players the ARL had to match what Super League was offering. The losers would be people like Puddy, Allen and me who opposed Super League.

While all this was happening the club was hit with a drug scandal. Laurie Puddy was at a board meeting in Sydney when the news broke of this scandal and the fact the coach was involved in setting up the Super League option in Perth. Puddy was advised by Ken Arthurson to return to Perth immediately and sack Mulholland.

When Puddy returned and called a meeting of the Reds board to discuss these issues, he found that Super League was the main point under discussion and the majority of directors agreed that the club should align itself with Super League rather than the ARL.

The writing was on the wall for Puddy and Allen once that vote was lost. Gordon Allen was then dismissed by the board and replaced by Brad Mellen, Newcastle Knights' chief executive. Then Laurie Puddy was removed as chairman.

Once again I found myself caught up in a situation much as I had been in at Wigan. I had been employed by Puddy and Allen so was perceived as a threat. The result was that I also was pushed out in order that Steve Rogers, a Super League supporter and good friend of John Ribot, could be installed as the new football manager.

The effect Super League had on Perth is clear from Laurie Puddy's recollections 15 years later. He says that the ARL spent $2million per year on the club, while Super League spent $4.5million per year. However, this was because of the vastly inflated salaries offered to the players. The Super League officials offered ridiculous amount of money to players to switch allegiance. All players were immediately offered between $10,000 and $50,000 if they signed on the night of the interviews. The players also had their contracts extended.

Ironically, the following season players were told that the payments could not be sustained, and cuts needed to occur. Having backed the players into a corner using financial incentives once, there was no way back for them so they cut their wages.

In Perth, in the end no one won from the divisions in the game over the next two years. Once the dust had settled, in 1997 it was decided that the club was no longer viable. The cost of running the club had more than doubled. In my opinion, the Perth Western Reds were sold down the river. The club ceased to exist at the end of the 1997 season as did some other clubs caught up in the debacle that was the Super League war.

The aftermath of that decision had and still has far reaching consequences for the game as a whole. In my opinion, the greed that overtook the game simply because of the need to control television rights ruined the game of rugby league in Western Australia. Many players were made instantly rich beyond their widest dreams and also beyond what their abilities warranted. A club that had been built on the love of the game and its communities was destroyed. The sponsors who had stood by the Reds were greatly disappointed. Today, as the talk once more is of expansion the game would do well to remember the manner in which the Reds were treated. Rugby league may have a short and selective memory for those events back in 1995 and on into 1997 the good folks and businesses of Western Australia have not. A great opportunity to extend the game and make it truly a national game was lost. I was simply one casualty and I was once again out of work, out of the game and wondering if I should get a proper job and get on with the rest of my life.

A Christmas family gathering

With Dane and Jason at the Illawarra Team of Steel presentation.

16. Warrington

Following the demise of my job at the Western Reds I made my way back to England. In January 1996 I had been told by my good friend at Halifax, Mick Scott, that Warrington's coach, Brian Johnson, was on his way out of the club after an 80–0 defeat at St Helens in the Regal Trophy.

I jumped on the phone and called Peter Higham, the Warrington chairman, who after speaking at length on the phone was interested in me as a coach. Peter asked me to hop on a plane, at my cost, and if I measured up in an interview Warrington's board would consider me to coach them in 1996. I packed enough clothes to stay for six months because I was confident I would achieve my goal of being the next Warrington coach. I then spoke to our good friends, the Stricklands of Wigan, who were willing to put us up in their home which was called 'The Old Nunnery'. This house is three stories high with a cellar to die for. There is some history around this old building. Initially I was there as a boarder until Linda and Cara arrived from Perth around March.

John Strickland was a terrific friend. He loaned me his car, a Rolls Royce, to run around in until the club could arrange for a vehicle from the local garage. It must have been quite a sight for the players when I arrived at training in a Roller. I did get some stick I must say.

After arriving in the cold of an English winter in January 1996, I met with Peter Higham and Alex Murphy, the club's newly appointed director of football, at Peter's home in Warrington. The meeting seemed to go well and it was comforting to have a person interview me who had also been sacked by Wigan. Yes, Alex Murphy had been dismissed in August 1984. There was a break in the meeting for Peter to take a business call. During this break, Alex confided in me that he would like to see me installed as coach and to leave it to him to speak to Peter once I had gone. Peter returned to the meeting and a little while later I left for the haven of John and Ann Strickland's home.

Peter called me the next day and asked me to drive across for a meeting. I believed I was going to receive an offer from Warrington and so it happened. Peter and Alex were both there and I was pleased to be able to stay on in England to coach Warrington. There was little hurdle I had to get over first and that was the need for a work permit from the Home Office. This could take days or weeks, and I would have to leave the country and return in two to three days. Peter and

Warrington packed me off to Paris for the few days it took to arrange for the permit. While staying in Paris, in the Montmarte area, I had the chance to walk around sightseeing and enjoying the time to prepare for the season ahead.

I received the phone call from Peter Higham to inform me the visa was through and I could return. Meetings were arranged to review the season ahead. I met several of the top players including Paul Cullen, who was the captain, Mark Forster, Paul Hulme, Gary Chambers, Jon Roper and Willie Swann. The season began well with several wins and a couple of losses meaning the Warrington faithful were happy. Plenty of try scoring came from Richard Henare, a speedy New Zealand left winger, and his centre, Toa Kohe-Love, who followed me from Perth.

One of the best moves by Peter Higham and the Warrington board had been to engage Alex Murphy as director of football. Alex's experience and football knowledge were second to none and vital in assisting me as a new coach at Warrington to bring the best out in the players. Alex and I would sit for some hours going over the players' strengths and weaknesses before deciding on a team for the weekend match. We became good friends even though we had been adversaries in 1989 when Alex coached St Helens and I was at Halifax competing in a Regal Trophy semi-final to see who would go through to the Cup Final against Wigan. Halifax won that day, but I remember Alex for far greater football exploits, having watched him when he was touring with the highly skilled Great Britain teams of the mid to late 1960s and listening intently to the radio when Australia played the Poms in England. Alex was a fantastic help to me at Warrington.

"I said at the time he was on a hiding to nothing [at Wigan]. There are certain times when you go to a club there are always people with a grudge to bear. For a coach the pressure is immediate. John was an intelligent man who knew good players, but he came into a club which in effect was coming down from heaven. They had won everything, but were coming to the end of their time. Maurice Lindsay had bought success by getting the top players into the club, but it was in financial trouble by the time John arrived. Those players did not think they had to change, but John realised they had to move on. Perhaps some did not like that.

When I went to Warrington I was instrumental in bringing John in as coach. He was highly rated by me and others as a coach and I think he did a first class job at Warrington. There was not a lot of money at the club and nor a great deal of stability and consistency within the

194

team. John brought a different style to the players and we began to improve. He certainly had very good man management skills and he needed them to sort out some of the problems we had. Harris was a case in point, I believe he thought he was a better player than we did, but to the board he was a 'golden boy' who could do no wrong. I believe he tried to set up a deal with another club, St Helens, behind the back of John and myself, something we were not prepared to allow. We made him train on his own at 6am each morning until he finally moved over to Leeds, a club I might add he was reluctant to go to initially.

The problem at Warrington was simple, the board expected John to come in and change things around and that the team would start to produce results instantly. As I said John improved things a great deal, but he needed more time. However, that was something the board was not prepared to allow. As we know it was the coach that was to suffer and John parted company with the club."

Alex Murphy

The assistant coach, Clive Griffiths, left soon after I arrived to move to South Wales, coaching their team, so it opened a space for someone new. As part of setting up a coaching team I brought in an unknown coach from Australia, Robert Tew from Newcastle Knights. When at Newcastle as assistant coach, I found Rob to be an astute coach and student of the game at the junior level. He was rising through the ranks. Someone of his ability I believed was needed in Warrington and would provide a springboard for young players to come through. Peter Higham was not keen at first, but along with Alex, saw the merit in bringing in someone like Rob Tew.

Warrington began well in the first year of Super League in England with some good wins mixed in with some losses against the top teams but we were around the top ourselves. The Warrington supporters were prepared to come and watch a winning team. The away supporters always disliked coming to Wilderspool. Of course, this worked to our advantage for much of the season.

Warrington had a kit man, Roy 'Ocker' Cunningham, who was a tough man, but loved his job like a man loves his woman. The lads loved Ocker because he was always able to conjure up various club memorabilia that no one could in their wildest dreams get anywhere. Of course, there was always a sting if you were after something, Ocker would want his pound of flesh, but let me say it was in the nicest possible way. Ocker was terrific with the lad's wives and partners and always called them 'Mrs'. He is related to Keiron Cunningham and sung his praises well before he was making a name for himself.

The family settled in and after they arrived we moved at long last into a lovely house in Westbrook. Dane and Jason had been training with the Adelaide Rams when the club was banned from the 1996 competition. The boys then went to stay with their maternal grandparents in Gloucester in NSW at the family hotel, the Avon Inn, for a little while. There they took up playing for the local Gloucester Magpies in the Group 3 competition. They were making a great fist of it against the tough country lads of Group 3 and were being sounded out by Sydney clubs because of their excellent performances.

It was one of those decisions that you regret when it was time for them to come over to England. Should they or shouldn't they? They could have done very well back in the NSW bush, but naturally they were keen to once again enjoy the English life. They both played for the academy team and thoroughly loved it in Warrington. Jason started a university course in Sports Science & Human Movement. Cara was again at Kirkham Grammar School which she enjoyed, seeing her friends again after an 18 month break.

I remember one play in particular during a home match against the high flying St Helens team. In the first 20 minutes of the match, a scrum was formed on our 10 yard line near the left touchline. We had only the winger standing on the left as the ball was being fed with Toa over on the right side of the scrum. As the ball came out our half-back, Willie Swann ran off to the left calling for the ball from the loose-forward who had picked up the ball from the winning scrum. The goal was to have the St Helens half follow Willie Swann across the pitch and not read the defensive pattern well enough with the Saints loose-forward breaking to chase the Warrington loose-forward which would then leave a gap between the scrum base and the defence moving to their right. It worked. At the very moment Richard Henare set off from his wing position for the hole left by the defenders he was passed the ball by our loose forward, Mike Wainwright, and set off on a 90 yard run to the try line. It had never been done before. The supporters were going wild with excitement of their team scoring such a wonderful try against their old enemy, St Helens.

Warrington finished the season in fifth place, just shy of fourth place which would have given them a place in the Premiership,

With Alex Murphy during my time at Warrington.

although it is doubtful the team would have progressed further than the first match. The chairman and the board were well pleased with the team's performance and were excitedly looking forward to the 1997 season.

At the beginning of the season Peter Higham, Alex Murphy and I decided we needed a couple of quality players to bolster the team's chances. I suggested a centre, Nigel Vagana. Peter and Alex agreed. So I packed a bag and headed down to Auckland to speak to Nigel. Nigel agreed to come and play in England for Warrington. He did a fantastic job before heading back down under to make a bigger name for himself playing in the NRL competition

Second season syndrome occurred in 1997 when the team faltered badly at the beginning of the campaign and after losing four games in a row the knives were well and truly out. Shame they couldn't remember the work that had been done to turn things around and that we were making significant improvements to the way the club operated that were also starting to have an impact. First, assistant coach Rob Tew was to go when the club wanted to save some money. The chief executive, John Smith, was a very tough fiscal manager and decided people had to go to save on wages. Not that the club was in financial trouble, it was his way and as a friend of Peter Higham it was interesting to note that John Smith had no rugby league background.

Within three weeks and coming into the Wigan match at home I was asked to a meeting with Peter Higham to consider my position. In a collaborative but ultimately disappointing meeting I stood down. After building a pretty good squad and looking forward to the match against Wigan I didn't quite make it. But it was gratifying to see Warrington win that game handsomely.

It would have been easy to stay and get another coaching job, but it was time for a major re-think on where to from here. After enjoying our time at Warrington and the life England provided us as a family and me as a player and coach, I believed it was time to return home and get on with life. Our daughter was turning 15 years old and I think that had we not returned to Australia then my little 'baby' would have wanted to stay in England for some time as she enjoyed the life, the people especially and the English system.

It was interesting to reflect on this as not long after we arrived and Cara was back at Kirkham Grammar, she wrote a note and told us that although she enjoyed coming back to England and catching up with her friends, she missed Perth and her cousins and friends from there. Also, she had had enough of travelling and wanted to return to Australia. Cara asked if she could return to Perth pronto.

She suggested that she could stay with her cousins the Kirk family, Barry, Lesley – my sister – their daughters Emma and Naomi and when we returned we could catch up with her then. Her comment "I will be okay at Aunty Lesley's" hit home. The only stipulation was that Cara "wanted to travel business class" on the way home. We were at the time concerned, but now we laugh often about the time Cara wanted to come back to Australia, business class no less!

In consideration of something like 22 moves to and from and in and around Australia it really hit home to both Linda and me that maybe we needed to settle in one place and stop the gypsy lifestyle as enjoyable as it was.

17. Finale in Australia

We moved back to Australia and again stayed at Linda's nan's house in Concord, Sydney for several weeks while the people in our house in Figtree moved out. This was a terrific opportunity for the family to be able to spend quality time with Linda's Nan. All the family loved her humour and home cooked meals. And with her being in her latter years it was a bonus for the kids to spend the time with her and learn all about her life in Gwabegar in north west NSW as a child before moving to Sydney with her husband. She helped all of us understand the hurdles faced coming from the bush compared to today.

I jumped straight back into the gaming industry with the Vidco Gaming Company. I was based in Milperra in Sydney, looking after the south east NSW region, a territory I knew well. Vidco was a small family operated company that was bought out by a chap named John Messara, a well known horse racing figure in Australia. I soon moved up the ranks and became the regional manager of Eastern NSW and soon moved into the role of NSW sales manager. I felt it was a good move to come home and was feeling much better about life away from football. For how long though?

Towards the end of 1997 I was approached to coach the Western Suburbs Red Devils for the 1998 season. Of course this was the club where it all began. We were by now living back in Figtree. The role involved just two nights training a week. I knew I could handle it as long as I had a good young coach assisting me because in my job I had to do plenty of travel to all parts of NSW, although I have never been to Cobar in western NSW. I brought in Wayne Rohoseink to coach the second team and he did a great job. When I couldn't be there, Wayne took over the coaching duties and with the captain held the fort. My captain that year was the son of a player I played with in 1971 when making my debut for the Devils, Matt Reh. His father, Klaus Reh, played in the second-row for the Devils from 1971 to 1973. Matt was a good captain and easy to work with. He drove the team well on the field and made sure the focus was on the game plan. However, he was also clever enough to change the plan on the field as the game went on should it be required. We had a good year, but fell short of our goal of winning the premiership.

Amazingly, it felt good to be back in the coaching arena. If there was one thing I would have liked to have seen improved in the game in the Illawarra Division, it was how the referees were trained and how they communicated with the coaches and players. Though the referees had an appointments committee member judging their performance and writing down their performance standards on a sheet of paper, I believed in referees having the same resources as coaches and to be able to watch a game video focused on their performance. I am sure it would have improved the way the game was officiated. My understanding of the game today in Illawarra is that there is still no referee video or DVD available unless one of the teams playing on the day provides one to them. Probably this is unlikely most of the time because coaches can be finicky people.

As the 1998 season was finishing, Tommy Raudonikis and I were chatting after a game in Sydney where Dane had a place in the under–23s team. Tommy asked if I would be interested in assisting him at Wests Magpies for the 1999 season. I was flattered that Tommy would ask me and after some deliberation I agreed to take on a role as his assistant coach because it meant that I wasn't at football all weekend. I was also disappointed to leave my post at Wests Red Devils, but had found that in 1998 I would go off and coach at Wests Red Devils, then the following day get in the car and go and watch Dane play for the Wests Magpies in Sydney. It meant I would only have to be involved with and watch one team on the weekend. The family was also happy because it meant going back to Wests Magpies.

Assisting Tommy Raudonikis at Western Suburbs Magpies in Sydney was always going to be a tough assignment. The club was still the pauper in the prince's playing field that is Australian rugby league and the quality of their players was not as high as most of the other clubs in the competition, without being derogatory to the club or the team. Tommy was a direct player and this came out in his coaching methods as well. Not that this was a bad thing, in fact some of the Wests players needed to instil Tommy's attitude into their game behaviour if they wanted to make it.

The team struggled and even the second team players in Col Murphy's squad were not putting enough pressure on for places to force a lift in performance to the level required to compete for competition points. There were some heavy losses and Wests were looking down the barrel of finishing in last place.

I remember the game that Tommy brought our Dane into the first team for a match at Penrith. It was quite exhilarating for the family and, of course, especially for Dane. He was so excited and in my opinion as a coach, not a father, I believe Dane was ready to taste first team duties. For the next 14 matches Dane played first team and acquitted himself well with Tommy saying that "Dane at least has balls and stands up to these b-st-rds".

I reckon Tommy's influence had Dane treading the fine line between aggressive play and being too aggressive. Dane was not one to get into fights on the field. He and Jason were always taught not to fight, probably because their father couldn't, but to laugh into the face of the opposition when they want you to fight. This means you have them thinking about other things than playing football at 100 per cent. And if you are playing without thinking about fighting you are a better chance to play well and help your team win. Unfortunately, with a team playing as tough as Wests Magpies did, often the referee's decision favoured the team that was expected to win.

It was a frustrating period for the Magpies team, with niggle getting into their game a little too much, and this made it easy for the referees to penalise them. One game that highlighted this was the Wests versus Souths match at Campbelltown. Dane went toe-to-toe with the Souths half-back Wes Patten. I was in the coaches' box with Tommy, who was shouting "Go Dane, give it to him, don't hold back son". And at half-time Tommy talked to Dane and congratulated him on his blue (fight) with Patten and told the team that they should take a leaf out of young Dane's book and "play tough and give it to these Souths mongrels".

It was also the final season for Western Suburbs Magpies in the Australian Rugby League competition, following the decision by the ARL to cut down the number of teams to 14. Personally, I did not believe this should have happened as an outcome of the Super League War. Of course, it is said the competition couldn't afford more teams, but when all is said and done in business companies come and go due to bad management practice or because of some catastrophic event. For Wests Magpies, it was neither of these because they were pushed into a merger with another club, the Balmain Tigers. Following the merger, it was difficult to put 60 players into one club and decisions had to be made on player selection from the two clubs of who would stay in the merged entity.

Unfortunately for Dane, though he was playing pretty well, I firmly believe that an injury sustained in the Cronulla match at Endeavour Field ultimately ended his chances of getting a start with the merged team. The injury occurred at the end of a scuffle between two Wests and Cronulla players. As it was ending, a Cronulla forward, who was standing on the outside of the fight ran in and grabbed Dane, who was standing outside the scuffle. He grabbed him by the scruff of the neck and dragged him away, then, like a rag doll, flung Dane head-over-heels into the ground. This injured his shoulder quite badly.

The biggest man on the field had made a target of the smallest man on the field. This injury forced Dane to leave the field. He was then sidelined for the rest of the season, and missed out on a strong chance to be a part of the Wests Tigers.

As the season finished, and the curtain came down on the Western Suburbs Rugby League Club's involvement in the premier rugby league competition in Australia, it was a sad finish to a once mighty proud club. As a former player and coaching assistant I can say it was an abominable situation that should never had arisen, and had through the greed of the corporate world wanting a piece of a very profitable sport. I believe the sport would have still continued to build strongly because the 1995 competition with 20 teams showed how strong the game was.

Dane headed off to England because he had enough Australian first team games to qualify for a work permit and went off for another four years of wonderful opportunities playing and living the dream as a professional rugby league player.

At the same time Jason had given up on league following the demise of the Adelaide Rams club and taken up rugby union, playing for the Western Suburbs Rugby Union club at Concord Oval, once the home of NSWRU. Jason had always been a clever player with a quick mind for opportunities, soft hands and a strong kicking game. Jason played in the first team for the Wests rugby union team in a strong competition. He was approached by Brian Smith, of rugby union fame, to move across to Eastern Suburbs club after two years at Wests. Unfortunately, like his father, he was dogged by injury and had to finally pull the curtain down on a promising career at a time when Brian Smith had nominated Jason for a position in the Australian RU 7s team. But Jason made up for all this by playing Oz Tag and playing for Australian Oz Tag over several seasons. At one event he met his future wife, Samantha Pagano, who was the daughter of a former player, Fred Pagano, a strong prop forward who was built like a tank. In 2007 Jason and Samantha presented us with our first grandchild, the beautiful Tameika Lee, followed by Brodie Jae, to keep us happy grandparents.

With the rise of the Wests Tigers, it was time to head back home and I was appointed coach at Wests Red Devils for the 2000 season. I completed the year, but work became too burdensome time wise to put in the right amount of effort to equal the players' needs. Again, we had a solid year, making the finals, but not quite doing what every team sets out to do and winning the competition.

Again, my captain was Matt Reh, and again he performed very well for the club as a player and captain. A couple of players in the team of English heritage sought my advice on the options available in England and how to get a run with a team there. They both went to England, played at the lower end of the second division competitions and eventually came home back to Australia having had a great time.

It was time to hang up the clip board, concentrate on the lovely Linda for a change and give something back to home life. This lasted a couple of years until I was approached to take up coaching again.

Towards the back end of 2005 I was approached by a director at Wests Magpies, Kevin Hammond, to see if I was interested in coaching the Wests Magpies in the NSWRL Premier League competition in 2006.

Initially, I said I was not interested, but Kevin persisted and I thought more about the opportunity and because it was Wests Magpies I relented and took on the coaching job for the 2006 season. Kevin informed me that the club was still a pauper and we had to be careful on how to attract players. There was some minor surprise about me being appointed because I wasn't in the game at that time, but the fact I was a former Wests Magpies player it was seen as a good fit and my background fitted the role. Importantly, I now had time to put into it. It was a good year to be involved as Wests Tigers had won the NRL competition in 2005, so the club was on a high.

I spoke to Tim Sheens, the Wests Tigers coach, about me joining Wests Magpies and how we fitted into the organisation of West Tigers,

Balmain Tigers and Wests Magpies. The meetings were very productive with Tim and his assistant coach, Royce Simmons, very helpful about how to further integrate the three teams. Tim was always going to be available for a talk. He also suggested Wests Magpies players could attend sessions at the Wests Tigers training or Balmain training sessions so all players knew it was competitive for spots at the top. The major point made by Tim was that for a club to be successful the second team coach had to have players pressing for selection in the first team. It was my role as second team coach to progress as many players to the first team as possible. I agreed because it was something I had spoken about to assistant coaches at previous clubs.

For me though, the major sticking point was the fact Wests Magpie players in the top squad who were not playing in the first team on game day did not come back to Wests Magpies to play, but went to the Balmain Tigers for a game. At the meetings with Tim the reasoning was that the Balmain team was aligned in their training with Wests Tigers and the coach of Balmain Tigers was assisting the Wests Tigers and understood all that was going on. This was a logical reason and I agreed. Unfortunately, this certainly had a detrimental effect on the Wests Magpies' performances. It was only right that the Wests Magpies chairman, Kevin Hammond, would be annoyed at not having the Wests Magpie players return to their club to play. I must say again I fully concurred with Tim that the reasoning was sound, but in reality it was not good for the Wests Magpies club because it meant we struggled for most of the 2005 and 2006 seasons. The Balmain Tigers received all the benefit of fielding the top players. They reached the finals and Wests Magpies ended up as wooden spooners.

I began by selecting my coaching and training support team. My first call was to Murray "Muzza" Whitehead who had been a coach at the Wests Red Devils for several years and won three second team competitions in succession. Muzza had a winning culture and was an astute coach in the Illawarra Division. The next stage was to ensure we had a good fitness trainer and someone who could run our messages onto the field correctly. The guy for the job was Cameron "Freddie" Thurgate, brother of Kendall Thurgate who played at the Steelers in the 1980s. The rest of the backroom staff came from within the Wests Magpies ranks and had been there for some years which gave the club some continuity.

Muzza, Freddie and I were from Wollongong and travelled together to and from Campbelltown, unless I was in Sydney on business and made my way directly to training. Otherwise it was a terrific drive where we would be planning and refining training and match plans. Kevin Hammond was happy all was going well. The club held selection trials at the Campbelltown Stadium in November and selected several players from this trial to play with the team for the forthcoming season. Training was run well under Freddie's direction and the team were whingeing about the high fitness levels we were trying to attain. This meant Freddie was doing a good job. There were occasions when the players would slack off and not do some drills correctly or at 100 per cent, so I jumped in, being as unfit as I was but fit enough to compete. There was one occasion when Freddie had introduced 'Farmers' Runs', a test of one's ability to run around a perimeter and back to the start carrying a heavy weight. I was not happy with how the players were doing this drill, so asked Freddie if I could do a run to show these young guys how to do it properly. The time to beat was 37 seconds. After picking up the weight I nearly collapsed there and then before on the shout of "Go" I took off as best I could. There were some shouts from the players "come on coach, you can do better than that". Well, I finished in a time of 34.5 seconds and didn't I give it to the players about the effort they needed to make if they wanted to have any chance of competing with the opposition.

I remember in the first week when Freddie, Muzza and I planning training we agreed that the player's core strength had to be highest priority. I had an idea that most of the players' abdominal strength was low. So at training that night I told the players that at the end of the session we would be doing 1,000 sit-ups. The players blew up and rebuked me with "How can you expect us to do that many?" Easy! At the end of the session the players were asked to take up a position on the ground and get ready for abdominal work. The players, Freddie and I got down while Muzza watched for slackers and started doing the first 100. It was apparent the players had very low endurance in the stomach region. Most of the players couldn't complete the session of sit-ups, let alone the first 100. I then gave them a week to improve, or be put in the additional training group doing sit-ups after training was completed. It soon improved and the number of additional sessions dropped significantly over the next few weeks.

The second year followed as the first year did, with much pain at not having the use of the former Wests Magpie players in the Wests Tigers squad. Wests again ended in last position.

My only claim to these two years was that the request by Tim Sheens for Wests Magpies to provide as many first team players as possible was fulfilled. In 2005 Wests Magpies provided five players to be selected in the top squad. In 2006 the Wests Magpies again had five players selected to play with Tim Sheen's team.

So job done! It was now September 2007. I left the Wests Magpies and Wests Tigers to return to a normal life, knowing I had left Wests Magpies in a much better position than when I arrived. Best wishes to Wests for a return to the big stage of rugby league.

Thank you rugby league

Thank you to the game of rugby league I played, coached and managed in for approximately 45 years. I loved you in the knowledge that history shows success doesn't come easy and that I was blessed to have the opportunity to share the love of this great game with my family and friends in Australia and England.

If I was to leave anything of myself in the sport of rugby league it would be that as someone plucked from obscurity of junior grade to become a professional player through the foresight of someone looking for a player to fill a void – I did okay.

I strongly suggest to all: enjoy the game first and foremost as it could be snatched away from you at the next step, tackle or decision made by others. All players should have the chance to first enjoy the game and not focus on the ultimate goal of playing a professional sport. To become a professional your skill, ability and tough approach to the knocks and bumps in a fast, fierce and physical game at all ages will be tested without letting up. If you are good enough and the rugby league scouts, coaches and management can identify the "flower in the seed of youth despite your physical stature" it will be you who proves your worthiness to play a game made for the ages.

"The big question is whether you are going to be able to say a hearty yes to your adventure." Joseph Campbell.

18. Our Dad, our hero

Our dad, our hero, we could finish this little piece right here! What a man! Father, grandfather, husband, businessman and what a footballer. John 'Joe Cool' Dorahy is the man in our lives who we look up to most. He is in the forefront of every living moment. If there is anyone in this world we would want to be like in the all rounded game and not just in football terms it would be dad.

Dad is a true gentleman and his love for our mother is second to none. We are constantly reminded of this with all the little (and big) things he does for her. Ours was a happy home; one our friends loved to visit. Yes Mum, it does take two to tango — without mum, dad wouldn't be the person he is today or where he is today. For mum to keep the family life as normal as possible while dad worked, trained and played football, all the while travelling from city to city, country to country is just amazing.

As a family we travelled all over the countryside and world following in dad's footsteps and this is why we find it so easy and enjoyable to meet people. The travel has given us a great life of constantly meeting different people from different backgrounds and countries.

How fortunate we feel to be born into this family, while not wanting to show disrespect to anyone else's family, this is the family we would choose over and over again.

Dad has succeeded at whatever he does and I think that is because he applies himself 150 per cent. His message to us has always been, "Whatever you are doing is worth doing well."

As twin boys trying to follow in dad's—Joe Cool's – footsteps, wow, what a job. All we could do is our best. Yes we were compared to John Dorahy, the player, but to us he was just dad, so the pressure was not from the outside. The pressure that we have, and had growing up, was from the inside as any other normal young lads growing up with the burn and desire to achieve and do great things. Football for me was great I enjoyed every moment of it, whether it was playing rugby league, both in Australia and England, or playing first grade rugby union in Sydney.

One of the greatest things I have done, made even more special to see the happiness in my father's eyes, was to get married to my beautiful wife Samantha Pagano. We have two beautiful children, Tameika Lee and Brodie Jae. When Sam and I found out the news of our first baby, we took a bottle of Grandfather's Port to dad, to say thank you for helping us move into our new house and at the same time drop the hint his first grandchild was on the way. Dad thanked us with a cuddle and a kiss for Sam and went back to watching the television. Well! That didn't go as planned! So we explained the significance of the Grandfather's Port to mum. When dad finally caught on, the emotions flowed — what a moment to cherish. The second time, with the impending birth of Brodie Jae was just as special.

As I have mentioned my wife's name, Samantha Pagano — this is where more fun and games began at family get-togethers with Joe Cool and the man mountain Freddy Pagano. Freddy, Sam's dad was a Sydney first grade footballer and played against dad in the Sydney competition. Freddy recalls how he would want the bomb to go up when playing dad so he could race through and smash this 'pretty boy', Joe Cool, as he was catching it. Who would ever have imagined after Freddy wanting to smash John all those years ago that their children would grow up and get married.

Well dad I will finish here, congratulations on a wonderful life and the journey you have had and thanks for taking our family with you. To me you are the greatest and always will be. You are my idol. You deserve this book about your life.

Congratulations mate.

Jason

Like most girls, I am very much a daddy's girl and have been since I can remember. Mum tells me I always wanted to be with dad and wanted him all to myself. If we were walking in town as a family, while mum and dad were walking along holding hands, I would apparently become most upset, beating mum and dad's hands loose and inserting myself in between them. We still walk together a couple a times a week when I visit mum and dad's after work. Dad and I put our trainers on and hit the pavement for a walk and chinwag and I still love having him all to myself, to talk and catch up or sometimes saying nothing at all.

Being the daughter of a footballer has definitely had its pros and cons. The pros include lifelong friendships, international travel and experiencing life living in another country, not to mention favourable

With Cara Lea.

attention from the lads at school — who just wanted tickets to the weekend matches. Cons would be lots of moving around and forever being the new girl at a new school, a new village, a new county or state, or a new country.

I moved backwards and forwards between schools 14 times, attending a total of 10 and never attending any one school for more than 18 months at a time, all before the age of 15. The constant moving to areas where we didn't know many people meant we spent a lot of time together as a family unit. Dad, mum, my brothers and I remain exceptionally close today and I think the nomadic lifestyle of football greatly contributed to this.

But when it came to moving to Wigan in 1993, the excitement of moving had worn off. I was settled and my friends were very important. My great aunts would say to me 'How lucky are you, moving to England?' I would reply, 'I'm not lucky, it's horrible'. The twins, no matter how old they got, never seem bothered – they always had each other to settle in with. I remember Pa and Nan D looking after us while you went off to England. Nan D spoilt us baking lots of yummy treats everyday for when we got back from school.

We were right in the heart of a village with sheep and cow farms which the boys and I would explore. We quickly made lots of friends – Mick down the lane for the boys, the Higginbottoms for me and Helen Reed whose parents owned the local store. We also rode quads and motorbikes in the fields with our new friends.

The boys and I would catch the bus into town every Saturday morning with our £5 pocket money – go to the local swimming bath where the boys would without fail every Saturday get us kicked out by climbing to the top 10m platform and running and jumping off. All the lifeguards would be yelling at them and blowing their whistles furiously signalling for them to not jump and get down. We'd then shower, and leave for some hot chips and shopping.

Having older friends in the village who wore make-up, I wanted to start wearing make-up too. Mum took me into the department store and bought me an entire kit of Clinque make up and skin care – how lucky did I feel.

I couldn't have asked for a more wonderful role model than dad. He is the most disciplined person I have ever come across. The way he applies himself to any task he turns his hand to is to honestly give 300 per cent every time and I believe this is why he has been so successful in every aspect of his life. Dad has always told my brothers and I that, as a teenager, he felt there were many young footballers who were more talented than he was – he is also extremely modest, so that could have been a little off the mark – however these talented young men weren't willing to put in the hard yards and make the sacrifices required to achieve on the field. My grandparents would tell us that dad was always at the field, practising his goalkicking over and over, putting in whatever time was needed to perfect his craft.

Dad being a professional footballer during his English League stints, I had the opportunity to spend more time with him during these periods — time that most children don't get to spend with their father, working nine to five, five days a week. I think having such time to spend with family is something special for today's current professional footballers to cherish. What a luxury to have had those years hanging out and building a solid father-daughter relationship, which we continue to share today.

My mother must have loved those times in England too, with dad always around. Back in Australia, she really was a football widow. When my older twin brothers were born, mum and dad were living in Burwood, Sydney, dad was working as a butcher leaving the house at 4.30 each morning, then training at night with the Western Suburbs team not returning home before 10.30pm. I'm not quite sure how she managed it, but I think she is amazing. It took a very special woman to be a footballer's wife back in those days.

My first memory of watching my dad play football is at North Sydney oval, sitting in the stands with mum. Being a daddy's girl, I was very protective of my father and, to my mother's embarrassment, would yell at the top of my lungs every time dad was tackled. "Don't you tackle my daddy like that or I will come down there and tackle you!" I certainly ruined her chances of going incognito in the stands. I would run down to the sheds at full time as I couldn't wait to see dad, and back then the kids were allowed in. Not sure they'd allow a seven-year-old girl in there these days.

My next most vivid football memory is from during our time in England. I loved going to the football in England. The atmosphere, the chanting fans, the sea of team colours throughout the crowd was intoxicating. Australia just doesn't have the same vibe, even though most games here have double the number of people compared to league games in the UK.

For myself and my brothers, going to school in England was a fantastic experience. Our schools were steeped in history dating back further than the history of our own country, Australia. Kirkham Grammar School, situated between Preston and Blackpool in North West England, which I attended for first, third and fourth year of high school and my brothers attended for their fourth and fifth years, was founded in 1549. The traditions, grounds, buildings, old school hall, the formal cape the headmaster wore each day, the morning assembly

211

where we sung hymns every day, along with the sick bay staffed by two matrons and the group of international boarding school students including a Middle Eastern Sheikh, Italians and Germans blew my mind. During the Easter holidays, my school ran skiing trips to Italy as well as bus tours to France for a week and I was fortunate enough to participate in two trips. I am so grateful to my parents for giving me the opportunity to participate in these incredible experiences.

While dad was coaching Warrington, Dane and Jason remained in Australia playing with the Adelaide Rams so it was just dad, mum and I at home. I really missed Dane and Jason when we were in Warrington. Even using the motorways, we were nearly an hour's drive from my school and my girlfriends were not just around the corner to hang out with. My two best friends would often come home with me on a Friday night for the weekend and we'd go off to the football and shop the rest of the weekend. I loved shopping in England and still miss the shops there. Depending on which day dad's match was, mum, dad and I would venture off to Manchester on a Saturday or Sunday for a day of shopping. Dad has always been such a great shopper with mum and I, helping me pick out clothes, shoes and whatever else. We would spend hours in Kendall's department store and the high streets of Manchester, always having lunch at my favourite Italian restaurant across the road from the department store. To finish, dad and I always shared our favourite desert, the Godfather, a delectable tower of chocolate fudge brownie, cream, ice cream and hot chocolate sauce.

We spent a lot of time growing up with the Eadie and Mortimer families, all us kids still get together and catch up regularly. I can't say I wasn't disappointed that they were all lads, with three Eadie boys and five Mortimer boys. Although mum tells me when I was five we visited the Eadies at Halifax and I asked Aunty Barb Eadie, "Why! Oh, why did you have to call them all boys' names? Couldn't you have called one a girl's name?" We were always playing football ... lucky after years of playing with boys I could hold my own.

Dad has achieved so much on the football field both in his playing and coaching career. I admire him so much for his determination, discipline, ethics and values. His hardworking attitude and application to his job has seen him succeed at all he turns his hand to. He gives blood, sweat and tears to each task, he is an inspiration and I am so proud of him.

212

Joe Cool is not just a character who comes to life on the football field. Dad has a way of calming a situation, sibling argument or hot headed moment, and offering clarity. No matter what has ever upset me, or how upset or cranky I've been, dad would sit down with me, talk things through, make sense of my feelings and emotions and bring me to a sense of peace. I can honestly say I've never once felt upset towards my dad. I know he's had this way with all of our family, not just me.

Dad is very generous and giving. I think he struggled to ever tell us kids no. I remember when we went on our American trip, after dad finished up at Wigan, the last stop on the way home was Hawaii and I found a beautiful heart knot shaped 14 carat gold ring at a jeweller's stall. It seemed a great price to my 12-year-old mind. I showed dad and asked if I could have it. He agreed it looked beautiful on me and went to find mum and get the money from her. Well, mum didn't think a 12-year-old girl needed a 14 carat gold ring. Dad persuaded her, however, he had to compromise and put it away for my 13th birthday. I still have and cherish that ring.

One of dad's greatest successes, and something I am sure has contributed to his achievements in football and life, is his and my mother's marriage. Since early high school years, my friends have always commented on how lucky I am to have such loving parents, who are so in love with each other and so lovely to be around. At the time I didn't realise how lucky I was, but now I do see how very special my parents' relationship is. My brothers and I openly say our goal in our own relationships is to emulate what they have. One night, my parents entertained my husband's best friend and his wife for dinner and the next time my husband and I caught up with them they told us that they were so touched by mum and dad's hospitality that they too decided their goal was to have a relationship and family life just like that, where everyone is welcomed warmly, where love and happiness is infectious. What a lovely compliment. Their love is inspiring not only to their children but to everyone they come in contact with.

I truly doubted that I would ever meet a man to marry. To me, my dad was and is so perfect and whilst it is of course a completely different kind of love, I couldn't imagine anyone coming close to my love for him. Luckily for me, my brothers introduced me to a lovely lad from their football team ... a man with a tough exterior and teddy bear insides who is more like my father than I had hoped — he also boasts a lovely bent broken nose!

Cara

Dad is, always has been, and always will be my hero. He has been a role model throughout my life and I feel blessed to have had John 'Joe Cool' Dorahy as my dad. Nothing is ever a problem, and he is my best friend, confidante and now a proud grandfather. To grow up and watch and learn from such an amazing person has been inspiring to say the least.

As a family we got to see the world both inside and outside Australia over and over again from such a young age. We were part of dad's career every step of the way. For Jason and I, mad keen footy fans, life could not have been better... we just about lived as professional footballers from the day I can first remember. Going training with Dad, going to games and hanging with his team mates in the dressing rooms after games. For both of us trying to follow in dad's footsteps was always going to be a big ask. However, what we did learn from dad was that nothing happens without dedication and sacrifice.

I have been fortunate to see first hand how highly dad is thought of as a footballer and person. I was lucky enough, when I started in my own professional career, to play for some of the clubs dad had played for, Wests Magpies, Illawarra Steelers, Hull Kingston Rovers and Halifax RLFC. Dad is a legend at these clubs. He was picked in the Team of the Century and Legends Team for the Magpies, selected as captain of the Steelers Team of Steel, and was one of the most successful players at Hull KR. Therefore to say the pressure from supporters and sponsors to perform as dad did was massive is an understatement!

Dad always taught us that pressure is what you make it. When I would be interviewed or when fans would compare me to him I would reply, "If I can be half as successful as dad then I would be more than happy."

Congratulations and well done on such an amazing career and life so far. I am blessed to be a part of it. Thank you.

Dane

19. And finally... a special thank you

My life would not have been complete if I didn't enjoy the game of rugby league over the years but there are a number of people I want to praise and say a BIG, BIG thank you for allowing me a chance to share the experience. I owe a great deal of gratitude and my success in life and rugby league to the following people.

The Hart family – Aunty Beatrice and Uncle Maurice (Morrie) from Sylvania who provided a loving home, bed and dinner when working in Kirrawee at the family wholesale meat depot while playing for the Wests Magpies during 1974 and 1975. It saved me many miles and heaps of time in travel. Aunty Beat would have my dinner on the table hot when I arrived home from training – a big T-bone steak, two eggs and chips – twice a week. If I went back to the pub with the lads and was to be late for dinner, and didn't call to inform her, boy did I receive the rounds of the kitchen. I only did this once because I loved my Aunty Beat like a mother, and was treated like a third son behind Ian and Phillip.

The Mitchell Family – Linda's family Don, Ida, John and Scott and Rita, Linda's Nan and her extended clan for welcoming me into their family and for the support they have provided to Linda and our family over the years. They were strong Wests Magpies supporters who encouraged both Linda and me to open the doors to an adventurous life in rugby league. The family matriarch Rita Mitchell (RIP), Linda's Nan was a rock and with her approval I was a welcomed addition into the family.

The Ryan family of Kingsford – Mr and Mrs Ryan who provided me lodgings for several months when I was working at Mascot in the family business as a trainee accountant after completing school in 1972. It was here that Warren taught me much about rugby league on the snooker table moving the balls around like players on a football pitch.

Warren Ryan – the best coach I have ever been under. Firstly, thank you Warren for taking the time out of your busy life to provide one of the two forewords to this book. I extend great appreciation to you for being a wonderful mentor in my formative years and a good friend and confidante over many years. Wok, as he came to be known was, as I found out, a student of the game of rugby league and this showed in his approach to coaching. Warren was instrumental in my formative years as a player, coaching me in the finesse of a first grade player, teaching me how to grow with the plaudits that come with a rising star, ensuring no bigheadedness evolved, learning how to compete with yourself and never doubting your ability to achieve what seems unattainable, being yourself and not having to live to someone else's standards be they good or bad. The most valuable component of any footballer's skill set is skill itself and I was blessed to have a coach of Warren's ability in those early years to extract mine and to have the opportunity to play with such a strong team as Wests Illawarra in the early 1970s

Laurie Puddy and his wife Rose – I would like to take this opportunity to provide special thanks for providing me and the family the chance to experience Perth. Our continuing friendship has been one of life's extraordinary positives. It is one of the best cities the family has lived in. We would have stayed, but as happens in rugby league, many things never stay the same and moves occur mostly out of necessity. Your pragmatism and vision in getting the new venture up and running and positioned successfully, only to have the rug pulled out from under, does nothing to show the efforts made to provide a springboard for local rugby league talent. I will always fondly remember the initial meeting at Coco's Restaurant in South Perth where we enjoyed a wonderful meal while you outlined the role I was to undertake for the Western Reds RL club.

Gordon Allen and his wife Brenda – many thanks for providing a place to stay in my early time in Perth and assisting my family's move across to the west. Gordon – thanks for being an excellent CEO and having the strength to make tough decisions for the best outcome of the club and the junior rugby league growth in Western Australia. Your friendship endures today and is a valued part of the Dorahy family.

ALL supporters of the game of rugby league who applauded my game and to the opposition supporters who booed me willingly on many occasions especially when taking those kicks at goal I thank all of you for being a part of my life's journey in rugby league. I particularly enjoyed the moments when young and not so young supporters from both sides would ask me for an autograph. It was important for you, it was important for me.

Peter Buchanan – Thanks go to 'Buch' as he was called for showing the foresight and confidence in suggesting I take the huge step up to play first grade at the age of 16. If Peter had not seen 'the rose in the

Five great Australian full-backs: Garry Jack, John Dorahy,
Ted Goodwin, Graeme Langlands and Keith Barnes

bud' or 'the flower in the seed' he was observing then I probably would never have had a similar chance to perform on the stage of rugby league as I had done. Peter is one of two people for whom I never signed a contract. It was always a handshake and their word is their bond. Warren Ryan and Peter had a salutation that showed the warmth of their relationship. Whenever they would greet they would say, "Hello old chap." I loved it.

Colin Hutton – former chairman of Hull Kingston Rovers RLFC. If it was not for Colin's friendship with the coach, Allan Fitzgibbon of the Illawarra Steelers club from his time playing at Rovers, the chance to play again in the UK may not have happened. To Colin I say thank you for taking the time to write the foreword from the English perspective. Your offer to play at Hull KR led without doubt to my and my family's most treasured time in the game of rugby league. I can never repay you for the time living in Thorngumbald outside of Hull, and the opportunity to play with such a great team under a terrific coach and having the chance to meet so many now long term close friends.

The Gale Family – Roger, Angela and their two young ladies Susan and Mandy. I cannot express enough gratitude to each of you for allowing my family to become a part of the Gale family from day one. Without the Gales our stay in England would never have been as wonderful or exciting as it was. We will always remember the home cooked meals with Yorkshire puddings, the apple pies for dessert and the many card nights at our homes. The love you extended to the Dorahys knows no bounds and is reciprocated across the 12,000 miles between Australia and England. Love you forever.

The Smiths – Mike and Jackie for being good mates and close friends since meeting in September 1983 at Hull KR. Playing alongside Mike was rewarding and long term friendship is vital in any time of life and shows what is good about having the chance to live and work in another country.

The Ounsworths – Jack and Pat and family. Jack allowed me, Linda and the family to become close friends away from rugby and Jack's unending love of the change room atmosphere to assist all players was openly there to behold. They were special times and great success for all of us to enjoy.

The Scotts from Halifax – Mick and Jane Scott with their daughters Emma and Faye remain close friends from our time in Halifax. I thank you for your close support and terrific friendship during the good times and some tough times at the back end of the 1989–90 season. Mick – thanks for your coaching assistance and strong support. Without it the club would not have survived as well as it did.

Ray and Ann Miller from Ashton-in-Makerfield near Wigan – without doubt, another one of the best things to happen during our visit to Wigan for a meeting with the board about the coaching position for the 1993–94 season was that Wigan had Ray Miller look after Linda and me during that week. Ray – you are the salt of the earth and a 'bloody good' bloke as we say in Australia. Your support and friendship at Wigan was a wonderful experience and I can only say a big thank you to you and your darling wife Ann 'Ma' Miller for the hospitality you provided and the friendship gained from our time at Wigan. I will always remember your greeting when asked, "How are you going?" your answer was, "Not three bad." I look forward to our next game of golf.

The Stricklands – our lives were blessed with the meeting of John and Ann which I firmly believe was a God-driven thing. Your friendship and unending support during and following our time in Wigan has been truly amazing. But John as you would say, "You do it for friends" and how true that is. Your fellowship had far reaching effects on our family and still rings true today.

Vaiaga 'Inga' Tuigamala – former All Black legend and the major recruit in my time as a coach. Inga, though we have met on several occasions since Wigan I would like to say a big thank you to a big man in God's eyes with incredible Christian power. The friendship our families have is unique and special and I thank you for allowing my family to be a part of your family and you providing a springboard to know how to not just 'talk the talk but to also walk the walk'. Our lives have been enriched by your friendship and support.

Kevin Hammond, former Western Suburbs Magpies chairman and general manager – for the special relationship and friendship you placed in our time working together at Wests 'The Mighty Magpies'. Your confidence in me to coach in 2006 to 2007 was much appreciated though the success we sought was limited only by the politics of rugby league. Kevin's passion for the Magpies was so strong it was astonishing. No one could deny Kevin's passion to see Wests Magpies succeed. You deserve a medal.

The Eadies – Barb and her family, Brook, Leah and girls, Todd and Clint became very close family friends over the years after joining Manly in 1980. Barb you have been a rock not only to your family but to all who are lucky enough to be your friends. Our families are closer now than ever and it is a blessing to count your friendship and enjoy the Christmas holidays together.

The Mortimers – thank you to Peter and Julie, Michael, James, Timothy, Daniel and Robbie for the wonderful friendship over the years. As competitors we respected each other, as friends we enjoy the opportunity to get together as often as time allows. Through a friendship borne from football our wives, who had never met, spoke on the phone for an hour talking about Hull KR and the positives and negatives of going to England. I am happy that you went to Hull KR and experienced the same joy that the Dorahy family did in their time there. We have enjoyed so many wonderful memories and nights on the Mortimers of Orange wine. Our children are close friends and our lives have been enriched by your friendship.

Many old friends in Wollongong during the formative years. A big thank you for being there in support. Time changes the way we communicate but you are always close to our hearts.

To all, thanks for the friendship and memories.

Appendix 1: Rugby league memories

My select team: 1971 to 1990
1. Graeme Langlands, St George and Australia
2. Martin Offiah, Wigan and Great Britain
3. Michael Cronin, Parramatta and Australia
4. Bob Fulton, Wests Red Devils, Manly and Australia
5. Va'aiga Tuigamala, Wigan and New Zealand
6. Wally Lewis, Brisbane and Australia
7. Tommy Raudonikis, Wests Magpies and Australia
8. Arthur Beetson, Balmain, Easts and Australia
9. Martin Dermott, Wigan and Great Britain
10. Steve Roach, Wests Red Devils and Balmain
11. Dennis Betts, Wigan and Great Britain
12. Les Boyd, Wests Magpies, Manly and Australia
13. Malcolm Reilly, Castleford, Manly and Great Britain
14. Mike Smith, Hull KR and Great Britain
15. Gene Miles, Brisbane and Australia
16. John Donnelly, Wests Magpies and Australia
17. Phil Clarke, Wigan and Great Britain
Coach: Warren Ryan

Favourite player: Arthur Beetson, Balmain and Eastern Suburbs
Best goalkicker: Frano Botica, Wigan RL 1993–94
Favourite defender: John Donnelly, Western Suburbs Magpies
Most feared attacking players: Bobby Fulton and Malcolm Reilly, Manly
Most influential player: Wally Lewis
Person I least wanted to play: Chris Mortimer
Best coach: Warren Ryan
Best fitness trainer: Ken Boothroyd, Illawarra Steelers
Most influential officials: Ken Arthurson, Manly and Australian Rugby
League and Maurice Lindsay, Wigan and Rugby Football League
Most respected officials: Bob Millward, Illawarra Steelers and Colin Hutton,
Hull Kingston Rovers, England
Favourite ground: Lidcombe Oval, Sydney
Least favourite ground: Whitehaven
Best ground to watch rugby league: Old Trafford, Manchester
Favourite club doctor: Dr. Robert McInerney, Western Suburbs Magpies
Favourite tour moment: Sydney tour to New Zealand 1976, watch two
players eat live gold fish before lunch
Favourite club moment: 1983–84 winning the Championship and
Premiership double at Hull KR
Disappointments: No Grand Final with Wests Magpies and missing selection
on a Kangaroo tour in 1978 and 1982 when I was informed before the
announcement I was picked to tour.

Appendix 2: Statistics and records

Born: 28 August 1954, Wollongong, NSW

	App	T	G	DG	Pts
Overall club career 1971 to 1989					
Wests (Wollongong) 1971 to 1973	28	Not known			
Leigh 1973–74	5	1	0	0	3
Western Suburbs 1974 to 1979	102	29	228	2	545
Manly-Warringah 1980 to 19881	27	6	19	1	57
Illawarra 1982 to 1985	73	14	204	5	463
Wests (Wollongong) 1986	10				
Hull Kingston Rovers 1983 to 1987	92+2	47	224	4	600
North Sydney 1987 to 1989	37	6	102	3	231
Halifax	22+1	5	10	0	40
TOTAL	**396+3**	**108**	**787**	**15**	**1939**

Representative career 1972 to 1988

	App	T	G	DG	Pts
City versus Country 1972 to 1988					
City Seconds 1979	1	1	6	0	15
City Firsts 1980	1	0	0	0	0
Country Firsts 1972-73	2	2	0	0	6
Country Origin 1988	1	0	7	0	14
TOTAL	**5**	**3**	**13**	**0**	**35**
New South Wales 1979					
versus Queensland 1979	1	0	6	0	12
versus Great Britain 1979	1	0	4	0	8
TOTAL	**2**	**0**	**10**	**0**	**20**
Australia 1978					
Tests 1978	2	1	0	0	3
Grand total – all matches	**405+3**	**112**	**810**	**15**	**1994**

With thanks to David Middleton of League Information Services for information on senior matches

Club records in Australia season by season from 1980

	App	T	G	DG	Pts
Manly 1980	6	2	1	0	8
Manly 1981	19	4	18	1	49
Illawarra 1982	25	6	70	1	159
Illawarra 1983	25	5	76	3	175
Illawarra 1984	7	0	22	0	44
Illawarra 1985	16	3	36	1	85
North Sydney 1987	13	1	40	2	86
North Sydney 1988	15	3	46	1	105
North Sydney 1989	9	1	16	0	36

Honours in Australia

1971
Premiers
1972
Illawarra Division
NSW Country Tour Queensland
NSW Country 1sts
NSW Country Vs NZ
Premiers
1973
Illawarra Division
NSW Country Tour Queensland
NSW Country 1sts
Grand Finalists
1974
Finalists
1976
Combined Sydney tour to New Zealand
1977
Amco Cup Winners, Wests Magpies
1978
Australia Two tests versus New Zealand
1979
City 2nds
NSW versus Queensland
NSW versus Great Britain
1980
City 1sts
1988
Country Origin

First captain of Illawarra Steelers
Wests Magpies Hall of Fame
Wests Magpies Team of the Century
Illawarra Team of Steel
Australian Sports Medal for services to rugby league

British rugby league records

Playing

Leigh	A	T	G	DG	Pts
1973–74	5	1	0	0	3

Hull KR					
1983–84	26+1	18	74	2	222
1985-86	37	8	99	2	232
1986–87	29+1	11	51	0	146
Total	**92+2**	**37**	**224**	**4**	**603**

Halifax					
1989–90	22+1	5	10	0	40

Overall totals	**119+3**	**43**	**234**	**4**	**643**

Honours

Hull KR

1983–84   Division One Champions
Premiership winners (Harry Sunderland Trophy winner)
1985–86   Yorkshire Cup winners
Challenge Cup runners-up
John Player Special Trophy runners-up

Halifax

1989–90   Regal Trophy runners-up
Yorkshire Cup semi-finalists

Coaching

Halifax 1989–90

	P	W	D	L	F	A	Pts
Second Division:	28	20	0	8	741	360	40

Finished fifth
Challenge Cup: Lost in first round
Regal Trophy: Runners-up
Second Division Premiership: Lost in first round
Yorkshire Cup: semi-finalists

Wigan 1993–94

	P	W	D	L	F	A	Pts
First Division	30	23	0	7	780	403	46

Won title on points difference from Bradford Northern and Warrington
Challenge Cup: Winners
Regal Trophy: Runners-up

Warrington 1996

	P	W	D	L	F	A	Pts
Super League	22	12	0	10	569	565	24

Finished fifth
Challenge Cup: Lost in fifth round

Warrington 1997: Played 3, lost 3 in Super League. Won 2, lost 1 in the Challenge Cup.

Best in the Northern Union

The pioneering 1910 Rugby League Lions tour of Australia and New Zealand

Tom Mather

Tom Mather's fascinating account of the first tour 'down under ' by the British Rugby League Lions, which helped establish the sport in Australia and New Zealand, and gave rugby league an international dimension. Published in 2010 at £12.95. Available direct from London League Publications Ltd for just £12.00 post free. For credit card payments visit www.llpshop.co.uk , cheque payments to PO Box 10441, London E14 8WR, payable to London League Publications Ltd. It can also be ordered from any bookshop for £12.95 (ISBN: 9781903659519).

Hunslet through and through

Geoff Gunney MBE, rugby league footballer

Maurice Bamford

Geoff Gunney was one of the great players of post-war rugby league and a stalwart of the Hunslet club. Former Great Britain coach Maurice Bamford outlines his career in an authorised biography published in 2010. Published at £13.95. Available direct from London League Publications Ltd for just £13.00. For credit card payments visit www.llpshop.co.uk , cheque payments to PO Box 10441, London E14 8WR, cheques payable to London League Publications Ltd. It can also be ordered from any bookshop for £13.95 (ISBN: 9781903659465).

No Sand Dunes in Featherstone

Memories of West Yorkshire Rugby League

Edited by Robert Light

Based on the *'Up and Under'* University of Huddersfield oral history project, this book includes memories from players, coaches, club officials, referees, journalists and supporters from the First World War to the present. Every rugby league supporter will enjoy this fascinating book.
Published in October 2010 at £12.95. Available direct from London League Publications Ltd for just £12.00. For credit card payments visit www.llpshop.co.uk , cheque payments to PO Box 10441, London E14 8WR, cheques payable to London League publications Ltd. It can also be ordered from any bookshop for £12.95
(ISBN: 9781903659533).

Braver than all the rest

A mother fights for her son

Philip Howard

Dave and Sarah Burgess are devastated when their young son Karl is found to have muscular dystrophy. Then another tragedy hits the family hard. But the family are committed to do the best they can for Karl, who has a passion for rugby league. Based in Castleton, a Yorkshire town near the border with Lancashire, Karl's determination to get the most out of life, despite his disability, inspires those around him, in particular Chris Anderton, one of the Castleton Rugby League Club players.

Philip Howard is a retired teacher who had responsibility for special needs at a sixth form college. He is a lifelong rugby league fan from St Helens, but now lives near Hull. This is his first novel.

Published in September 2010 at £9.95. Available direct from London League Publications Ltd for just £9.00 post free. For credit card payments visit www.llpshop.co.uk , cheque payments to PO Box 10441, London E14 8WR, payable to London League publications Ltd. It can also be ordered from any bookshop for £9.95 (ISBN: 9781903659526).

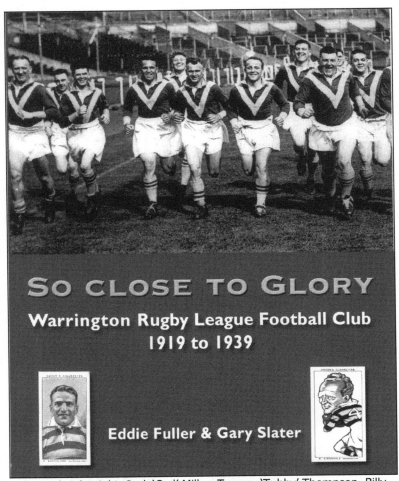

SO CLOSE TO GLORY
**Warrington Rugby League Football Club
1919 to 1939**

Eddie Fuller & Gary Slater

Big Jack Arkwright, Jack 'Cod' Miller, Tommy 'Tubby' Thompson, Billy Dingsdale and Bill Shankland are rugby league legends. All five made their names at Wilderspool and are in the Warrington Wolves Hall of Fame.
So close to Glory is the story of how they and their team-mates in the club's famous primrose and blue colours helped the club to grow in size and popularity during the 1920s and 1930s. In this period the team played in three Challenge Cup Finals and three Championship Finals.
This was a time of poverty, economic hardship and mass unemployment, but Warrington RLFC became a focal point for the town and prospered.
This is the untold story of those two decades and is lavishly illustrated with photographs, cartoons, caricatures and cigarette cards from the period.
So close to Glory also shows what Warrington was like between the wars.
Published in March 2008 at £12.95. Available direct from London League Publications Ltd for just £10.00 post free. For credit card payments visit www.llpshop.co.uk , cheque payments to PO Box 10441, London E14 8WR, payable to London League publications Ltd. It can also be ordered from any bookshop for £12.95 (ISBN: 9781903659373).

Liverpool City RLFC

Rugby league in a football city

Mike Brocken

Rugby league in Liverpool has a long history. Older fans have memories of visits to watch Liverpool Stanley before the war and Liverpool City in the 1950s and 1960s. This history of rugby league in Liverpool covers from the 1850s to the present day. It includes the first Liverpool City RLFC, Wigan Highfield and London Highfield, the forerunners to Liverpool Stanley RLFC, and the club after it moved to Huyton in 1969 until it was wound up in 1997.

Published in October 2008 at £14.95. Order from London League Publications for £14.00 post free. Credit card orders via www.llpshop.co.uk or by cheque payable to London League Publications Ltd to PO Box 10441, London E14 8WR. Or order from any bookshop for £14.95 (ISBN: 9781903659403)

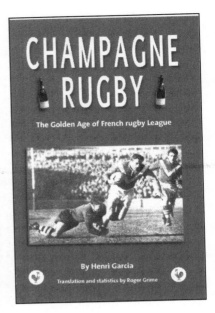

Two fascinating books available from London League Publications Ltd. *Snuff out the Moon* describes the origins of floodlit rugby in the nineteenth century, when sport was used to promote electricity, to the development of modern floodlit rugby league. *Champagne Rugby* is the first English translation of Henri Garcia's book on the historic French tours to Australia and New Zealand in the 1950s, when they were the most exciting team in the world.

Both books are available from London League Publications Ltd at £5.00 each. Cheques payable to London League Publications Ltd, credit card orders via www.llpshop.co.uk

Published in 2008, the authorised biography of one of the game's most successful coaches is available for just £5.00 direct from London League Publications Ltd. For credit card payments visit www.llpshop.co.uk , cheque payments to PO Box 10441, London E14 8WR; cheques payable to London League Publications Ltd.